In loving memory of my father, Sergeant James Arthur Darke,
who proudly defended Darwin as a member of the 2nd AIF.

HEREDITY

I am the family face;
Flesh perishes, I live on,
Projecting trait and trace
Through time to times anon,
And leaping from place to place
Over oblivion.

The years—heired feature that can
In curve and voice and eye
Despise the human span
Of durance—that is I;
The eternal thing in man
That heeds no call to die.

Thomas Hardy

THE MEN BEHIND THE MYTH

THE FIGHTING LEANES
OF PROSPECT

CAROL
ROSENHAIN

First published in 2019 by Barrallier Books Pty Ltd,
trading as Echo Books

Registered Office: 35—37 Gordon Avenue, West Geelong, Victoria 3220, Australia.

www.echobooks.com.au

Copyright ©Carol Rosenhain

Creator: Rosenhain, Carol.

Title: The Men Behind the Myth: The Fighting Leanes of Prospect/Carol Rosenhain

ISBN: 9780648554011: Paperback

A catalogue record for this book is available from the National Library of Australia

NATIONAL LIBRARY OF AUSTRALIA

Book layout and design by Peter Gamble, Canberra.
Set in Garamond Premier Pro Display, 12/17 and/Trajan Pro3.

www.echobooks.com.au

(((echo)))
BOOKS

CONTENTS

LIST OF ILLUSTRATIONS

PREFACE

After the publication of *The Man Who Carried the Nation's Grief*, which had been my 'baby' for 20 years, I was as lost as a mother whose children had flown the family home. I kept gravitating to the computer in search of a new focus. My genealogical assistant, Nola Russell, was also feeling singularly bereft. One day she emailed me and asked if I had any more research that demanded attention and, in a rather cavalier fashion, I suggested that she help me unearth more of my family history. My maiden name is Darke and I knew that James Bennett Darke and his wife Martha had arrived in Adelaide on *Westminster* in 1848. They had settled in Prospect and produced a large family of a temperate and hard-working disposition. I had been thrilled to visit their grave in the North Road Cemetery some years ago which clearly recorded them as early pioneers of the utopian settlement of Adelaide. Other than my direct lineage through Henry, Arthur and my father, James Darke, I knew little about the other members of the family and the associations they had formed in the early days of that small but vibrant colony.

After a few weeks, I was stunned and intrigued when Nola posted the question, 'Don't you know who you are related to?' This of course begged the question of 'Who?' Her answer directed me to google the 'Fighting Leanes of Prospect'. So that is what I did, opening up a whole new vista of World War I names that I had never heard before. While reading of their exploits, additional information revealed that Charles Bean had called them 'the most famous family of soldiers in Australian history'. Fascinated, I read on, unsure of the relationship and significance to my own family history. Finally a word loomed large on the page. That name was 'Short'. The mother of these famous men was Alice Leane, née Short. My great-grandfather Henry had married her half-sister, Elizabeth Jane Short. That relationship meant that I was, in effect, a first cousin twice removed from the famous 'Fighting Leanes of Prospect'!

At first I was amazed, incredulous and then consumed with excitement. Surely, in this quirk of fate lay a possible focus for my next undertaking. I began to read widely, marshalling as much material as possible on this famous family and its men. The internet provided a foundation and from that I gravitated to the Australian War Memorial and the National Archives. Naturally most of that material pertained to the World War I service history of the five brothers and the six of their sons who had enlisted. I read details of their exploits in war diaries and books documenting their deeds and meritorious service. Wider research suggested intriguing and unusual paths followed by those who returned in their post-war lives. I was spellbound. I was hooked. Here was the source of my new passion, the extended family history of those famous Leanes. Inevitably, even the most superficial of enquiries posed questions. What brought these Leanes to Australia? Where were their origins? How did they manage to establish a foothold in the new settlement of Adelaide? What were the values that motivated such a united commitment from one family to sublimate self and sacrifice security to take up arms? These questions and of course that very strong personal connection, directed my research. I yearned to unravel what was virtually a myth that had endured for nearly a century. What mettle of people made these men and their family so famous? Was the sobriquet justified or were Bean's words patriotic hyperbole? This book is my way of answering these questions.

Carol Rosenhain

February 2018

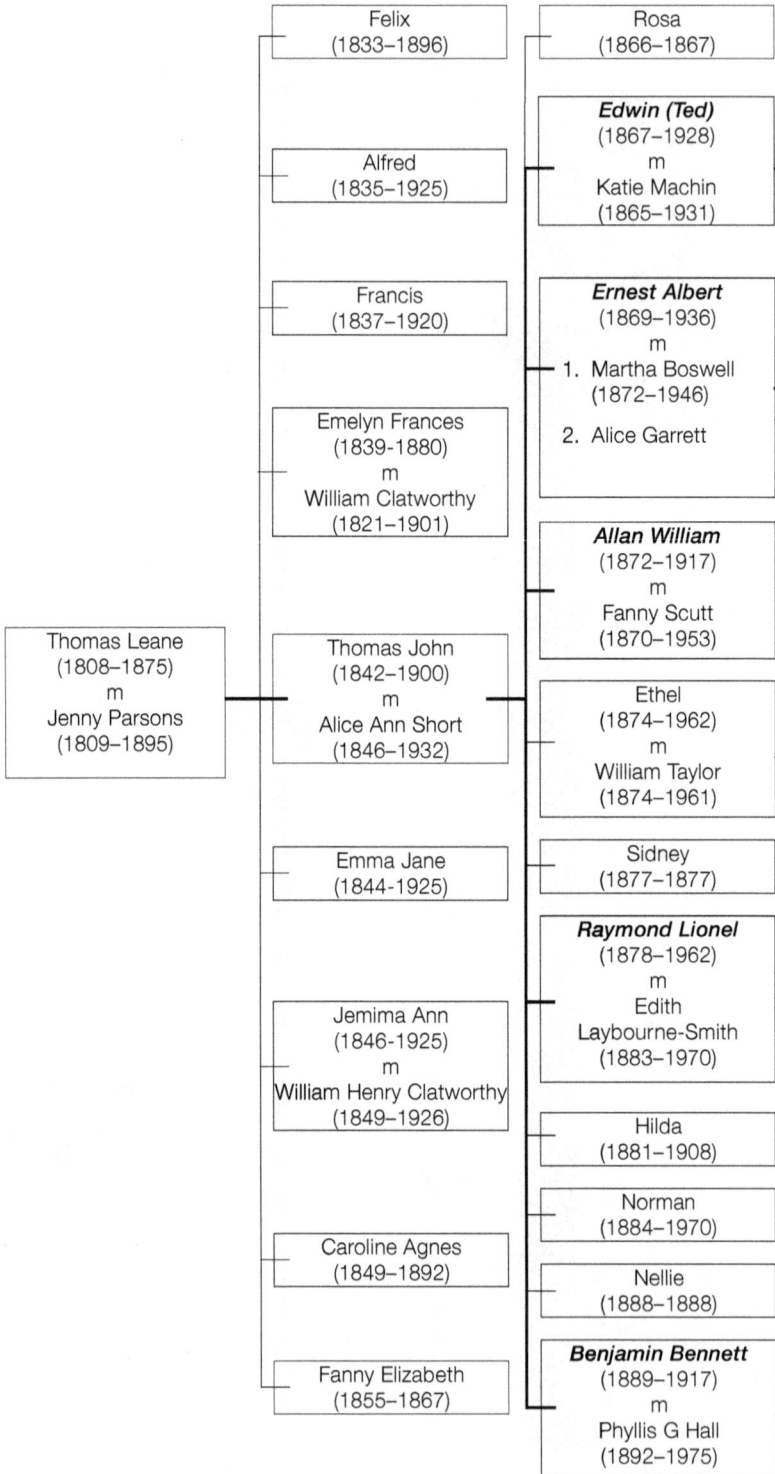

Thomas Leane
(1808–1875)
m
Jenny Parsons
(1809–1895)

- Felix
(1833–1896)
  - Rosa
(1866–1867)

- Alfred
(1835–1925)
  - **Edwin (Ted)**
(1867–1928)
m
Katie Machin
(1865–1931)

- Francis
(1837–1920)
  - **Ernest Albert**
(1869–1936)
m
1. Martha Boswell
(1872–1946)

2. Alice Garrett

- Emelyn Frances
(1839–1880)
m
William Clatworthy
(1821–1901)

- Thomas John
(1842–1900)
m
Alice Ann Short
(1846–1932)
  - **Allan William**
(1872–1917)
m
Fanny Scutt
(1870–1953)
  - Ethel
(1874–1962)
m
William Taylor
(1874–1961)
  - Sidney
(1877–1877)
  - **Raymond Lionel**
(1878–1962)
m
Edith
Laybourne-Smith
(1883–1970)
  - Hilda
(1881–1908)
  - Norman
(1884–1970)
  - Nellie
(1888–1888)
  - **Benjamin Bennett**
(1889–1917)
m
Phyllis G Hall
(1892–1975)

- Emma Jane
(1844-1925)

- Jemima Ann
(1846-1925)
m
William Henry Clatworthy
(1849–1926)

- Caroline Agnes
(1849–1892)

- Fanny Elizabeth
(1855–1867)

Doris (1892–1970)	Jack (1895–1896)		Peter (1929)
Allan Edwin (1894–1917)		Geoffrey Paul (1897–1963) m Beryl Pride	Edwin (1933)
Reuben Ernest (1898–1971)	Marjorie (1899–1979)		Margaret (1935)
Maxwell (1899–1979)	Hatherley (Babs) (1904–1974)		

Ethel (1894)	Arnold Harry (1896–1916)	William Ernest (1897–1964) m 1. Lillian Musselwhite 2. Vera Davis 3. Eleanor Wadham.
Frank Harold (1898–1899)	Jack (1899–1970)	
Thomas (1901–1970)	Allan (1904–1985)	
Ivy (1905–1968)	Lawrence (1907–1990)	Glenda Rae Leane (1942)
Thelma (1909–1992)	Elsie (1911–1984)	

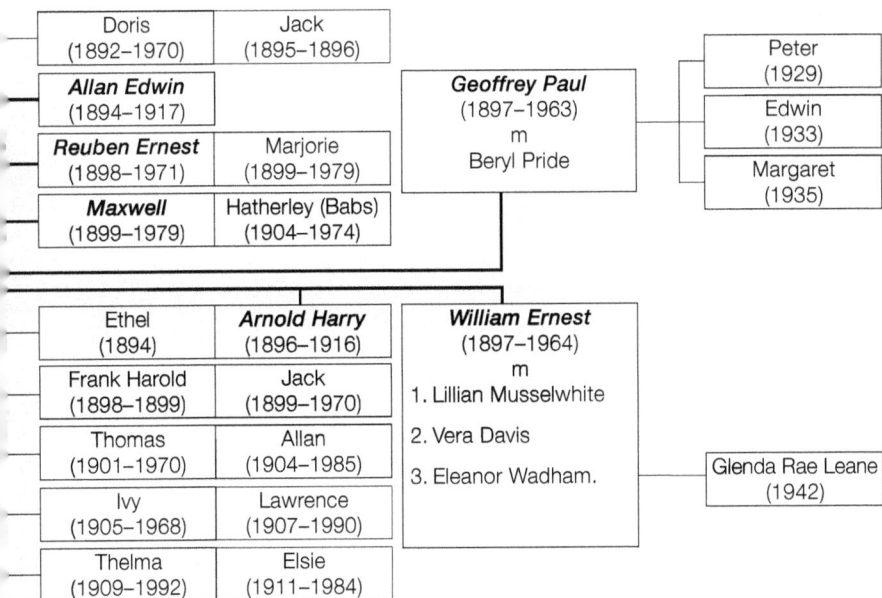

Eric Allan Leane (1896-1963)

Thomas Clarence Fairley (1894–1964) Adopted	
William Taylor (1903 -1985)	Donovan Taylor (1905 -1990)

Lionel (1903–1979)	Kenneth (1904–1965)
Geoffrey (1907–1990)	Betty (1812– ?)
Allan (1920–1971)	Benjamin (1920–1969)

Gwenyth (1913)	Marjory (1915)

Leane Family Tree

1. GENESIS

When Ellis Ashmead Bartlett's account of the Gallipoli landings was first published in the Melbourne *Argus* on 8 May 1915, no-one could have realised that he had laid the foundation for what would become known as the 'Anzac legend'. His evocative descriptions of 'the race of athletes' as they scaled the perilous cliffs and their good humour in spite of horrific wounds inspired him to write, 'I have never seen anything like the wounded colonials in war before ... they were happy because they knew they had been tried for the first time and had not been found wanting'.

Such approbation was readily embraced by Australia's Official War Correspondent, Charles E. W. Bean. Born in Bathurst in 1879, Bean was initially educated at All Saints College where his father was Headmaster. When he was only nine, the family relocated to England to enable his father to take up a new appointment at Brentwood School in Essex. Naturally, Charles became a student there, after which he moved to Clifton College, Bristol, as a boarder. His outstanding results at secondary school and his service in the Volunteer Corps readily secured Bean a position at Oxford where he read Law and Classics. During the formative years of his childhood Bean had developed a love of the Australian bush, while in adolescence, he became absorbed in all things military. In 1904 he returned to Australia where he taught Greek while awaiting admission to the New South Wales (NSW) Bar. In 1908 he obtained a position as a journalist with the *Sydney Morning Herald* where he quickly cemented his identity as a hard-working features writer. A brief secondment to London in 1910 exposed him to international events and the rising unrest in Europe. His recall to Australia was to open the door to a career path and a lifetime of dedicated work that was to leave Australians a lasting legacy—a comprehensive and detailed history of 'the war to end all wars'.

Bean's opportunity arose from the decision by the British government to nominate one Australian as an Official War Correspondent. Much to the chagrin of fellow journalist, Keith Murdoch, the sensitive and erudite Charles E. W. Bean was nominated by the *Sydney Morning Herald*, which led to an appointment which he secured with relish. When Bean embarked with the senior officers of the Australian Imperial Force (AIF) on the troopship *Orvieto* to leave for Egypt in November 1914, he could never have imagined that over the next four years he was to witness some of the bloodiest battles in military history. In this initial period he would spend eight months with the Anzacs at Gallipoli where the subsequent publication of the *ANZAC Book* sowed the seeds of the Anzac legend. This legend would be embellished during the three years of the brutal conflict which Bean witnessed on the Western Front. He felt his mandate was tantamount to a sacred duty, to record for posterity the courage and sacrifice that Australian soldiers had displayed in loyalty to a distant empire. As he spent most days observing military manoeuvres and troop movements, he wrote up his observations that very day and well into the night to ensure accuracy. In his role he mixed not only with enlisted men, but officers whose names and actions he would record after the war in his seminal 12-volume *Official History of Australia in the War of 1914-1918*. This unashamedly popularised the Anzac legend which was readily embraced in a wave of public nostalgia.

In this work, which consumed his lifetime, Bean lauded the Anzac as a fighter second to none who could always be relied on in a crisis. In many ways, the Anzac legend fulfilled an emerging sense of nationalism which was readily adopted by both the Australian people and the nation's military. In addition, it served as a potent resource for powerful interests, be they politicians, churches, recruitment centres or simply bereft families. This seminal work not only recorded the exploits of the AIF, but ascribed to its members a distinctive, almost mythical set of characteristics. From Bean's first-hand perspective, the Australian and New Zealand soldiers exemplified raw courage, ingenuity, contempt for danger, good humour, larrikinism and mateship. All were ideal attributes which echoed much of what he had witnessed in the bush as a child, and singled out the 'digger' from servicemen of other nations. To many Australians such qualities became central to a new and distinctive national image that Bean did his utmost to support.

In the century since World War I however, there has been much criticism and rejection of what is now regarded as the 'Anzac myth'. Historians, with the benefit of hindsight, suggest that such a perspective is purely fanciful, while new-age thinking regards such ideals as anachronistic. The volatility of this seminal legend therefore challenges historians to question some of the other key assertions Bean makes. One such question surrounds the Leane family and Bean's belief that its members constituted 'the most famous family of soldiers in Australian history'. Although written in the middle of the 20th century, this statement, with the vision of hindsight needs questioning. Undoubtedly, such a title is all the more extraordinary given the fact that the members of this family were not descended from British aristocracy whose sons, by virtue of their wealth and privilege, were ushered into military careers through Sandhurst and via paid commissions.

Instead, the five fathers and their six sons who enlisted to serve in the AIF came from humble origins. They were all descendants of working-class families who had been raised with strict Christian principles and a strong sense of duty. As such they were not dissimilar to the thousands of other men who were prepared to take up arms in defence of the Empire. Yet amid the 331,000 soldiers who served in World War I, the Leanes managed to distinguish themselves sufficiently to be aligned with the great names of Australian military history. In ascribing fame to this family name, Charles Bean clearly felt that this single group of men had embraced and represented all that was characteristically Australian and unique to the Anzac legend.

It is both ambitious and complex to house the qualities of a nation under one umbrella, charging historians with the task of investigating whether a single family deserves shelter there too. Who then were these famous Leanes who were dubbed by the Adelaide press 'The Fighting Leanes of Prospect'? Do they remain today, a century since they fought, 'The most famous family of soldiers in Australia's military history?' Since the cessation of hostilities in 1918, Australian servicemen have been engaged in numerous conflicts in which they have continued to distinguish themselves. Obviously Charles Bean could not have anticipated or known of these conflicts when he penned his sobriquet, which begs the question, 'Are there other more worthy families, whose service has been overlooked in the course of the century?' In order to assess and evaluate Bean's claim, it is necessary to examine the Leanes' record of service in World War I and, if possible, compare it with that of other families whose menfolk made a commitment of similar magnitude. A valid starting point is obviously the Leanes' service records which are readily accessible through the National Archives. These tattered pages, now digitised, yield names of family members, battles fought and honours won. Yet, such records do little to animate the personality and nature of the individuals in this family. Instead, they remain shadowy figures shrouded in an unquestioned myth of Bean's own construction.

In order to explore the legendary status ascribed to the Leanes we need to demystify them. Who are the individuals involved? What did they do that singled them out from others? What were their origins? What motivated them? Did they all fight? What distinguished them from other families from which multiple sons enlisted? How did their post-war lives embellish their image? All of these questions need to be answered if we are to truly understand 'The Men Behind the Myth' and Bean's enduring declaration of their fame.

'The Fighting Leanes of Prospect' were the children and grandchildren of Thomas John Leane and Alice Ann Short, who had established their family and shoemaking business in Prospect, an inner suburb of Adelaide. Apart from their son, Norman Short, the example of Edwin Thomas and his brothers Ernest Albert, Allan William, Raymond Lionel and Benjamin Bennett, inspired their sons, Allan Edward, Geoffrey Paul, Reuben Ernest, Maxwell, Arnold Harry and William Ernest, to take up arms. Edwin Thomas and Allan William had previously fought in the Boer War and, as the eldest members of the family, theirs was an example that was envied by all and which many sought to emulate. All except Maxwell embarked for Egypt before deployment to Gallipoli and the Western Front. Four never made the homeward journey.

While the call to arms, the allure of the uniform and the prospect of adventure have historically drawn men to enlist, the seeds of the Leanes' distinguished service are far more complex and this in many ways distances them from Bean's typical Anzac. It may be perfectly normal for some siblings to follow in an older brother's footsteps, but it is unusual for all to follow, along with their sons. Clearly such a circumstance suggests a common background and unity of purpose that may not have existed in other families. In order to understand how the Leanes embraced this universal commitment, we need to explore their origins and the fundamental forces that shaped their destiny. Removed from fame and fortune, the Leanes trace their humble origins back to one of the most isolated and remote counties of England—Cornwall.

Cornwall is almost an island unto itself, for the River Tamar flows along all but five miles of its border with Devon. It is a county covered in drowned valleys, bogs and creeks, interspersed with rugged cliffs and quaint fishing villages. In a sense it is a marine county, as the sea is never more than 20 miles away from any given point. The county is dotted with small hamlets where, for centuries, life was focused around the church and the labours of a largely illiterate folk who worked the land, the sea, or the trades passed down from their forebears. Doubtless most Cornish people would have had some inkling of neighbouring Plymouth in Devon which, since the 13th century, has been a large commercial port. They would, in many cases, have been aware of Plymouth's importance on the world stage. It was from Plymouth that the Pilgrim Fathers sailed for the new world on *Mayflower* in 1620 and in 1772 James Cook departed on his great, three-year circumnavigation of the globe. Ventures from Plymouth proved visionary journeys that not only shaped knowledge of distant lands but the rich and rewarding lives of the people who settled them.

However, the horizons of most working folk living in Britain in the 19th century were limited. Life in small villages had become very bleak. The Industrial Revolution had all but destroyed cottage industry and encouraged thousands of village labourers to flood to the cities of the north to work in the burgeoning factories. Consequently, rural Britain fell into disrepair for want of labour. Poverty and unemployment were rife and families struggled to feed and clothe their children. Gaols were filled with debtors and the destitute and, with transportation losing favour, the government was faced with a multiplicity of social problems. Oddly enough, a vision for the future of the impoverished working classes emerged not from the government or its politicians, but from a man who was himself a prisoner in Newgate Prison.

This man was Edward Gibbon Wakefield. Born into a comfortable Quaker family and well educated, Wakefield had served as secretary to the British envoy at Turin. However his ambition had exceeded his salary. At just 20 he eloped with and married a 16-year-old heiress with whom he had two children. Her premature death ensured that he inherited a substantial income. Marriage, it seemed, had the potential to be lucrative and, at 30, Wakefield next abducted and married a 15-year-old schoolgirl from a well-credentialled family. The marriage, which was promptly annulled by parliament, caused outrage and a public scandal. As a consequence, on 14 May 1827, Wakefield was sentenced to the ignominy of a three-year term in Newgate Prison. This proved a seminal experience which was to shape his whole career and the lives of thousands of people who would be the beneficiaries of his thinking. Incarcerated in Newgate, Wakefield was exposed to a class of people with which his privileged upbringing had denied him contact. Here he met the poor and the dispossessed who were forced into crime and imprisonment because they had no land or employment to sustain them. Wakefield was profoundly moved by their plight and quickly formed the belief that their situation must and could be remedied. In response, he formulated a plan—a plan for systematic colonisation.

Wakefield's proposal was first printed anonymously in 1829 as *A Sketch of a Proposal for Colonising Australasia.* It was later reprinted as 'A Letter to Sydney, the Principal Town of Australasia' in the *Morning Chronicle* which was edited by Robert Gouger, a well-known Dissenter. He had spent time in Newgate as a debtor, and this had shaped his own philanthropic views. Wakefield argued that, if crown wastelands in colonies such as Australia were to be sold by the government, the proceeds could fund the emigration of labour from Britain. The benefits would be twofold. Impoverished, unemployed British workers could be encouraged to begin a new life and the colony could reduce its dependence on convict labour. He believed in 'limiting the quantity of land as to give the cheapest land a market value that would have the effect of compelling labourers to work for some considerable time for wages before they became landowners.'[1] As such, selling land should be the rule, replacing the practice of bestowing it gratis as had been the custom earlier in the colony's history. He believed that 'a sufficiency of labour and a congenial society would attract capital, encourage emigration, assure prosperity and justify the rights of the colony to elect representatives to its own legislature.'[2]

Further to this, Wakefield stipulated strict conditions for the selection of emigrants:

> It would be advisable to select as emigrants young persons only and especially young couples of both sexes... Secondly, young men would be more willing than old ones to make a venture of immigration

and young women would prefer crossing the world in couples, to migrating singly across the channel. Thirdly, young persons of both sexes would most readily accommodate their habits to the new climate and embrace a new model of cultivation and general labour. Lastly, having families to raise they would be more industrious than other persons and probably more apt to save part of their earnings whereby they would promote a more rapid increase in colonial capital. In a nutshell they would make the best members of a new society.[3]

Putting it plainly, Wakefield envisaged that the best of British society could be transplanted to the colony, devoid of the convict stain.

Convinced that his proposal for systematic colonisation was more than simply a panacea for population problems, Wakefield took every opportunity to promote his belief. He became an assiduous propagandist, plaguing newspapers and parliamentary dignitaries with endless articles and tracts on his system. By 1831 the British government had accepted Wakefield's proposal, agreeing that 'British Labourers would be of real and essential service [while proving] the most useful class of emigrants.'[4]

Wakefield's proposal continued to gain momentum. Given that all Australian settlement had previously been dictated by convict needs, it was believed in some circles that the associated ills of that system had 'created wealth it was said on a moral dunghill.'[5] Therefore another location had to be found which could allow decent people to flourish. In 1831, news of Sturt's discovery of fertile land between the mouth of the Murray River and the Gulf of St Vincent provided Wakefield an ideal location in which to apply his plan of systematic colonisation. Historian Manning Clarke remarks acidly of Wakefield that 'he was just as quick in stealing ideas as in stealing a child wife.'[6] Yet it was Gouger's initiative in 1833 that saw the formation of the South Australian Association. In June of that year, over 2500 people interested in the formation of a settlement on the southern coast of Australia gathered at a meeting. 'They were told there was to be equality of opportunity, and appropriate rewards for those who worked and remained sober, there was to be no aristocratic patronage, and nobody was to have a single inch of land for nothing.'[7] Commitment and hard work were the tools for success in this new utopia.

Such sound ideals encouraged the British government to establish South Australia as a British province and to provide for its government. This was formalised by an Act passed on 15 August 1834. The Act outlined processes by which laws for the peace, order and good government should be maintained in the settlement. The Crown was to appoint resident commissioners to ensure that land was sold and the proceeds directed to pay for the passages of migrants. Needless to say, those nominated and subsequently appointed as commissioners were men whose names remain etched in South Australian history—men such as Robert Gouger, Robert Torrens, George Fife Angas and James Hurtle Fisher. In spite of the fact that the management of the association was marked by diverse opinions and considerable dissention, the financial structure and the religious tone of the settlement were ideals that were maintained. Settlement plans now proceeded apace.

Early choices and abortive settlements were attempted at Kangaroo Island and Encounter Bay, but after the Surveyor General, Colonel William Light, discovered the harbour of the Gulf of St Vincent, 'one of the loveliest spots a man could behold', a final site was accepted.[8] Although Governor Hindmarsh had preferred a site closer to the sea, he nonetheless agreed to name the place 'Adelaide' in honour of Queen Adelaide, consort to King William IV. While the British government issued Letters Patent that established South Australia as a geopolitical reality on 19 February 1836, the date on which the first Governor arrived in South Australia and proclaimed a colony—28 December 1836—is celebrated as Proclamation Day. From the people's perspective, this marked the birth of South Australia.

Back in Britain, emigration agents were appointed in England, Scotland and Ireland to select migrants. They were instructed to choose men and women who were capable of becoming members of a virtuous and enlightened community. They were to discourage all those of a reckless or roving disposition. Above all, they were to weed out anyone they considered might be tempted by idleness and drink and select only those who were capable of frugality and industry.[9]

In the sleepy Cornish village of Crafthole (parish of Sheviock) some 9 miles west of Plymouth, Thomas Leane was largely unaware of the momentous developments in the antipodes. Having been born in Crafthole on 9 September 1808, he had relocated to Crafthole on his marriage to Jenny Parsons at Sheviock on 25 October 1832. Jenny, the daughter of John and Jane Parsons who resided in the parish, was born on 21 July 1809. Thomas followed his father, John Leane, in serving an apprenticeship as a shoe and boot maker.

Thomas' small workshop in the village of Crafthole was no doubt always busy. The village, forming the western end of Plymouth Harbour, is bounded in the north by the tidal waters of the Lynher River and in the south by Whitsand Bay. Naturally, fishing was its main occupation. While shoes were a luxury item for most working classes, durable and practical footwear were essential for fishermen and the agricultural labourers of the region. Fishermen's boots were in constant demand, or in regular need of repair given the corrosive effect of salt water. They were made of strong leather sourced from a local currier and were generally knee high with a folded cuff. Agricultural labourers' boots were basic, sturdy shoes with a leather tie or, alternatively, a simple pair of clogs. Each clog was hollowed out of a block of wood and sanded inside to provide a degree of comfort. The outside was then pared and rasped to form the distinctive shape.

Boots and shoes were an equally challenging item to make. First the feet were measured for size before the sole was cut from the hardest, most durable leather. The uppers were cut from a softer leather and the sole was then secured to the upper with tacks. Heels were attached with wooden pegs. The finishing operation then included rasping, scraping and smoothing before blacking and burnishing. Then the shoe would be removed from the last and the shoemaker would carefully run his hand around the inside, feeling for any pegs or tacks which might have pierced the inner sole. These would be cleaned out or sanded back. Many shoes were made with a basic sole pattern so that the shoe would fit either foot. Shoe and boot making was a labour-intensive craft, but one which provided an essential product for all men of the labouring class. Thomas Leane would have had little call for the ribbons or shiny buckles of middle-class footwear, but he would have proven adept at crafting comfortable and practical shoes for everyday needs.

Thomas Leane and his wife Jenny, like most people of the time, began their family soon after their marriage. Their first child, son Felix Leane, was born on 9 April 1833 in Crafthole. He was followed by Alfred, born on 11 February 1835 and Francis, who arrived on 4 January 1837. Following Francis' birth, Thomas and Jenny moved with their young family to London, relocating to 7 Finsbury Street in the parish of St Luke in Middlesex where Thomas found work as a porter. Given that most people of that era rarely moved beyond a radius of 10 miles of their village, such a family relocation was both monumental and most unusual. The reason for this move is not entirely clear, although itinerant Wesleyan preachers had developed a strong foothold in Cornwall at the time and it is not unreasonable to believe that they had found receptive hearts in Thomas and Jenny. It is therefore highly likely that the couple felt inspired to follow the call of their Nonconformist faith. The Nonconformists belonged to an evangelical Protestant denomination of the Christian faith strongly aligned with the Methodist Movement. Its founder, John Wesley, promoted a breakaway from the Church of England in the belief that personal discipline and a life of Christian holiness could lead to a closer relationship with God through 'sanctification or sinless perfection in life'.[10] The Wesleyans believed in the sacraments of baptism and communion. They believed in the Holy Trinity and that the Bible was the word of God.

In the early 19th century the Wesleyans established themselves strongly in the Middlesex area which became the cradle of Methodism.

In Finsbury, Moorfields and Hoxton, their ambitions saw them establish an extensive network of chapels and school buildings. More importantly, they founded the Hoxton Academy as a training school for aspiring ministers. Wesleyans encouraged people who had full-time jobs to become lay preachers. This gave working people experience of speaking in public and so the faith developed very much into a working-class religion. The Wesleyans were very supportive of women's roles in the church and focused on family and service to the community. Not surprisingly, Nonconformists abhorred gambling and alcohol. I suspect it was to the company of like-minded souls that the Leanes were drawn to London, in order to enrich their faith and equip themselves with the life skills to proselytise.

On 20 March 1839 their daughter, Emelyn Frances, was born and in the 1841 census, Thomas and Jenny were living with their children, Felix, Francis and Emelyn, at 5 Union Place in the Parish of St Luke, Middlesex. By 1842 the Leanes had returned to Crafthole where a son, Thomas John, was born on 13 February 1842. Yet by 1844 the family was back in Middlesex residing at 5 Amien Place, Tabernacle Walk, in Shoreditch. Here their second daughter, Emma Jane, was born on 13 March 1844, followed by a third girl, Jemima Ann, on 12 September 1846. All three children were baptised at the Wesleyan Methodist Chapel in City Road, Middlesex. In the same year the Leane family returned to Sheviock, where Caroline was born on 5 January 1849.

Living between Cornwall and London over the 1840s, Thomas and Jenny had plenty of time to evaluate their lifestyle in the different communities and to form a vision of the life they wanted for themselves and their children. Perhaps it was in the more cosmopolitan London setting that Thomas Leane may have heard tidings of the new settlement in South Australia or the work of the South Australian Association. The colony was growing rapidly and word may have spread that the population of 546 in 1836 had expanded to 23,904 by 1848.[11] Another development may have proven confronting and made Thomas Leane more receptive to information about South Australia—the decline of the traditional role of the shoemaker in London.

Since the Napoleonic Wars, the establishment of mechanised shoe and boot production by Marc Brinel had gained currency and English factories were beginning to appear. These facilities were capable of mass-producing shoes on an assembly line using unskilled labour, with each man trained only in the specific task for his stage of production. Lengthy and demanding apprenticeships were no longer necessary or *de rigeur*. Having witnessed the growth of the factories and the popularity of mass-produced shoes, it is likely that Thomas and Jenny returned to Cornwall where hand-crafted shoes were still valued and where they could plan for possible emigration to South Australia.

Although driven by practicality and a significant sense of adventure, the prospect of emigration must have been daunting and by no means guaranteed of success. Thomas and Jenny Leane also had the welfare of eight children to consider. They were aware that only the outward passage was funded, and that the length of the journey would make it unlikely that they would ever see their extended families again. It would be a dramatic and heart-wrenching severance from a way of life that the Leanes had pursued in Cornwall for generations. Nonetheless, with remarkable courage and hope in their hearts, Thomas and Jenny committed themselves to the venture and began making plans for a life in the antipodes in a little-known frontier town.

Thomas Leane's first step in qualifying for an assisted passage was to meet the conditions outlined by the visiting Emigration Agent. These demanded that a certificate of good character and circumstances be submitted to the Commissioners for their approval. Thomas Leane would have had little difficulty in presenting such a document. He and his family were regular attendees at church. He was proficient in an essential trade, was sober and industrious and was married to a woman of equally good character. No doubt a letter from the local minister would have attested to these facts. Furthermore, with eight children to support, it was unlikely that he would behave irresponsibly, either on the voyage or in Adelaide. Although the passage was funded by the government, before an embarkation order could be issued, specific payments of £1 were required for each person, to provision the passengers with bedding and mess utensils.

Once informed of their success in applying for an assisted passage, Thomas and Jenny had to carefully plan the carriage of items that would serve their immediate needs in their new land, as familiar essentials were likely to be unobtainable. While Thomas' tools of trade were essential, Jenny had to consider household items to feed her growing brood. Then, of course, suitable clothing had to be sewn in anticipation of a hot climate, although warm attire would be essential during the long sea voyage. With everything made by hand, even the men's suits, this was a monumental undertaking in terms of both cost and time.

Finally, after nearly two years of planning and preparation, Thomas and Jenny Leane and their eight children boarded the sailing ship *Gloucester* in Plymouth Harbour in late April 1852. *Gloucester*, at 531 tonnes, was exceedingly small for her task of transporting a crew, 57 families, 28 single men and 19 single females.[12] All non-essential items and luggage were stored and inaccessible in the hold, so that the passengers had to be circumspect in choosing items to accompany them. By 1 May, the ship duly loaded, the Master, Captain Marshall, waited for high tide before ordering the crew to hoist the sails. On hearing that command, the passengers rushed to the rails on the top deck for their last glimpse of their native land as it gradually disappeared into the haze. No doubt members of the extended Leane and Parsons families farewelled their children and grandchildren, fighting the realisation that they would probably never see them again.

With the ropes creaking and under the strain of the sails as they began to billow, *Gloucester* eased her way down the River Tamar into the estuary of Plymouth Sound. Passing the headland that enclosed the sound, the ship began to lurch as she hit open water. In spite of his optimism and solid preparations, Thomas must have felt his heart almost bursting with restrained grief as he transferred his gaze to the horizon of dark blue water laced with white caps that lay before him. Some 11,500 nautical miles of horrendous seas had to be weathered before they reached the family's future home in South Australia. *Gloucester*, like most ships heading for Australia, would have followed the traditional route down the east Atlantic Ocean to the Equator, crossing somewhere around St Peter and St Paul Rocks, approximately 20 degrees west. From that point the route ran south through the western South Atlantic, following the natural circulation of winds and currents, passing close to Trinidad before heading for the Cape of Good Hope.[13] Here fresh supplies would have been taken on board before the passengers braced themselves for the journey across the Indian Ocean. Having departed England in May, those aboard would have faced the strongest winds and roughest seas of the roaring forties in winter. It would not have been a pleasant passage and those clad in winter clothing must have reflected on the wisdom of their decision.

The family's quarters for the next three months were anything but salubrious. Families were crowded into steerage class which was only one deck above the hold. Tiered un-planed wooden berths, which resembled large hen coops piled one above the other, were built alongside the ship's hull. A thin mattress lay upon the wooden gridirons in the hope of some small comfort for each passenger. Inside, large communal tables were placed in the centre with benches for seating. Personal storage space was miniscule and privacy was only achieved by draping a blanket or tablecloth from the top bunk. For passengers, particularly females schooled in Victorian modesty, such public exposure among men and strangers to their most intimate functions must have been humiliating. In rough weather, with the hatches battened down, the area was unventilated and lit only by a central lamp. With seasickness, body odour and cooking smells, this main living area must have been an utterly foul environment for such a long voyage.

In good weather the passengers needed no encouragement to exercise on deck. There was pleasure in the interesting birds and fish glimpsed over the railings and relaxed conversation and singing shared with fellow travellers. Nonetheless, emigrants had to work for their passage, and strict rules were established to maintain both harmony and hygiene. A typical daily regime specified that every passenger had to rise by 7.00 am. Breakfast was held between 8.00 am and 9.00 am, with dinner at 1.00 pm and supper at 6.00 pm. In order to accommodate these meal times, fires were to be lit by the passenger cook at 7.00 am and were to remain alight only until 7.00 pm when they were extinguished. In the dark bowels of steerage, only three safety lamps were allowed, with just one remaining alight after 10.00 pm.

Owing to the fear of disease, the maintenance of sound hygiene was enforced with a rigorous cleaning regime. After rising, and before breakfast, the passengers were expected to roll up their bedding and sweep the deck and areas underneath their bunks. After breakfast, sweepers were rostered each day to maintain other areas of the ship. For this task, males above the age of 14, in a ratio of five to every 100 passengers, worked around the ship cleaning ladders, the hospital and dining room, after which they dry-stoned the decking. The women were not exempt from arduous tasks, as Mondays and Tuesdays were designated clothes-washing days. This must have been a tedious and backbreaking occupation in the confined space of steerage, amid the pitching and tossing of the vessel. Bad weather would exacerbate the hardship of this duty and would add to the difficulty of drying newly washed clothes. No washing was permitted to hang between decks though, so clothes lines in steerage would not only limit space, but add to the inevitable body odours and cooking smells that permeated the environment.

Sunday was of course holy and passengers were required to muster at 10.00 am in clean and decent apparel for worship. The Leanes and other devout families must have rejoiced in a formal and collective opportunity to offer prayerful thanks for their present wellbeing and hope for their future. No doubt Thomas, and the older members of his family, participated actively in worship with readings and sermons. After worship, the rest of the day was to be observed as religiously as circumstances would permit. On a passenger ship such as *Gloucester*, order was easily maintained with spirits, gunpowder and gambling, forbidden along with the clear demarcation between passengers and crew areas.

Clearly the migrant ships were no holiday cruise. The days must have been monotonous, the weather unpredictable and the company on some voyages insufferable. However these hardy folk weathered all manner of adversity and privation in the belief that a more prosperous future awaited them at the end of the journey. After 105 days, *Gloucester* arrived in Port Adelaide on 13 August 1852. The ship's Surgeon Superintendent, Dr James Reed, reported that it had been a comparatively safe crossing, with one birth and the loss of only 23 lives.[14]

We will never know Thomas Leane's first thoughts on arriving in South Australia, but there is no doubt they were dominated by enormous relief at the family's safe passage. *Gloucester* was the thirteenth ship carrying emigrants from Britain to South Australia. This meant that, by 1852, some provision had been made to tide the passengers over until they could find work and accommodation for themselves. Fortunately for the Leanes, 'There was a row of cottages built at Port Adelaide for the temporary accommodation of emigrant families. 14 days [were] allowed on ship after reaching port and provisioned. The Colonial Labour Office established in Adelaide opposite the Post Office in King William St [was] open for the hiring of servants and labourers.'[15]

Over the coming fortnight, Thomas Leane assessed his opportunities and bent his back to making a new life in South Australia. With infinite resourcefulness and sheer hard work, he and Jenny continued to raise their family on the firm foundation of the Wesleyan religion, a social conscience and a strong work ethic.

2. HEAVEN AND HARD WORK

B y 1853 the Leane family had established itself in a cottage by the
Torrens River before moving to a farm at Two Wells on the Gawler
River in 1854. Prior to embarkation for South Australia, Thomas and Jenny
had arranged for two blocks of land to be reserved for them by the South
Australia Company at Chain of Ponds near Gawler. As they did not have
the money to improve their land, they leased 62 acres from a Mr. J Sparshott
at Gawler River which they farmed for several years with their children.[16]
Here they were instrumental in establishing The Ebenezer Bible Christian
Church at Angle Vale and in providing the land for the Reverend Samuel
Keen's Mission House.[17] Although government officials replicated the
British class system, hardworking and skilled settlers were usually quick
to gain employment and carve a future for themselves and their families.
Crown surveyors had begun to open up the country and many migrants
longed to acquire land of their own, thereby putting the old class systems
and religious intolerance of Europe behind them. This was particularly true
of the Lutherans and a group of 162 political and economic refugees who
arrived from Germany. A number of these German arrivals, known as the
'Forty Niners', formed a company and acquired section 44 in the Hundred
of Mudla Wirra.[18] This land was located some four miles from Gawler
Town on the Gawler River and there the Forty Niners established a town

to be called Buchfelde. Many were university graduates and founded a lively intellectual community that made substantial and innovative contributions to South Australian agriculture and viticulture over the next four decades. No doubt this progressive and deeply religious community also added to the attraction of the region for the Leane family.

The Wesleyan religion was central to the lives of the Leanes. Deeply rooted in Christianity, the Bible and the church, the practice was simple and unostentatious. In worshipping according to Christ's teachings, its disciples were called to be holy in character and conduct. Its followers were characterised by a loving and willing heart of obedience that served God and mankind gladly and they developed a rich spiritual life based on fidelity, duty and service. The Wesleyans had strong teachings on leadership and drew their inspiration from St Mark's Gospel. It was a leadership that demanded humility and service, espousing the principle that, 'Whoever wants to be great among you must be your servant and whoever wants to be first among you, must be servant of all. For even the Son of Man did not come to be served, but to serve, and to give his life as a ransom for many.'[19] Under the umbrella of the Wesleyan faith were two splinter groups: the Bible Christians and the Primitive Methodists. The Bible Christians had strong roots in Devon and Cornwall and it was to this group that Thomas and Jenny pledged their allegiance. Evangelism, devout piety and the primacy of consecration over all worldly attainments were the hallmarks of the Bible Christian Methodists. Such commitment to service before self was the foundation on which Thomas and Jenny and their descendants established the family name in the new colony.

At Mudla Wirra on 10 March 1855, Jenny Leane gave birth to a daughter, Fanny Eliza Elizabeth Leane. She was the family's ninth living child. With this addition to the family, Thomas continued to work as a boot and shoe maker, while his three eldest boys were engaged in apprenticeships. On 20 August 1857 Edwin Bennett Edgecombe conveyed one acre of Section 7562 in the Hundred of Munno Para to 'Joseph Kenner, Joseph Collins,

Ebenezer Church Angle Vale Road. Angle Vale, South Australia.
Ancestry.com.au. Leanetracker originally shared 6/1/2016 by Catherine Croll

John Patterson, Hugh Stephens, James Clements, Thomas Edmund Keen and Thomas Leane (As Trustees) upon the trusts of the Model Deed of The Bible Christian Society.' This land lay on what is now the corner of Angle Vale Road and Bubner Road, Angle Vale.[20]

In the first years of their existence in South Australia, the Bible Christians expanded more rapidly than any other faith and the region of greatest influence was in Angle Vale. The congregation generally comprised farmers and families on the Gawler Plains and was sustained by the insatiable passion of the Reverend Samuel Keen. In the seven years of his ministry in the region he formed 15 congregations and built over a dozen churches.[21] The ancient history of Israel inspired the names of his churches, and his congregations were drawn not only to his outstanding oratory, but the joy of song that Methodism nurtured in its hymns. In lives that were filled with hard work and few comforts, the church brought colour to otherwise drab lives. Although Bible Christians believed that 'God can enable a woman as well as a man to speak to edification and exhortation and comfort', few female evangelists were present on the preaching circuit.[22] With a growing family, it is probable that Jenny, like most mothers, did her teaching within the home.

Felix was the first to leave the family home in South Australia. Having begun his working life as a mill servant to a Richard Clement in Sheviock, Felix was quick to put his experience to good use, seeking an apprenticeship to a miller in Mount Gambier. Alfred initially leased farming land from William Griffin, supposedly for 21 years, but he relinquished that lease in August 1857 and moved to a lease owned by the estate of the late James Guppy at Keresbrook.[23] He also followed his father's trade as a shoe and boot maker and both father and son became well-known lay preachers in the area. Francis began work with a storekeeper in Adelaide while young Thomas John remained at home to join his brother and father as an apprentice boot and shoe maker. The girls, Emma, Jemima and Caroline, would probably have received their education at the local Wesleyan school, later to be joined by Fanny.

In 1858 the Leanes moved to Old Blumberg (renamed Birdwood after World War I). On 20 October of that year, Thomas Leane purchased a half-acre parcel of land in Section 6578 in the Western Sources of The Torrens Special Survey.[24] From there the family relocated to Philptown, later renamed Chain of Ponds. Here Thomas and Jenny and their extended family took advantage of the land they had preselected and were quick to purchase 'land on the hill, the shop, the post office and two houses'. This consisted of Lot 32, Main Road, Chain of Ponds, adjacent to the Gumeracha-Keresbrook road junction.[25] With their strong family bond and their abiding faith, the Leanes worked hard in those early years of settlement to secure a living and a stake in the future of the new colony for their family. They constructed a small church behind the post office and the whole family actively embraced the church and its local affairs. In travelling the circuit as a lay preacher, Thomas was to establish a fortuitous and abiding friendship with one William Clatworthy.

William Clatworthy, his wife Rebecca and two children, Elizabeth aged four and William Henry aged two, had arrived in South Australia from Cornwall in November 1851 aboard *Lysander.* The family's early years in the colony had been hard. On 11 October 1853, William had purchased Section 2328 in the Hundred of Kondoparinga for £180 but had been forced to sell it on 20 June 1855 for £150.[26] In 1854 his wife had given birth to a son, Alexander. Rebecca never recovered from the birth and had little to comfort her when Alexander died in 1855. The family then relocated to Mt Torrens, where Rebecca passed away on 11 August 1859. The church and the Bible Christian Society were to provide the strength and succour so desperately needed by the grieving family and it was through his religion that William Clatworthy met Thomas Leane. On 25 April 1859 both men were reported as having addressed the congregation at the Mt Torrens Bible Christian School.[27]

The personal and devotional friendship between the two men provided William Clatworthy with the fillip to start afresh when he was introduced to the Leane family. With two dependent children he could not help but be attracted to the gentle piety of Thomas and Jenny's 30-year-old daughter, Emelyn. It did not take either party long to acknowledge their affections and, accordingly, they were married on 31 May 1860 in Adelaide. The bond between the two families was firmly cemented on 19 December of that year when the Clatworthys' first child, Emmeline Francis, was born. Ill fortune continued to dog William Clatworthy however, as Emmeline died in 1865. On a brighter note, the births of Louis Thomas in 1863, Emma May in 1866 and Fanny in 1868 offered cause for combined celebration. The two families were to work harmoniously over the next decade, travelling the local circuit to preach and bring the Wesleyan faith to isolated communities.

On 21 August 1865 William Clatworthy took a seven-year lease on Section 6136 of Parra Wirra. Thomas and his son Alfred later joined the venture to become trustees of the land and begin construction of the Sunninghill Wesleyan Methodist Church, adjacent to the Sunninghill Bridge and vineyard at Millbrook.[28] On 19 May 1867, the Sunninghill Sabbath School celebrated its first anniversary and William Clatworthy delivered the keynote address.[29] In the 1866 Index of Assessments of the Para Wirra District Council, Thomas is named as the owner/occupier of a house and post office on Lot 39, Main Road, Chain of Ponds. The Index also records Thomas John, now married, as the occupier of a house on Lot 32 and Alfred as resident at the Sunninghill House on the Sunninghill Vineyard at Millbrook.[30] It seems somewhat incongruous that members of a temperance-based religion should acquire skills in wine production. However, the first Bible Christian minister in the region, the Reverend Francis Symonds, made his own wine and his family consumed it at mealtimes. Following his example, Alfred was to become a vintner and Thomas was granted a wine licence in 1868.[31]

The nucleus of the family remained at the small settlement of Chain of Ponds until after Thomas' premature death following surgery on 21 December 1875. By this time all of the male members of the family had set out to forge a life of their own in marriage and trade. In 1876 the bonds between the Leanes and the Clatworthys were further strengthened when William's son, William Henry, married Jemima Ann Leane. William Henry was 28 and Jemima 29, and the close interactions of both families through church-related activities provided each with ample time to assess the merits of prospective partners. This couple was also blessed with four children: Ivy Agnes, born in 1878, Hilda Fanny in 1879, Hedley Thomas in 1880 and Olive in 1883. In 1876 the title of Lot 39 was transferred to a mortgagee and sold for unpaid monies to Oliver Philip of Chain of Ponds who was a victualler.[32] Without Thomas' income and support, Jenny and her unmarried daughters, Caroline and Emma, moved to the more civilised domain of Adelaide. There, the three women occupied a number of residences ranging from Angas Street, Chesser Street and finally 'Linna Cottage' in Tucker Street.[33] From these locations all were able to engage in a reflective and Christian life revolving around the Pirie Street Methodist Church.

Caroline, who wrote under the *nom de plume* Agnes Neale, became a prolific writer and one of the earliest female members of the Adelaide Literary Society, which met in the Stow Hall Congregational Church.[34]

Her work was published in a range of Methodist journals and publications, as well as the *Christian Chronicle* and the *South Australian Chronicle* and *Daily Explorer*. After her death a number of small anthologies of her poems were printed, the best known of these, *Shadows and Sunbeams*. In this book her poems explore the majesty of nature, her pride in Adelaide and her commitment to Christ. Her devotional poetry reflected not only her abiding Christian faith, but the Methodist values of temperance, duty and service, to which the whole family subscribed. In one of her obituaries she was lauded as 'The Adelaide Proctor of South Australia by Douglas Slader who incorporated some of her poetry in his book on Australian poetry.'[35]

Caroline was also a passionate public speaker. Accepting the evangelical and feminist mission of the Wesleyan faith, she presented papers entitled 'Women's Work' in 1885 at the Pirie Street Methodist Church. Her central premise, that a woman's true place was in the home, nurturing children and addressing the needs of her husband, is not surprising. However this conviction was diametrically opposed to the emerging feminist beliefs of Catherine Helen Spence, whose egalitarian views rapidly gained momentum and currency over the latter decades of the 19th century. Catherine Helen Spence was a Scottish-born Australian author, teacher, journalist and suffragist. Her insight into the broad-ranging and previously untapped potential of women challenged the traditional image of a woman's place at the hearth. Her advocacy and writings laid the foundations for South Australian women to be among the first in the world to be accorded the political power of the vote. It was against the views of this highly intelligent and articulate public figure that Caroline Leane resolutely promoted traditional family roles. Caroline may have been fighting a groundswell of popular opposition, but her faith and strength of character ensured that she sustained her crusade.

In spite of recurrent ill health, Caroline remained a valued member of The Rose of Adelaide Union Daughter of Temperance Benefit Society, promoting sobriety and a pure life.[36] Her strong Christian faith imbued her speaking and writings with a celebration of the cornucopia of Christ's Kingdom that had been given man and with which the family had been blessed in South Australia. In those hard and difficult years of early settlement, Caroline's writings were to prove her solace during her illness, and a compass and inspiration to those who suffered hardship and isolation in the new colony. Her poor health was to limit Caroline's contribution to the literary life of South Australia as she died prematurely on 22 September 1892 at the age of 43. A large funeral saw not only the attendance of immediate family, but representatives from the many walks of life with which she engaged in spite of constant sickness. She was laid to rest at West Terrace Cemetery on the edge of the city.

Amid Thomas and Jenny's determination to carve a future for their family and Caroline's celebration of the bounty they had shared, Felix—Thomas and Jenny's first born—was quick to shape a life for himself in the new colony. On 17 May 1857 he married Emma Batchelor at Gawler. Emma was a fellow migrant, having been born in Kent in 1839. In a devastating blow to Felix, his young wife died just four years later. Undaunted and imbued with the strong Christian values of his parents, Felix also chose to serve the Lord in the integrity of his profession and his devotion to family and community. Striking out as a young widower and having found his independence as a miller in Mount Gambier, Felix next married Mary Anne Bishop on 5 August 1866. She had arrived in the colony with her family aboard *Sir Thomas Gresham* on 19 March 1854. Felix then cemented his employment at Thomas Williams' Flour Mills at Mount Gambier. Between 1869 and 1894 the couple were to have 10 children: Herbert, born in 1869, Arthur in 1872, Edgar in 1875, Maude in 1877, Mary Violet Jane in 1880, Ivy in 1882, Annie in 1884, Frederick in 1887, Mary Violet Harwood in 1893 and Edith. All lived long lives except Mary Violet Jane, who died aged one. Mount Gambier was a clean and attractive settlement in which Felix and Mary Anne could raise their large family and they lived there for 34 years before Felix's sudden death on 2 April 1896. During the 1870s, Felix had purchased a number of blocks of land at Mount Gambier and Beachport. He had been a highly respected and industrious member of the community who was renowned as a thorough master of his trade and an expert in milling machinery.

Felix's sudden death at his residence shocked the town—particularly his unfortunate wife, who still had a large brood to nurture. There was a considerable outpouring of grief among the many friends Felix had made through his involvement in Temperance Lodges. He had been a past officer of The Grand United Order of Oddfellows and a member of Court Marion A.O.F.[37] His funeral generated a huge assembly, foremost of which were 30 members of the Forester's Court who processed in formal regalia in front of the hearse. Felix was just 63 years of age at the time of his death.

Alfred, the second-born child of Thomas and Jenny, was the first of the children to wed in Australia, marrying Eliza Griffin on 1 January 1854 in St Matthew's Church of England in Kensington. Eliza had been born in Limehouse, London, and had been working as a maid in Tavistock Street, Adelaide, when Alfred once again made her acquaintance. She had also been a passenger on *Gloucester* and the couple had obviously enjoyed each other's company in the confines of the ship. With his marriage, having served his apprenticeship with his father as a boot and shoe maker, Alfred sought to establish himself in business in Adelaide in June 1859. But the enterprise was undermined by Alfred's protracted periods of poor health, and he found himself in the Insolvency Court as a consequence. The court assessed that his books were well maintained and that there was no reason to believe that any possessions or property had been withheld. Alfred was subsequently awarded a First Class Certificate.[38] His problems were compounded when his first-born son, Alfred, who was born in 1854, drowned in 1862 aged seven. But Alfred had no time to grieve given his ongoing responsibilities—he had other children who needed to be fed and clothed. Felix was born in 1857, Frank in 1858, Emily in 1861, Alice in 1863, Frederick in 1865, Jenny in 1868, Minnie in 1870, Florence in 1873 and Annie in 1876. With the failure of his business, Alfred was forced to secure employment as a Sanitary Inspector which he supplemented with gardening jobs. Since arriving in Adelaide in 1852, Alfred had moved between Hackney, Gawler River, Gumeracha, Birdwood, Chain of Ponds, Millbrook, Mt Torrens and Adelaide.[39] His was an extraordinarily tough life.

Later, Alfred and his wife Eliza sustained their family by jointly running a boarding house at 212–214 Rundle Street in Adelaide. However, it was at these premises that the harmony of Alfred's world truly began to crumble. His wife Eliza was accused of being involved in an adulterous relationship with a lodger named Carl Gustav Altmann, an upholsterer. For a man of Alfred's religious standards and moral scrupulousness, this must have been a shattering disclosure. Such was the basis for Alfred's petition for divorce in June 1881 which was heard in the Supreme Court in Adelaide. Alfred, as plaintiff, alleged that, 'during the past twelve months [his wife] had been addicted to drink and was of intemperate habits. And that in January and February, the respondent and co-respondent had committed adultery together.'[40] Eliza denied all allegations. In her defence, she explained that Altmann had taken ill in the boarding house and that she had entered his room to attend to him. However, a witness stated that the defendant was frequently seen entering Altmann's room in a furtive manner after her husband left for work each morning and that the couple were often seen walking together. Alfred declared that he had found his wife in a 'rumpled state' after leaving Altmann's room and that 'one evening after midnight he had found his wife and Altmann together in the back yard.'[41] In relation to the 'allegation of drunkenness, the petitioner said it was a rare thing for the respondent to be soberly sane and that on one occasion, when he remonstrated with her, she replied, it was his damned meanness; he did not mind how much she drank, he only objected to having to pay for it.'[42]

Having confronted his wife and ordered her out of the house, Alfred alleged that she broke several things and took other items to sell. This was verified by members of her own family, lodgers and domestics.

His honour, Mr Justice Boucaut, after consulting with the Chief Justice, determined the application for divorce as a 'nonsuit'. He declared that, while Eliza's behaviour might have been injudicious, the petitioner had not proved that she had been guilty of adultery. He did not believe the allegation that Eliza was 'rarely soberly sane', as it was absurd that, in an establishment with more than 20 boarders and only one servant, she could have attended to the comforts of the lodgers and managed a house if she drank to excess. The petition was dismissed and Alfred was charged with leaving his wife without adequate means of support and ordered to pay 17s 6d per week and costs of £4 6d overall.[43]

It is possible that Eliza drank and perhaps flirted, and Alfred may have been parsimonious with his money, but it is more likely that his commitment to various temperance movements made him an intolerable old bore. Since his arrival in South Australia in 1852, Alfred had been actively engaged with a number of Friendly Societies. Given that the young colony had no social welfare policies or a philanthropic class to care for the infirm, poor or destitute, South Australian Friendly societies evolved to fill very real social needs. They endeavoured to offer the fellowship of like-minded souls, support in times of hardship and loss and, in modern parlance, an avenue for 'networking'. In addition, the social functions, the pageantry and the mystique of such organisations offered a legitimate form of escape for men in a community devoid of colour and diverse social interaction. Given his strong social conscience, Alfred joined the Grand United Lodge soon after its formation, the Good Samaritan Lodge and the Independent Order of Oddfellows by 1878. In all of these institutions he had held high office as Grand Master, Grand Treasurer, Grand Scribe, Grand Secretary and Grand Patriarch. It was through Alfred's initiative with the Patriarchal Branch that he 'thought it desirable to introduce a "Display Branch" called "Patriarch Militant" and to facilitate its organisation in South Australia. At his own cost he communicated with the parent body, and obtained a Commission with the rank of Lieutenant Colonel and special A.D.O. for Australia.'[44]

He was instrumental in establishing the Rebecca Lodges for women as a part of the Grand Lodge which offered membership to women of the industrial classes.[45] His commitment to the lodges and the offices he held within them would have consumed a great deal of his time and perhaps made Eliza feel lonely and isolated within their marriage.

Given Alfred's commitment to Temperance Societies and of course his high standing in the close-knit Adelaide community, it is not surprising that he refused to allow his wife's behaviour to remain unchallenged. His grievances reappeared in 1884 when he lodged a second suit for divorce. The *South Australian Advertiser* reported the proceedings on 25 July 1884:

> Mr G Moore appeared for the petitioner and read the petition which prayed for a dissolution of the marriage between his client and Eliza Leane on the grounds of the latter's adultery with one Carl Gustav Altmann. ... The petition also set out that the respondents committed adultery on various occasions during 1881, 1882, 1883 and 1884. Affidavits read showed that [the] respondent and Altmann had been living together as man and wife in August 1883 and January and February of the following year. It was stated that on one occasion the respondent said, 'My husband could not get a divorce when he tried before. He can get it now, and I hope he will, as I wish to get married again.' His honour said he would report 'the allegations proved'.[46]

Members of the Independent Order of Odd Fellows with Alfred Leane Centre.
State Library of South Australia PRG 280/1/9/30

The widespread publicity of these two divorce proceedings must have been deeply mortifying for Alfred, especially when contrasted with the insouciance of his wife. From Alfred's perspective, the sanctity of the marriage vow had been violated and his firm Christian platform demanded the dissolution of the relationship, albeit in a public forum.

Following the divorce, Alfred subsequently married Mary Jane Harris. In February 1895 the couple welcomed a new daughter, Dorothy. Another daughter, Alfreda, was born on 22 April 1899. Reinvigorated by a new relationship, Alfred's good name and temperate habits saw him become a Justice of the Peace as he settled in Fullarton, South Australia. Surprisingly, the poor health which had compromised his early working life was not apparent in his mature years and he lived until 1 October 1925 when he died aged 90. Following the death of Altmann, Alfred's former wife Eliza died on 25 October 1895, having been cared for in deteriorating health by her son Frank who was estranged from his father. Family history suggests that she died an alcoholic, but perhaps after raising 10 children and running a boarding house for many years, sheer misery and exhaustion contributed to her death. Frank's care and compassion for his mother prevented a reconciliation between father and son for many years.[47]

Thomas and Jenny's third son, Francis, was the second to marry. He married Rebecca Weeks Hosking on 21 July 1863 in Athelstone, South Australia. There were no children from this marriage. Francis, like his brother Alfred, was committed to Temperance Societies and also held high office with the Grand Lodge of South Australia. His social and religious conscience saw his involvement in the Board of St Margaret's Convalescent Hospital for many years. In the 1885 Sands MacDougal inventory he is listed as a storekeeper of Beulah Road, Norwood.

Clearly three of the sons of Thomas and Jenny Leane carried the tenets of their faith into their adult and community life. They embraced a commitment to serve and through this service augmented their social status. Similarly, Caroline's ardour and intelligence established her as a leading light in Adelaide. All achieved a standing in South Australia that would most likely have been unattainable in Great Britain. The promise of the new land was blended with the values of the old. All family members embraced new callings, but for old purposes.

3. THOMAS JOHN LEANE
AND FAMILY

The youngest of Thomas and Jenny's sons, Thomas John Leane, married Alice Ann Short in June 1865. Alice had arrived in Adelaide, South Australia on the *Samuel Boddington* with her sister Ann, her father William and her stepmother Susannah in 1851. Although a shoemaker by trade, William Short, who was also a committed Wesleyan, was to make a name for himself in the new colony as an evangelical lay preacher. The family settled in Nailsworth and William opened the first Methodist church in the district in his own house in California Street. He became a driving force in the establishment of the Enfield Methodist Church, the first in the area. Born in Quethiock, Cornwall, in 1819, William lived in Adelaide until 1912, dying at the age of 92. He conducted his last service when over 90 years of age. Of that service the Rev. T. B. Angwin wrote,

> His farewell service at Enfield ere he retired from the pulpit was historical; the age of the preacher, his long period of service, his clearness of mind and fervour of soul, all tended to make it such. He seemed to possess not so much the beauty of age as the freshness of youth. Attitude, manner and force of delivery all indicated youth rather than age. Who; that was permitted to be present can ever forget the service? After that he passed into retirement, sitting beside 'the silent sea waiting the muffled oar', assured that no harm could come from God to him.

This lengthy and notable obituary was published in the *Australian Christian Commonwealth* which, among other comments concluded that 'He was a man of God—a stalwart among the spiritual minded. Had he in early life entered the ministry he would have taken his place in the front rank. As it was he took a foremost position as preacher, counsellor and pastor. His services as local preacher, the influence of his life and character, have left their mark upon the district of Nailsworth and the City of Adelaide.'[48]

Alice, like many of the Leanes, was also born in Quethiock and her family clearly had strong Wesleyan and Cornish connections. With their Nonconformist background, Thomas John and Alice were an ideal match and were married at the Pirie Street Methodist Church in Adelaide in June 1865. This church became the centre of their own family worship and they soon occupied a family pew. The couple's strong Nonconformist beliefs were the foundation of their relationship and it was on this rock that they nurtured and imbued their children with faith, a sense of duty and strong moral principles. Thomas John and Alice's marriage was to produce 11 children, the men of whom would later form the nucleus of Australia's most famous military family.

The Family Methodist Chuch on Pirie Street.
State Library of South Australia PRG-631-2-1292

Initially, the young couple established themselves in the small settlement of Chain of Ponds, where Thomas's father worked and his mother ran the post office. The town was approximately 30 kilometres from Adelaide, its site initially described as a creek which ran from beyond Kersbrook to the confluence of the River Torrens in the Adelaide Hills. The aptly named Chain of Ponds area was dotted with small ponds that had no visible connection above the ground and which never dried up. Thus settled, Thomas John and Alice's first child, Rosa Alice Leane, arrived on 16 April 1866, but died within the year. Ill fortune was to follow the Leane family into 1867 when Thomas and Jenny's last-born child and Thomas John's youngest sister, Fanny Eliza, died aged 12 on 6 August. Her death must have been a prolonged and traumatic passing, as her death certificate describes the cause of death as an 'ulcerous throat'.[49]

It would seem that Chain of Ponds was neither salubrious nor economically viable for Thomas John and Alice as, by the time their second child, son Edwin Thomas Leane, was born on 25 August 1867, the couple had re-established themselves and settled at 2 Rose Street, Prospect, in Adelaide, which remained the family home for the rest of their lives. Although two of their family were to be born in Mt Gambier, where they relocated from 1870 to 1875, it was in this humble stone cottage in Prospect that Thomas John and Alice were to nurture and raise all of their children. These were: Ernest Albert born in 1869, Allan William born in 1872, Ethel Alice born in 1874, Sidney Rowland born and died in 1877, Raymond Lionel born in 1878, Hilda Violet born in 1881, Norman Short born in 1884, Nellie born and died in 1888, and finally Benjamin Bennett born in 1889. These children amounted to 11 births in 23 years for Alice Leane, with six sons and two daughters surviving. It was indeed a large brood to raise in a small home and life could have descended into chaos but for disciplined parenting and constant reference to the pathways directed by the church.

During the years in which Thomas John and Alice raised their children, entertainment revolved around the family and the church community.

Leane Family Home. 2 Rose Street Prospect.

Sunday was wholly devoted to worship and strict Wesleyans would not even taint the sanctity of the day with an exchange of money. Administration of the church and its affairs would be conducted by the menfolk during weekly meetings, while various women's groups worked to raise money to further the cause of Christian education and worship. Social life revolved around church gatherings, picnics, presentation nights and talks by evangelical lay preachers. The other essential part of the fabric of social life was, of course, the extended family—uncles, aunts and numerous cousins. For the Leanes, this remained a pivotal part of their life, as the family had grown markedly since those tentative days of the early settlement.

Even these family gatherings reinforced their religious principles as all members of the family were regular worshippers. The children of Thomas John and Alice would have spent a great deal of time listening to and learning from their maternal grandfather, whose preaching had established his fame and virtue around Adelaide. They would also have come into regular contact with their aunt Jemima and cousin Hedley Thomas Clatworthy.

Like her sister Caroline, Jemima was an accomplished devotional writer and was published under the *nom de plume* Coral J. Thwyat. Her son Hedley, born in 1880, was roughly in the same age bracket as the sons of Thomas John and Alice. The values instilled in Hedley during his childhood inspired him to promote God's love and become a minister. He was to marry Nellie May Allanson in April 1912. Like the Leanes, she too had been blessed with god-fearing parents. Her father had worked assiduously for the Methodist cause and for years had been superintendent of the local Sunday School. As a minister's wife, Nellie was actively engaged as a Sunday School teacher, Christian Endeavour Leader, organist and chorister. The *Australian Christian Commonwealth* wrote a fulsome obituary on her premature death in 1923 at the age of only 33. 'Of her it may be said that she was a loyal friend, a devoted wife and an untiring worker. It is a life of Christian service cut off early.'[50]

If we consider the religious milieu in which Thomas John and Alice's family grew up, it is impossible to overestimate the influence of the church in shaping the children's views and values. However, for each of the boys, as one of six in the family, there were other forces at play too. Unlike their cousin Hedley, who only had sisters for siblings, the Leane boys always had conspirators to join in typical boys' games. Edwin, as the eldest, assumed the mantle of responsibility for and leadership over his brothers. Like so many first-born sons he lived with the high expectations of his parents, and Edwin seemed to deliver much promise during his early education at the North Adelaide Public School in Tynte Street. The modern, bluestone school was established in 1877 and is one of the oldest schools in South Australia. The school's motto, '*esse quam videri*'—'to be, rather than be seen'—promotes values of service and selflessness and, in classes of some 50 pupils, there were few opportunities to be selfish. In those days, teaching was not considered a worthy career path, with pupil teacher cadetships, rigid discipline and inspectors enforcing an examination-based curriculum. Discipline was rigid and physically enforced. For boys, the curriculum would have consisted of reading, spelling, arithmetic, English, history, poetry and drill.[51]

Tynte St Public School C1880.
State Library of South Australia B-10677

Edwin must have responded to this regime with gusto, for his parents later enrolled him in Whinham College, which is now North Adelaide Grammar School. The school was founded by John Whinham in 1854 with the aim of developing moral, physical and mental training—in that order. It also prepared students for university and civil service examinations. On leaving school, Edwin became a bookkeeper before moving into insurance, although he appears to have had little love for the tedium of sedentary office work. In his leisure time he followed the example of his cousin, Frederick Thomas Leane, and enlisted in the Volunteer Forces.

Frederick Thomas, son of Alfred and Eliza Leane, was born in 1865 at Chain of Ponds. He was quick to enlist to fight in the Boer War as No 75 in the First South Australian Mounted Rifles. He embarked on *Medic* for South Africa on 2 November 1899 and disembarked at Cape Town on 25 November 1899. In correspondence to a Mr J.J. Ogilvy of Port Pirie, Trooper Leane appears to be revelling in the conflict and has no pricking of conscience in recounting how 'we have driven the Boers back to within two miles of our old position, taken several of their guns and killed from 800 to 1000 of them while our loss was eight killed.'[52] Of particular interest is Frederick's pride in the 4th Mounted Infantry Brigade 'which the Tommies call the "Fighting Fourth".' He delighted in boasting of the apparent superiority of the South Australian troopers over their British counterparts. According to Frederick, such superiority extended from the scouting and horse-riding skills of his comrades, to their adaptability and resourcefulness in preparing an edible meal:

> We have been trying for some weeks to teach Tommy Atkins Esquire, how to live on a pound of flour a day, and as he has never been initiated into the mysteries of devil-among-the-coals, flapjacks or donuts, and has never indulged in the luxury of damper, the results are somewhat disappointing, and while we are living in luxury on meat and flour, poor Tommy is lining his innards with what he calls porridge, but what is nothing else but bill-stickers paste and all the time he is cursing the Army Service Corps as only Tommy can curse. The Pirie boys are all pretty well ... while I have a touch of rheumatics.[53]

Inspired by correspondence such as this, those of an adventurous spirit were soon intrigued by the world and events beyond the small settlement of Adelaide. Long before anyone could have imagined that the Empire would call on Australian troops to support it in a global conflict, Australian soldiers had established themselves as a unique fighting force in the minds of those who watched on from home. Imbued with initiative and the resilience to 'rough it', those early units of mounted bushmen displayed a degree of expertise and exhibited enormous courage and dash, garnering both praise and pride.

Rheumatic fever saw Trooper Leane invalided home in September 1900. He then spent five months recuperating before departing for South Africa again on the troopship *Ormazaon* on 9 February 1901. During his convalescence, it is highly likely that Frederick had ample time to share his exploits with his immediate and extended family who no doubt hung on every word. His second period of service saw Frederick promoted to Regimental Sergeant Major and enjoy more action before returning to Port Pirie on the troopship *Manchester Merchant* on 27 April 1902.

Although none of Edwin's correspondence from this period appears to have survived, it is reasonable to assume that he would have shared his cousin's sentiments. It was grist to his mill. From his days at Whinham College, Edwin too was imbued with a similar love of order and a sense of adventure. Accordingly, he had joined the South Australian Garrison Artillery as a gunner in 1888 and transferred to the 3rd South Australian Regiment in 1890, reaching the rank of captain.

On 15 June 1891 Edwin married Catherine Mary Walker Machin at St Paul's Church in Adelaide. She had been born in Adelaide in 1865 to English immigrants James Fox Machin and his wife Ellen Howard. Edwin and Katie, as she became known, were to have eight children, seven of whom were born in Adelaide: Doris Katie born in 1892, Allan Edwin born in 1894, Jack Donovan born in 1895 and died in 1896, Geoffrey Paul born in 1897, Reuben Ernest born in 1898, and twins Marjorie and Maxwell born in 1899. Their eighth child, daughter Hatherley Heather, was born on 20 January 1904 in Pretoria, South Africa. But more of that later.

Given the physical and financial commitment of a wife and seven children it is difficult for a modern reader to understand how both Edwin and his wife agreed to his decision to volunteer for service in the Boer War. Perhaps he was inspired by his cousin Frederick Thomas Leane who was so quick to enlist. Perhaps he was seduced by the fact that this was the first South Australian contingent which would receive full imperial pay. It is also not impossible to imagine that responsibility for such a large family proved uninspiring, compared to the excitement of his service with the Volunteer Forces. Such experience was suddenly valuable and, having volunteered his services, Edwin was welcomed as a lieutenant with the 4th South Australian Contingent of Imperial Bushmen. Formal farewells such as that of the 4th Contingent at the Thebarton Town Hall on Saturday 28 April 1900 explain the social milieu of the time and the values that were endorsed. In addressing the large gathering, the Mayor declared that 'the Colonial troops had given to the world the best possible demonstration of solidarity to the Empire—

the English blood which coursed through their veins had not deteriorated since the days when their forefathers left the dear old motherland over sixty years ago.'[54] The contingent comprised 12 officers, 222 other ranks and 240 horses and left Port Adelaide on 1 May 1900 aboard *Manhattan*.[55]

Lieutenant Edwin Leane served in the Cape Colony from June 1900 to June 1901. His deployment saw him engaged in the Charge of Bakerkop, the skirmish at Stinkhoutboon, in which three men were killed, the Battle of Rhenosterkop and the advance on Pietersburg and into East Transvaal. His service and character under fire were clearly exemplary as he was Mentioned in Despatches three times by Lord Roberts and awarded the Queen's South Africa Medal with three clasps.

As the Boer War ground to a halt, Lieutenant Leane seemed reluctant to return to a less exhilarating existence in Australia. He was offered and accepted a position with the Imperial Military Railways, although the appointment was viewed with suspicion in some circles in Adelaide. News of this disquiet reached Lieutenant Leane, prompting him to pen a letter to the *Advertiser* to clarify any misconceptions. In his missive he stated,

> Letters received from Adelaide today make it appear ... that I have left my corps for the purpose of accepting civil employment, and I shall deem it a favour if you will allow me the opportunity of contradicting this ... I was transferred at my own request to the Imperial Military Railways, having been offered a responsible appointment, which promised and has proved a sphere of greater activity and usefulness; but I still remain a member of the contingent, and shall remain so until it is disbanded. I draw no pay from the I.M.R., but am paid by Colonel Rowell, in ordinary course. I am liable to retransfer at any time on the order of Colonel Rowell, but I may say that this is not likely to happen, as I have accepted the appointment of adjutant of the I.M.R Volunteer Corps. My appointment is distinctly a military one and I retain my rank and shall do so even after the bushmen are disbanded, and I desire to make these facts known to you, so that no charge of surrendering my commission for the sake of civil employment may be entertained by you. Under no other circumstances than the above would I have parted with the command of my squadron and I trust this explanation will satisfy

you that I have not in any way failed in my duty to the colony which
honoured me by sending me out here, and shall ever bear in grateful
remembrance those who have afforded me a chance to have some
active service.[56]

While the letter appears both diplomatic and patriotic, it is arguably
self-justifying and a tad contradictory. It also reflects Edwin's prickly
defensiveness and smacks of an inability to cope with personal criticism.
This arrogance and innate sense of superiority would become the hallmarks
of Edwin's military career and also sow the seeds of his fall from grace.

Clearly Edwin Thomas Leane had enjoyed his time in South Africa and
was in no hurry to return home. According to family rumour, his wife Katie
was also concerned about his delay in returning to Adelaide—so much so that
she bundled up all of her children and, with her sister, boarded a ship, arriving
unannounced at Edwin's residence in South Africa.[57] Katie was evidently of a
similarly forthright bent to Edwin. She was an assertive and decisive partner
who was disinclined to take a back seat. Like Edwin, she regarded whites
as superior to coloured peoples and appears to have considered their lives
of lesser value. On one occasion in South Africa, Edwin was confronted at
his home by a group of angry natives. Perhaps frightened but nonetheless
undaunted, Katie burst out of the house brandishing Edwin's service
revolver exclaiming, 'Shall I shoot them Ted?' His response was equally
urgent. 'Put the bloody gun away Katie or you'll kill us all!'[58] This was strong
language from an avowedly conservative Methodist and is some testament
to the heat of the confrontation. In spite of such trials, Edwin continued to
work with the Imperial Military Railways until 1904. Then, with the birth
of his daughter Hatherley on 20 January 1904, the whole family returned to
Australia on *Wilcannia*, arriving in Adelaide on 8 April.

On his return to Australia, Edwin was unsettled and either unable or
reluctant to re-engage with life in the very small Adelaide circle. He moved
to Melbourne and then accepted a position as Secretary to the Colonial
and Mutual Life Society in Sydney in 1906. This peripatetic lifestyle is

suggestive of an aspirational man dissatisfied with the tedium and the routine of a mundane existence. However, in this larger role, he developed a full knowledge of ordinary, industrial and accident branches of the insurance business and acquired a high level of managerial skill. Yet even this life was not sufficiently fulfilling and, although the family had relocated to Burwood in NSW, Edwin continued his involvement with the military through the Volunteer Forces. The regular sight of their father in military regalia and the esteem in which he was held, were to have a profound effect on his sons. Their father epitomised the honour and duty of faithful military service and they viewed him with both reverence and awe.

Edwin's love of all things military understandably proved a potent example to his impressionable younger brothers. His younger brother, Allan William, also joined him in the 4th Contingent of Imperial Bushmen and served with distinction. Raymond Lionel had tried to enlist for the Boer War but was rejected on medical grounds. The rejection did not sit well on his shoulders. All family members, brothers and sons, were inspired by Edwin's example and admired the trappings of his uniform and the honour accorded to military success. Edwin's eager participation in the Boer War and the plaudits and awards he obtained, branded military life as a glamorous and highly prized experience. As his siblings and children matured and began to shape their own lives, the threat of global war and the thrall of action grasped each one of them. By 1914, the sons and grandsons of Thomas John and Alice Leane could hardly wait to enlist.

The Fighting Leanes of Prospect.
Back Row, Benjamin, Raymond, Ernest.
Seated, Edwin and Allan.
Australian War Memorial, P02136.001

4. THE SWORD
AND THE CROSS

Every one of Thomas John and Alice Leane's sons enlisted immediately on the outset of the First World War. All of them had been enthusiastic participants in Lord Kitchener's Universal Training Scheme, a system of compulsory military training introduced in 1911. As such, they had a firm grasp of military principles, army routines and discipline. They were not uneducated and illiterate yokels who were tempted from remote settlements with the promise of adventure. They were not the larrikins of Charles Bean's vision, yet their collective contribution to the conflict earned Bean's praise and the sobriquet that 'the Fighting Leanes of Prospect were the most famous family of soldiers in Australian history.' All but Norman Short Leane were accepted for overseas service. In 1915 Edwin was aged 47, while Ernest Albert and Allan William were 45 and 42 respectively. Raymond Lionel was 36, and the youngest, Benjamin Bennett, was a mere 25 years of age. All were fathers of substantial families and, with the exception of Benjamin, all were realistically too old for active service. Nonetheless, their example encouraged their sons to enlist. Edwin's sons, Allan William, Geoffrey Paul and Reuben Ernest, enlisted in the AIF, while his fourth son, Maxwell, enlisted in the Royal Australian Navy. Ernest Albert's sons, Arnold Harry and William Ernest, of similar ages to their cousins, were also quick to enlist.

This willingness to volunteer their services at the potential cost of their lives to defend a nation that their family had left to pursue religious and social freedom poses fundamental questions. What would encourage middle-aged men to offer not only their own lives, but those of their young sons, to engage in a war on the other side of the globe? Patriotism? Hubris perhaps? Ironically, much of their impetus was derived from their religious faith, which dictated the fundamental tenets of their upbringing. The foundations of most global religions honour the sanctity of human life. Christianity as practised by the Wesleyan/ Methodists was no different. Nonetheless, Christians have managed to justify going to war since the Crusades, in spite of the moral and religious questions raised by active service. Still the question remains. How did an avowedly Christian family such as the Leanes reconcile the sixth commandment with a decision to enlist? Such participation needed strong justification and, in examining the attitudes of the Methodist Church leading up to and during the First World War, it is not difficult to find. At an official level there was a consistent effort to add religious reason to patriotism and the grounds for supporting war. The Conference of Ministers and Lay Representatives which assembled in 1915 issued a series of fundamental principles:

- Its steadfast loyalty to the throne and the person of His Majesty the King.
- Its profound conviction of the righteousness of the cause for which the Empire has sprung to arms, and its unbounded faith that the conflict will issue in the triumph of freedom and truth over an organised system of oppression.
- Its gratification at the loyal response in manhood and in the treasure which the Commonwealth is making to the call of the Empire and its confidence that Australia's sons will prove worthy of the best traditions of the race from which they sprang.[59]

The Methodist Church sought its justification in terms of good and evil and the duty of the strong to help the weak. Initially, the propaganda surrounding Germany's invasion of 'poor little Belgium' provided the moral catalyst for the church to mount its justification. In a sermon delivered just after the war began, the Rev. W.T. Shapely declared that "The strong must help the weak [which is] a Christian law which applies to nations as much as individuals. At this time, we Britishers must needs maintain the inviolability of smaller nations which have a moral right to their own independence and their self respect.'[60]

Further moral justification that consolidated the belief in German perfidy was supported by a series of widely documented outrages that included the rape of Belgian women, the execution of nurse Edith Cavell in October 1915 and the sinking of the passenger liner *Lusitania*, with its civilian cargo of women and children, in May 1915. Added to this list of atrocities was the use of poison gas in May 1915 and the bombing of the east coast of England including civilian targets. A lengthy article by Arthur T. Guttery, published in the *Australian Christian Commonwealth*, argued that the Kaiser was not only evil, but mad:

> Is the Kaiser mad? Has Europe been set aflame by a lunatic? Is civilisation plunged into chaos by a modern Caligula? Has our peace been shattered by armed millions who obey a maniac? ... The suspicion of insanity is well founded ... The whisper has been heard in Germany for years, and the world stands aghast at crimes that seem impossible, unless they are the result of a perverted will and deranged mind. ... The heredity of the house of Hohenzollern makes madness easy. Professor Quidde has drawn an impressive parallel between the Kaiser and Caligula the degenerate. There are pathological facts that indicate a similarity between the German Emperor and the tragic Louis of Bavaria; and Dr. Sarolea, in his masterly analysis, shows how distinct are the symptoms of mania in the Prussian King.[61]

All of these points were manifestations of a kingdom of evil that had to be overthrown. Who better to make the necessary sacrifice than Christians, whose saviour, Jesus Christ, had made the ultimate sacrifice for man? Fiercely evangelical preachers such as Henry Howard, who was at the height of his legendary reign at the Pirie Street Methodist Church, and the Reverend Octavius Lake, a trenchant speaker and writer, inspired congregations with their rhetoric. Furthermore, their views and values were disseminated weekly to over 2500 South Australian homes in the *Australian Christian Commonwealth*. This publication had been founded in 1901, its title reflecting not only the Federation of the Australian Commonwealth but also the Methodist Union, which saw the amalgamation of the Wesleyan Primitive Methodists and the Bible Christian Church. A string of Methodist ministers edited the newspaper, beginning with founding editor Joseph Berry. Sermons, snippets and general news of individual churches and circuits (districts) as well as events at church schools and obituaries filled the pages of the magazine. It usually ran to some 16 pages, cost just 1d per week and was published for the church by Hussey and Gillingham.[62]

To encourage recruitment, the Reverend Octavius Lake wrote in the magazine in 1915 that he wished to:

> Direct the attention of our Ministers and the officers of our Church to the recruiting campaign by the Government in the Town Hall. There is a call to heed throughout the Empire to men who are fit to go forth as soldiers in our nation's defence and in defence of small nations like Belgium and Serbia. The time is critical and one in which the Church should lend assistance to the State. Our Master is the Prince of Peace, but he is righteous in all his ways. His kingdom is not meat and drink, not a materialistic one, but righteousness, peace and joy in the Holy Ghost. When righteousness is established, peace and joy will appear and abide.
>
> This matter is urgent beyond words and with our Church throughout the Empire we must take our part in dealing with it. We are up against a mighty combination of force and fraud, of organised tyranny and cruelty, that aims particularly at the humiliation of Great Britain. Methodists are loyal with more than wordy loyalty, and I have no manner of doubt this latest appeal of their King and country will have their prayerful consideration.[63]

With such a focus, Methodism developed into the purest form of evangelical or reformist faith in South Australia. The war became a struggle of cosmic proportions in which history would be affected by the outcome. 'This war is one of the most tremendous things in the history of the world. We believe it will tell on the future history of the world as no event has been told since the birth of Jesus Christ.'[64]

Inspirational patriotic poetry was also published in the *Australian Christian Commonwealth*. In it the Germans were identified as Huns, barbarians, brutes, hordes and swine, against whom the Australians upheld righteous moral principles. Such graphic rhyming couplets may have been an affront to the sensibilities of the time, but the simplicity of the dichotomy could not fail to be understood. This material would have been read, shared and perhaps recited around fireplaces and kitchen tables by families keen to uphold the church's fight against Satan:

OVER THE TOP

Over the top where the bullets fly,
Out of the trench to kill or die:
Freed are their hearts of a passing fear
Their arms are strong and their brains are clear.

Brooding of home and loved ones there,
Their 'Merrie England' caped with care,
Their savage foes and shameful deeds
That match so well with their inhuman creeds.

They thought of the raids on 'London Town,'
The seas where women and children drown
The hospitals bombed, the hospital ship,
Crushed in the merciless German grip.

The thought of women by Huns outraged,
Of captured mate by those monsters caged.
The insulted soldiers in their sties
Who starved and maltreated, die like flies.

A righteous wrath our lads inspired,
As the bombs they threw or their rifles fired;
And a flock of German souls that night
From those muddy trenches took their flight.

'Tis a fearful road, but the only way
You can meet the hordes who rob and slay,
What would you call the craven who can
Meekly submit? He is not a man!

Over the top, where the death birds fly,
Out of the trench to win or die;
Swept from their souls is the passing fear;
Their cause is right and their brains are clear.[65]

As the war years dragged on and the mounting casualty lists were published daily, the church was forced to address the natural outpourings of grief. Ministers of religion were often the first to break the news to distraught relatives, and many did so employing terms such as 'duty' and 'sacrifice' which held cold comfort for families who had often suffered multiple losses. Ministers knew that the fallen of their parishes had to be honoured and so various committees were established to raise funds for Honour Rolls to be erected in their churches. While each provided an enduring earthly memorial, ministers such as the Reverend Howard lauded a higher purpose and sought to sanctify the soldiers who lost their lives. This was very much the case in his sermon of 8 October 1915 when he spoke of the loss of No. 965 Private Percy William Venning who had died of wounds at Gallipoli that year. A 20-year-old farm labourer who had enlisted in the 10th Battalion in September 1914, he was one of the first casualties from the tiny South Australian town of Pinnaroo. Such exultant rhetoric would have little currency in the 21st century, but for the bereaved in that small church, the Reverend Howard may have succeeded in transforming the mindless loss of their son's life into ennobling sacrifice:

> The most dull and commonplace life by such sacrifice became transfigured. In this world it was made to rank with the true aristocracy of the race, while in the next it was classed with those comrades of the Lamb, who followed Him witherso ever He went. Their voluntary service and sacrifice in the cause of the world's freedom included them all among the elect of God. Every man who battled for the true and just and sought to make the world a better and brighter place was fighting the battle of God, and to all such would be extended, the hand that was pierced and the welcoming words, "Come ye blessed of my Father."[66]

The churches, in particular the Methodists, ably supported the propaganda that the politicians espoused. In response to a welcome luncheon by the Lord Mayor of London while visiting England, Prime Minister Billy Hughes' reply bore echoes of the transfigurative nature of combat sacrifice for both the soldier and the victorious nations. Replete with obsequious jingoism, he declared:

You are the guardians of the citadel. It is good that we should justly determine never to lay down our arms, whatever the sacrifices may be, until we emerge from the struggle triumphantly. The war has saved us from moral and physical decay. We were in danger of losing our greatness and of becoming flabby. We were almost beginning to lose the ancient qualities of our forefathers. But the war has been the sun that has dried up the mists of suspicion with which class regarded class and the war has enabled us to find ourselves. The overseas dominions have been enabled to know England and England to know her dominions. The Empire before the war was merely a name which found no echo in our hearts, but which now has an abiding place in our souls. The war which threatened our destruction has been the means of our salvation.[67]

In spite of horrendous casualties and the grief that was gradually consuming one in five Australian families, the Methodist Church continued its crusade to sustain support for the cause. The church was an avid supporter of conscription and directed its vitriol against the Catholics. Their primate, Archbishop Daniel Mannix, was to become the scapegoat for the bill's defeat in the two referenda. Archbishop Mannix only publicly addressed the issue twice, but he argued that the government was already doing enough to help the British. Anti-British sentiment was already rife among the Catholic population as a consequence of the ruthless suppression of the 1916 Easter Rebellion by the Crown. Against this opposition, the Methodists remained fast. Women's groups and committees were constantly entreated to raise money or provide comforts for the troops, thus maintaining the fire in the hearts of congregations. The German people became the focus of vilification in order to justify the cause and hold firm the faith. Anti-German sentiment filtered throughout the community, and towns and families with Germanic names were forced to Anglicise those names. The condemnation articulated in the *Australian Christian Commonwealth* would have added fuel to this fire:

The successful resistance of the brute force of the Kaiser's legions is not all that is at stake. In their triumph would be a victory that would put back immeasurably the moral progress of the world. In the German initiation of this campaign and in their entire conduct of it, all moral restraints and humane considerations have been set aside. Hunnish and Hellish have become interchangeable terms.[68]

As the war ground to a halt in November 1918 and people began to count the cost, the *Australian Christian Commonwealth* continued to view the conflict in simplistic black and white terms:

> It must be remembered, that in all that is wasteful and wicked and cruel and irreparably destructive in this war against civilisation, the German people were solid in their support of their Emperor and his lords and on the German people the execration of the rest of the world should rest. Germany stands out before the world as a nation of robbers, of robbers under arms, and in carrying out their burglarious purposes they have shrunk from no possible villainy and enormity. The remembrance on broken men will bring us the thought of our more than 50 000 young Australians sacrificed on the altar of German ambition will make for this generation at least the name German to be abhorred.[69]

Having been deeply entrenched in militant beliefs for the duration of the war, the Methodist Church had to reconsider its role in post-war society. It maintained its high-blown rhetoric, maintaining that an evil regime had been dethroned. It was up to the Lord now to comfort His people and look to the future. As the *Australian Christian Commonwealth* asserted: 'The Church built on the foundation of the apostles and prophets with Jesus Christ himself being the chief corner stone, feels that she has come to the birth of a new age, that there is opening before her the doors of unparalleled opportunity, and the password among all of the evangelical sects and denominations is:

'Let us go up at once and possess the land, for we are well able.'[70]

Adelaide is not called the 'City of Churches' for nothing. Multitudes of faiths were drawn to the new colony when it was established. Devoid of convicts, it offered earnest, hard-working, family-oriented citizens the opportunity to live in a community that had a Christian framework as its spine. There were Anglicans, Roman Catholics, Lutherans and Protestants of all persuasions. Being largely of British extraction, all were quick to respond to a call to the colours. All could see that defeat by Germany would render them a Germanic colony under the yoke of a militaristic Emperor.

For the Wesleyans/Methodists who had travelled so far to practise their reformist faith, such consequences would have amounted to a loss of all that they had struggled for and which they held dear. Ironically, fearing a militaristic power, the Methodists chose to fight fire with fire. They employed words as their own form of inflammatory warfare and, initially, they appear to have succeeded. In 1914, full membership of the Methodist Church was 20,765. It rose 10% over the following five years to reach 22,926 in 1919.[71] However, in the men returning, shell shocked and irreparably damaged from the catastrophic conflict that had consumed the best years of their youth, faith had taken a battering. With post-war austerity and then the Great Depression, many returned servicemen dropped out of church life. The promise of 'a future of transcendent greatness and peace' proved elusive for so many returned servicemen.[72] Religion and patriotism had left them ill equipped to cope with the harsh economic challenges they would face in the 1920s and 30s.

5. COLONEL EDWIN THOMAS LEANE

I n order to evaluate the validity of Bean's claim, it is essential to examine the contributions of each of the Leanes in terms of their service. Certainly the conservative Methodist sons of Thomas and Alice did not fit the national stereotype of the Anzac. While in June 1915 the enlistment requirements applied to men between the ages of 19 and 38, it is obvious that three of the Leane sons did not fall within these parameters. However, with a dearth of military experience, the essentially youthful army demanded seasoned and intelligent leaders and the older Leanes certainly fitted that requirement. At the outbreak of hostilities in Europe, Lieutenant Edwin Leane was in Western Australia where he enlisted in the AIF on 14 August 1914. He was immediately promoted to captain in command of H Company of the 12th Battalion. When G and H companies were combined, he became second in command to Captain Joe Lalor. Given that he had experienced the carnage of war in South Africa, it is difficult to understand what compelled a man of his years to enlist and endure further hardship and absence from his family. His commitment to the Empire and the greater good of the Empire's territory sounds and no doubt sat well, but the camaraderie of the army obviously had a stronger pull than family. Yet, as Edwin's battalion embarked at Fremantle aboard HMAT A7 *Medic* on 2 November 1914, his diary records his loving thoughts of his family:

> The cabins are very small, but Annear (with whom I share a cabin) and myself have got about as good a cabin as there is on the ship. Fixed up cabin as comfortably as possible with shelf for military books and put up photos of all at home—miss them all very much, and am afraid I come into the cabin more often than necessary, just to have a look at them. Am keeping in touch with the difference in time so that I can concentrate my thoughts on the dear ones at home as near as I can to 12 noon Sydney time.[73]

Nonetheless such nostalgia was overtaken the next day as he described the magnificent spectacle of the fleet steaming in convoy:

> 38 magnificent liners, some up to 15 000 tons filled with Australian troops going to fight for the Empire ... As they came up it looked as if there were hundreds of them and they all fell into their places—a big 4 funnelled British Warship has now taken the lead. We are steaming in three columns of vessels at about a half a mile between the columns and about a quarter of a mile between the vessels in the same line. It is a most wonderful spectacle to stand on the bridge deck and see the surface of the ocean covered with ships, and it is a remarkable feeling to think that we are all going to war. It is good to be one of such a crowd, even if we never get a chance to make history and whatever the result may be, so far as I am concerned, I feel that I have done something to make those who love me, proud to give me up in such a cause. Even if I pass out, although they will grieve for me sorely I know they can but be glad that one of their very own died in such a great moment in the history of the world.[74]

Edwin's deep-seated need to achieve honour and esteem is consistent with the high expectations he felt were placed on him as the eldest of Thomas John and Alice's sons. Unconsciously, these same expectations flowed to his own sons. In supporting and encouraging their enlistment, like Abraham, it seems he too was prepared to offer his sons as a sacrifice.

On his arrival in Egypt, Edwin's excitement and enthusiasm were soon tempered. Ego, rather than common sense had driven his enlistment. In spite of his experience and obvious leadership qualities, at 47 years of age, the rigours of military training proved totally beyond Captain Edwin Leane's physical capabilities. The soft desert sands presented a gruelling training environment and he quickly developed severe and debilitating varicose veins. He was admitted to Mena Hospital in Egypt on 26 December 1914 for surgery which, although successful, could not rejuvenate ageing legs. On discharge on 21 January 1915, Edwin's hopes of participating in further action were dashed when he was declared medically unfit for service. Dismayed, he then made representation to the Chief of Staff, General Sir William Birdwood, to serve in a different sphere of operations by utilising his business knowledge and organisational skill. He had a point and Birdwood was quick to recognise his worth. Edwin Leane's expertise proved invaluable and he was promoted to major on 26 April 1915 and appointed Deputy Assistant Director of Ordnance Services (DADOS). With the troops now on Gallipoli, Major Edwin Leane was responsible for the organisation of the Cairo Base Ordnance before he was himself deployed to Gallipoli with the 2nd Division in September 1915.

However brave, no war is won purely on the efforts of its infantry. Essential to the efficiency of those at the front is a ready supply of equipment and supplies. Initially, this was the role that Major Edwin Leane was to fulfil at Gallipoli and then Egypt, France and Belgium for the next 12 months. At Gallipoli he faced the first of many challenges—to adequately clothe and shelter the troops, who were ill equipped to face the rigours of a Turkish winter in the remnants of ragged clothing that they had worn for months. Boots were falling apart and needed replacing. Underwear, sheepskins, greatcoats, blankets and gumboots were ordered, but insufficient numbers were available to address the needs of all the troops. The problems were compounded when 'the blighters started shelling us [in the Ordnance Yard] and put in about 100 altogether and boots and clothing and all was flying in the air.'[75] This was equipment the Australians could ill afford to lose as 'the temperature dropped degrees below zero last night and this morning the ground was frozen hard, but lumpy and uncomfortable. Last night I could not sleep for hours on account of the cold. I am in a dugout and comparatively comfortable and have plenty of covering. It must be HELL for the poor fellows who are fully exposed and have not more than two blankets to cover them.'[76] Damaged artillery also came under his purview and Edwin desperately tried to organise repairs with minimal replacement parts. The awful reality of provisioning and sustaining an army from the other side of the world must have hung heavily on Major Edwin Leane during those final, perishing months on the peninsula.

The withdrawal proved just as painful for Edwin. Having done his utmost for months to acquire necessary supplies and support the men to the best of his ability, he was overcome with despair at the waste of lives and the millions of pounds expended on the Gallipoli campaign. A vast quantity of supplies was to be left at Gallipoli and this grieved him sorely. On December 14 he reflected: 'What muddlers we are. I thought South Africa was bad and I thought that we had learned a lesson there, but it seems to me now that South Africa was a systematically conducted campaign compared to this. When the war is over and facts can be dealt with, the responsibility for this fearful bungle will be fitted to the shoulders of those who are responsible for it. I am ashamed of the whole show!'[77] As a man who took pride in his work and whose faith valued the sanctity of human life, the failure of the Gallipoli campaign must have been excruciating.

In the days leading up to his own withdrawal, Edwin moved among the men, seeking out family members to bid them farewell. As the eldest member of the family, he felt acutely his responsibility for the welfare of them all. He was glad that his son Geoff was still in Egypt and felt 'that I have been under Providence of doing so much for others of my family, that I cannot expect too much for myself and I am not going to complain at anything that happens to me.'[78] Edwin was eventually evacuated from Gallipoli on 17 December and, along with the rest of the force, transited at Mudros before being shipped to Egypt. On Mudros, Edwin was able to catch up with his brothers, Allan William, Raymond Lionel and Benjamin Bennett. No doubt their opinions concurred on the appalling management of the Dardanelles campaign by the British. Christmas Day however, drew Edwin's thoughts to his family:

I wonder how my dear ones at home spent the day. I do hope they had a real good day and were all happy. I am afraid however that Australians generally have not had a good day if the news of our evacuation from the Peninsula has been made public. Just think of the thousands who would think of those dear to them left behind at ANZAC, buried there to get a country which was not thought to be worth keeping. What an awful waste of good lives and good money. I am very glad that none of my family have been left behind.[79]

On 30 December Edwin embarked from Mudros for Egypt where he was to be reunited with his sons, Allan Edwin and Geoffrey Paul. Not long after his return, Edwin records from Tel el Kebir that he was 'Interviewed with ADOS and discussed proposition for running this depot and for me to act as DADOS 2nd Division and also as Ordnance Officer ANZAC afterwards. Discussed with AA and QMG [Assistant Adjutant and Quartermaster General] 2nd Division and he approves.'[80] Consequently Edwin accompanied the 2nd Division to France with the Army Ordnance Corps, but was then ordered to proceed from Albert to AIF Headquarters at Horseferry Road, London, on 30 July 1916. In August 1916 he was promoted to lieutenant colonel and became responsible for the organisation of Ordnance Depots in the United Kingdom. In his capacity as DADOS, Edwin's organisational skills and his extensive military knowledge proved invaluable. He served in this appointment until February 1917 when he was granted home leave to Australia, arriving in Melbourne on 9 April 1917.

While no doubt anxious to see his wife and family, these months became a period of inconsolable compassionate leave. During Edwin's absence from the front, his two brothers, Lieutenant Colonel Allan William, who was Commanding Officer (CO) of the 28th Battalion, and Major Benjamin Bennett of the 48th Battalion, were killed in major assaults at Bullecourt, while Edwin's son, Captain Allan Edwin, also of the 48th Battalion died some months before at Deville Wood. The news must have been shattering for both the immediate and extended families. For Edwin, no solace was to be found at home. In his heart he felt that he should have been in Europe. Lieutenant Colonel Edwin Leane knew that his place was back with the troops and that one of his major tasks was to discover the details of his son's death and final resting place. Accordingly, he embarked on *Shropshire* on 12 May, returning to London in July to report to General Birdwood at AIF Headquarters. Edwin was posted to France on 31 July to report on Ordnance Depots on the Western Front. By December 1917 he had been appointed Assistant Director of Ordnance Services (ADOS) for I Anzac Corps Headquarters in France where he remained until the Armistice. He was promoted to substantive colonel on 1 November 1918.

In spite of his enormous personal loss, Colonel Edwin Leane sublimated his grief to his duty. As a soldier who had served in two wars, he knew full well the finality of death and the imperative of continuing the battle to seek justification of such loss. Gone was the initial excitement of finding a place in history, of enjoying the camaraderie of men. Now it was replaced by a grim determination to bring order and organisation to the AIF. Edwin was determined that efficiency and clear communication should overcome the British 'muddle' to ensure that Australian servicemen were supported by whatever means possible. This was to be one of his greatest challenges and a task he was admirably equipped to handle.

Irrespective of his efficiency and the organisational roles Edwin fulfilled in his appointment as ADOS, possibly his greatest service to the AIF occurred after the war. 'When General Monash was appointed as Director General of Repatriation and Demobilisation, he was quick to identify Colonel Leane's expertise and appointed him as Deputy Director in the AIF Repatriation and Demobilisation Department in France, Egypt and England.'[81] On 16 November 1918 the Demobilisation and Repatriation Branch was formally constituted in London. Its task was unprecedented in history and a totally new infrastructure had to be developed. With over 200,000 men, women and children requiring a passage to Australia, it was anticipated that repatriation would take at least a year. Apart from the sheer logistics of the task, demobilisation and repatriation presented a monumental exercise in terms of controlling a force whose motivation for existence had disappeared.

In a masterstroke of essential organisation, the Demobilisation and Repatriation Branch was organised into five departments. These were:

- 1D Non-military employment and education. This department identified the existing skills of servicemen and provided education and training for the repatriated servicemen to assist them to find employment on their return to Australia.

- 2D Shipping, Movements, Quartering and Supply. This department assessed available shipping and organised lists of troops, wives and children according to the strict criteria for return to Australia.

- 3D Administration. This department was entirely involved in administration.

- 4D Ordnance. This department arranged the retrieval, audit, inspection and care of equipment prior to embarkation for Australia. This covered ordnance in Europe, the Middle East and Egypt. Loading and care of equipment during transport and the disposal of surplus equipment stores and salvage was also part of this department's remit.

- 5D Finance and Pay. This department was charged with costing and funding the logistics previously described. The Finance Department, acting on advice from the Ordnance Department, was responsible for ensuring that special transactions were negotiated with the imperial authorities concerning equipment for the maintenance of a post-bellum army in Australia. Australia was entitled to receive new or serviceable equipment to replace what she had used to equip the AIF.

In this remarkably efficient organisation, Colonel Edwin Leane's expertise in ordnance and proven business management skills saw him appointed Deputy Director of Ordnance and Equipment under Brigadier General W.A. Coxen CB, CMG, DSO. This position required him to review various depots in France and establish protocols for the auditing, return and storage of equipment through the Australian Army Ordnance Corps. General equipment, heavy and field artillery, ammunition, light horse, engineers, signals and veterinary stores all came under his purview. In addition, and no less important, was the ordering and distribution of new uniforms and basic equipment for the thousands of troops who were clad

Colonel Edwin Thomas Leane.
Australian War Memorial, P02136.001

in uniforms so damaged and tattered by the effects of the weather and the fighting that they almost resembled rags. New clothing had to be provided for the return to Australia. One important element of the duties of this branch was the preparation of indents for all arms of the post-war army in Australia. Under the guidance of defence authorities, a satisfactory arrangement for the issue of ordnance and equipment was agreed and the proposed period of adjustments was accepted by the War Office.

The department proved extremely efficient in auditing its resources and organising the transfer of ordnance. By June 1919 Brigadier General Coxen had returned to Australia and Colonel Edwin Leane had been promoted to Director of Branch 4D. It is interesting to note the detail in the weekly record of activities undertaken by the department under Colonel Leane's tenure. Every communication, every concern is meticulously recorded in the weekly minutes. Finally, on 13 July 1919, Colonel Leane and seven staff left England on HMAT *Persec* bound for Australia, the bulk of their work completed.

In human terms alone, the department organised the logistics for the repatriation of at least 185,000 servicemen, of whom 95,000 were in France and Belgium, 60,000 in Great Britain and 30,000 in Egypt and Mesopotamia.[82] There were now also wives and children to consider as the long years abroad had seen many Australian troops marry and start families. Colonel Edward Leane eventually returned to Australia in September 1919 and was demobilised in November that year. In addition to his three service medals, he had been Mentioned in Despatches five times. He was awarded the Belgian Croix de Guerre and was made a Commander of the Order of the British Empire, the latter award gazetted on 15 September 1919. His citation for his knighthood stated: 'From its original formation in July 1915 until July 1916, this officer was DADOS of the 2nd Australian Division and from December 1917 until November 1918 he discharged the duties of ADOS of the corps. He has been in Egypt, Gallipoli and France and carried out his duties with great judgement, energy and ability.'[83] The awards were testament to Colonel Edwin Leane's decisive leadership, commanding disposition, and total commitment to the cause.

While front-line combat was beyond Edwin's ageing body, his work was of monumental importance to the war effort. For him, ordnance was a comfortable field and well within the scope of his meticulous management skills. It was also a fillip to his already inflated ego. He was given responsibility within his expertise as an organiser of materials and logistics. He was accorded rank and privilege and his contribution was recognised at the highest level. Edwin probably considered that he had fought a good war, although his efforts were not the stuff of the Anzac legend. Apart from his time at Gallipoli, he had avoided having to 'muck in with the lads at the front' and, in his own words, an officer had comforts that were far removed from those experienced by the enlisted man in the trenches. In terms of age, duties, rank and experience of front-line action, Colonel Edwin Leane was not one of Bean's quintessential Anzacs.

6. THE SONS OF COLONEL EDWIN THOMAS LEANE

While managing his own enormous responsibility during the war Edwin, as his diary indicates, remained acutely mindful of the deployment and welfare of his four sons, who had all enlisted. His eldest son, Allan Edwin, was 19 when he enlisted on 22 April 1915 at Liverpool in NSW, having resigned from the militia 39th Infantry Battalion. He embarked from Sydney on 16 June 1915 aboard HMAT A63 *Karoola*. As a prolific correspondent to his mother and family at home and writing occasional missives to his father, Allan's letters, preserved at the Australian War Memorial, offer a candid insight into this sensitive and dutiful young man. Clearly he adored his parents. His love, esteem and concern for their welfare permeate every letter. Yet he was an anxious young man, mindful of childhood infirmity, anxious over his 'weedy constitution', and hopeful of overcoming an embarrassing tendency to sleepwalk.[84] Of greater concern however, was his earnest desire to honour the family name, obtain a commission and live up to the military standards of his father and uncles. As a mere lad on his enlistment and arrival in Egypt, it is evident that Edwin, his father, pulled administrative strings to have Allan and his other son, Geoffrey, join him in the Ordnance Corps in Cairo. This ensured their safety until Edwin and Allan were deployed to Gallipoli in early September with the 2nd Division. While in Cairo,

Allan expressed his frustration with his desk job in a letter to his mother, in which he wrote, 'I would not like to return home to say that I had never been under fire. I came over here to go to the front and the sooner the better, as it is getting on my nerves at this place and Geoff's are raw, he and I both are getting sour, and bad tempered for no other reason than we have abandoned soldiering for pen and typewriter.'[85]

By September Allan's wish had been fulfilled and he was sent to Gallipoli as a sergeant clerk alongside his father, who was by then Major Edwin Leane. Allan's October letter to his mother must have reassured her that Edwin continued to monitor their children's wellbeing. Allan wrote about the perishing conditions on the peninsula, stating rather naïvely, 'I had returned from my work at father's office and turned in, the time was about 9.30. When the show (the storm) started, my being in bed so early is accounted for by the fact that father shooed me off early to enable me to get home before it.'[86]

Edwin's concern for his son's potential frailty appears to have been well founded as, with the onset of the colder weather in October 1915, Allan was admitted to the field ambulance with influenza. His condition obviously deteriorated and, by 7 November, he had been transferred to No. 3 Australian General Hospital (AGH) at Heliopolis (Egypt) with Pyrexia (fever) and general debility, which he referred to in his letters home as 'Enteric Fever'. In December he was transferred to No. 2 AGH at Gezirah Palace, Egypt, with yet another bout of influenza. By this stage the Australian troops had been evacuated from Gallipoli, but Edwin's concern for his son did not end there. Allan wrote to his mother of his despair at discovering his father's well-intentioned plans to protect him if the force had remained at Gallipoli over winter:

> Captain Maxted had a letter from father telling him that I am to be kept in Egypt till the winter is over and telling him to take me on the strength at the Base. I protested but was overruled on every point, and as far as I can see, I am to be put on light duties in Egypt and the pity of it is that my having had Enteric they can

do it. They can keep me away from the Peninsula for six months if father says the word, his letter adds the postscript that he does not suppose they will be able to keep me after the cold weather is over. I judge from this that the Dad guessed how I would perform when I found what he had done and knows that the moment I am able to move on my own again, I'll go back whether they like it or not, my place is near to him and the Devil himself shall not keep me from it. Of course, as Father said when we argued the question out on the Peninsula, he tried to get me to promise that when I got back here and got better I would take a job in Egypt. For which purpose he wrote letters of recommendation to the Ordnance Pay Corps etc, at least till the snow and bad season was over for as he said, he being an Officer on the staff was sure of good food, a roof, a bed, a nip of scotch, all of which would keep him in comparative comfort through out the short but rigorous winter, while I would have none of these.

He would always be worried about me. He explained that I had done my bit. I admitted that it was for my own good, but agreed that my place was by his side, that I was, in a way personally responsible to those at home for him. All of this may sound very ungrateful and silly to you, but put yourself in my place. This is the first time that I have actually stood in opposition to Father's will and he took it like a good sort. If only you knew how I hate that phrase (all for my own good) anyone would think that I was a weakly puling invalid, instead of six feet of India rubber that has shaken off the Enteric Fever, which has got men who caught it before me still on their backs. I am hard as nails.[87]

With the evacuation of Gallipoli, January and February saw the AIF recuperating and regrouping in Egypt. The original depleted battalions were amalgamated and new ones were formed. By March, Allan had met up with his uncles, Ernest Albert, Allan William, Raymond Lionel, Benjamin Bennett, brothers Geoffrey Paul and Reuben Ernest, and cousins, Arnold Harry and William Ernest. In such company, Sergeant Allan Leane was no doubt quick to pick up the whispers that his uncle, Raymond Lionel Leane, was about to be appointed CO of the newly formed 48th Battalion. Immediately Allan Edwin saw this as his opportunity and, pleading his case with his father and his current CO, Colonel Sellheim, successfully transferred on 3 March 1916. In spite of the fact that his Uncle Ray was CO of the newly formed battalion, the aspiring recruit was granted no favours.

Although delighted with the promotion to 2nd Lieutenant, Allan Edwin was immediately confronted by his appointment as company quartermaster. This was a responsibility that kept him on a knife edge of anxiety, as he later described to his mother:

> I was going to a new battalion, new uncle as CO, new work, new everything and you can imagine that I was more than a trifle nervous as to the result, not for my own sake but for fear that I might let the uncle down. I have always striven to emulate the Dad and his brothers who are all universally recognised as white men, which as you know is the Australian limit of perfection and although now striving, I hope to be a success.[88]

Within weeks of Allan's appointment, the AIF and the CO had decided that the 48th Battalion should embark on a four-day desert march from Tel el Kebir to Serapeum. This was a monumental undertaking, with marches of approximately 17 miles per day through soft desert sand, the men weighed down with full packs. It was designed to toughen the troops for the Western Front and it certainly tested the resilience and resources of the newly appointed quartermaster. Allan was under no illusion as to the gruelling nature of the task and regaled his mother with details of the logistics of catering for over 1100 men with unpredictable camels over the duration of the trek. From the outset he was determined to form a separate column of his platoon of 25 men consisting of himself, his own cook sergeant, 17 cooks, guards, horses and limbers and 12 camels carrying all provisions, plus blankets, dixies and wood. In his determination to stay ahead of the battalion and have food ready whenever the troops bivouacked, young Allan pushed himself close to exhaustion with no more than six hours' sleep and little to eat over the four days.

In spite of his enormous levels of anxiety, Allan's endeavours proved a great success and he reported to his mother that:

The experience has I am sure taken years off my life, but it was worth it I assure you, as my reputation as a competent and capable Quartermaster is assured. I have accomplished my purpose, that is to make good and have the satisfaction of knowing that I am now one of the Leanes who can do things. It is for father's sake and for your sake mother that I am glad that the 48th was the best fed and looked after regiment that marched here and that I as QM am spoken highly of. The CO put me up for my second star over the affair but ANZAC say that the promotion would be too rapid and that I must wait my turn.[89]

Like a child who has won his first prize and seeks the affirmation of his parents, Allan also described his exploits to his father. 'We arrived here at Serapeum the most fresh and the best fed battalion in the line and I am glad to tell you father that I have had a chance to make good, and I have not spared my self in order to make surety of coming out on top, and when you receive a letter from Ray, I am confident that it will contain the news that justifies any confidence you may have had in me, or set any lingering doubt that I may have tackled something above my weight, namely that I have made good.'[90] Clearly proud of the esteem in which he was held in the AIF, Allan wanted to reassure his mother that not only was he efficient, he was also honourable. He had continued to live according to the moral and religious standards which had been central to the family's values. In concluding one letter to her, he stated, 'If anything should happen to me here, I want you all to know that I have lived cleanly and straightly and always striven to be a Leane.'[91] As a reader of his letters the issue is never in doubt. In spite of adversity and living with diverse people from all walks of life, there is a total absence of offensive language, blasphemy or ribald humour in 18 months of detailed correspondence. Allan Edwin makes no reference to the unsavoury behaviour of many of the Australian troops and speaks ill of no man.

Back at Tel el Kebir, Allan rejoiced in his new posting and the news that his Uncle Ben was to be Uncle Ray's adjutant, which would make the 48th quite 'a family affair'. This proved 'all the more reason for determination on [his] part to make a name on a par with them for they all set a high standard.'[92] Allan's new appointment filled him with pride for he believed that he was 'someone at last as I had always striven to be, since holding Major Kimpson's job for a while on the Peninsula and I find lively satisfaction in the fact. Under my control is the QM store and all that therein lies, the cooks, butchers, pioneers, transport and so on. I am responsible to the CO, for the comfort and equipment, provisioning and general wellbeing of the regiment, the cleanliness of the battalion lines and the sanitation of conveniences and a host of other things.'[93] His pride and excitement knew no bounds and, in writing to his sister Doris, he acknowledged his father's influence in training him for the responsibility he now held. For, 'I was trained by the right man, to accomplish all these things, that is the dear old Dad and I very often bless the hard work and methodical methods that he imbued into me which have enabled me, now that I have a job that calls for organisation of a big scale, to carry on to the CO's satisfaction and believe me, Uncle Ray, though a white man in every sense of the word takes a lot of pleasing. My training first in the Volunteers, later in the Militia and finally in the AIF enables me to keep the hundred or so men who come under my direct command well in hand.'[94]

In letters to both his mother and sister, Allan is at pains to reassure them of his acceptance of possible death, and the honour of dutiful service. His writings and reflections are typical of an idealistic adolescent suffused with altruistic imperialism. In anticipation of a move to France he wrote:

> I am sufficient of a fatalist to believe that I will go when it is written, and it does not matter whether I am in the trenches with my regiment, or a hundred miles away when my appointed time comes, I will go. This is not a skin deep conviction either, for I proved that on Gallipoli. I give you my word of honour that I never felt the slightest fear and although as I have written to you from there, my poor chappies were knocked over continually, something inside told me that it was alright and I never worried and after all Dear, when you come to think, those lines of Rudyard Kipling's express the sentiments of us all:

'How can a man die better
Than facing fearful odds
For the ashes of his father
And the temples of his Gods.'

I am not going into heroics for I badly want to come home to you all again, but if I must die, for God's sake let it be in action and not of illness, and I should die knowing that whoever had failed in their duty to our country, I at least had done what lay to my hand with the best that I could put into it. That the men of our family have and are doing more than their fair share of the work, and that no reproach could be thrown on the memory of any of us that face, as face we must, for we can't always be as lucky as we were at ANZAC where although several of us were knocked over, we all recovered and came up smiling for the next round. Some day when you learn how near the Enteric came to getting me, you will be surprised that I am still going strong and take back all you used to say regarding my weedy constitution. Do you remember how big Uncle Ray was? Well if you can believe it, I am as big as he is now, of course not so broad, but that will come. I am glad I am getting the makings of a man as I was a weed long enough.[95]

Allan Edwin duly reached France and, by 15 June 1916, had been promoted to lieutenant. He harboured hopes of further promotion with the possibility of platoon command. This became increasingly likely with the battalion's horrendous losses between July and November at Pozières. In spite of the casualties, Allan continued to delight in the battalion's success. Remaining positive as always, he reported to his father that:

Our regiment was mentioned in all sorts of places and orders for its heroic stand. The Colonel gets great kudos out of it as indeed he ought, his courage and daring being superb. He is the talk of the division. We got three Military Medals and two Military Crosses out of it, there are to be others we hope. Clarrie has been sent on by General Cox for one of the Crosses doing wonderful work.[96] I tell you the regiment covered itself with glory. I got nothing of course! QM's don't but the CO spoke a few words that pleased me as much as any decoration for he said, 'You have done your job QM and I am satisfied.'

As to your questions about my joining a company, it is very likely but not as a Platoon Commander. I am now Senior Sub and we are three Captains and a Major short so that I am likely to get a second in command and my Captaincy. I am not breaking my neck though, as I am giving every satisfaction as QM and TO [Training Officer] combined and fear that if I fly as high as Second in Command I may yet fall down in the CO's estimation and would much rather not take the responsibility on my shoulders. However we shall see! Regarding your remark re my being as likely to get cracked as QM as in the Coys, I concur. I went into Pozières with 15 cooks, butchers, storemen, 4 CQM's, RQM and 4 Coy storemen, 28 OR and a Sergeant in my transport section that made the strength of my command 55. I came out with 3 cooks, no Coy QM's, no butcher, no Coy storemen and 25 transport men making a total of 30 so we certainly get our share of it.[97]

Allan's report to his mother on Pozières was much less graphic, reassuring her that he had simply been mildly shaken up by concussion. Again his admiration of Uncle Ray prevails, as he writes that Ray 'has distinguished himself again, getting several of our wounded in himself from the craters, walking about the place as though he were on his own lawn at home despite everyone's entreaties to keep down. Ben did great work and all three of us are unhurt. There's no doubt about it that we Leanes must be guided by a special providence.'[98]

Captain Allan Edwin Leane.
Australian War Memorial, PO1723.001

After months of receiving no mail and becoming quite depressed by the fact, Allan finally received a newsy letter from his mother in late September in Belgium. Whatever she wrote about the love of Allan's life, his long-time friend 'Dutch', he responded in a playful manner wondering, 'I fear to think what it will mean, if God willing I return and she is promised, yet I dare not declare myself for fear of hurting the friendship that now exists, and oh, hell!'[99] With extraordinary faith in his mother's diplomacy and positive intervention, he then remarked, 'I must leave it to you Mother mine, knowing that no one can pull me out of my dilemma if you cannot.'[100] While timid and uncertain in love, Allan was confident in his belief that:

> My Captaincy is now a positive certainty, so that I can tell you without fear of disappointment, it is only a matter of days and I will be a full blown Captain and Second in Command of a Company. This marks another step up mummy and is another feather in your cap. I said that I would not rest till I attained the Dad's Boer War rank and I have I think redeemed my promise, a Majority is a bit to expect. I am tremendously bucked over this last promotion, I did not think I was capable of it. Still there you are, I've got it and the CO must consider me good enough or he would never do it.
>
> I tell you what has occurred to me now, this minute! All things being well and God willing, and if I am spared to obtain a Majority, that day I write a proposal of marriage to the colleen I adore and put my fate to the final test. (you will notice that every promotion I attain, I immediately book myself for one higher! If that is not too swank I'll eat my tin hat.) Write me by return and tell me if you would think the scheme too hare brained or not. I'll be guided by you in this matter, but would dearly like to know how I stand, though I dread the answer knowing what it must be. I have lived a straight life and have endeavoured to do you all credit since coming away, and have succeeded in the first and had far to make a go of the second for two reasons. 1. For the sake of the finest father and mother, sisters and brothers, uncles and cousins that ever God blessed a man with. 2. For the girl, whom God being good, I will make my wife. I am not a religious man mother, but these in themselves constitute a religion for me to live up to them. One must play the game, which is I hope somewhere in the neighbourhood of Godliness.[101]

While such personal and intimate confessions were readily made to his mother, matters of a military concern dominated Allan's correspondence to his father. On 1 October he informed his father of his captaincy, although no doubt his senior position in DADOS had made him privy to such information. He wrote to his father that:

> Ben takes a company shortly and that he is going to take me as his Second in Command. There is no man after yourself living that I would sooner scrap alongside than Ben and the arrangement would be a great idea, what say? I hope and pray that I am not taking over a job too big for me to handle Dad, to fall down in the CO's estimation after such a length of time would settle me altogether, as to face with him would cause you to regret ever having trusted your good name in my fool hands. I do not mean that I will squib it, I will be scared stiff for sure, but am convinced that I've guts enough to hide it, but that I might make a mess of some work. However, I'll do my best! I cannot promise more and if I let you down, it will not be for want of trying to keep my end up be sure of that.[102]

Having enlisted full of self-doubts and emotional insecurity, young Allan's promotion to captain seemed to imbue him with a degree of satisfaction and a measure of self-confidence. It was only with his mother that he could share this new-found certainty, for she had known him for all of his foibles and would never regard his descriptions as bragging. In his letter of 31 October 1916, a much more assured Allan reflected on the remarkable journey he had travelled from boy to man over the previous 16 months. She had clearly been his 'mother confessor' and he was devoid of inhibition when he recounted his personal evaluation of his performance as a member of the 48th Battalion:

> At times I lie awake at night (this is when I go to bed) and review my life since joining the 48th Battalion and I say to Allan, old son, you've had a hell of a time you know, and though worried out of your mind and driven nearly crazy, you've got them every time and you've enjoyed the uphill fight. You have tackled the well nigh impossible and brought it off, not once but every day, just out of sheer cussedness. You have a CO who is a man in all senses, yet who takes a savage delight in heaping the most impossible tasks upon

you, just to see what you can get over. You've received the most unreasonable commands and carried them out inside contract time and have felt like a king in your own right, when you have been able to click your heels together and report. You ordered so and so to be done by sunset, I wish to report OK.

You've been strafed and badgered, as surely never sub was strafed before, you have come up smiling after every round. What odds! We all get strafed at times, you have been told that you're no b—good and are to be sent to Australia and on top of that commanded to make bricks out of straw. You have not believed the first and accomplished the latter, thereby proving the error in the statement. You've got a perfectly fiendish temper which you are slowly, but surely learning to curb; you came to this regiment a complete grouch, you were soured and disheartened, you are now a confirmed optimist, you had to be. Others were busy enough trying to break your heart without you lending a hand yourself etc. and tons of other things equally silly, yet with a little pride in the job, well done! I can say with the fullest confidence and the CO's backing that I have been tried harder, more continuously and exhaustively than any other officers in the regiment and have come out on top. In other words, the CO determined to either thoroughly make or properly break me and through some inherent doggedness and tenacity of purpose, I thank God that I was not broken. I was made and made well.

When I first joined I had a hell of time, a little of which you know, a little more than the Dad knows, but the worst of which you will never know. I have been so done up at times that in the privacy of my tent I have howled like a big kid and have been utterly and hopelessly miserable. Oh! Mummy. I had a bad bitter time in my initial stages. At first I used to resent the CO's demands and though despairing, was prepared to go to the last extreme in order to achieve the things demanded in order to show that I could not be beaten. After a while, this resentment faded and was replaced by a grim determination to show him that I was capable of anything, and I went to any extreme in order to carry out my intentions. This afterwards endowed me with a tenacity of purpose such as I would never have possessed had I not been strained to the utmost. Though an iron hard man, he has a great affection for me I am sure and only does these things to me for two purposes, one inevitably being relationship and the other a grim curiosity to see just what I am capable of. He hides his real feelings well, but I am sure that I stand well with him and that he gives me full credit for my outcomes, this connection being borne out by my recent promotion, yet to hear him you would imagine that I was the one dud in the outfit.

After Pozières when he was satisfied as to my conduct under fire, as you know my promotion came, and believe me Mummy he never entrusts his precious men to any but those in whom he reposes fullest confidence. I went into the fire a raw boy and came out a man. The ordeal was a bitter one, but for dear old Ben my heart must have been inevitably broken and he has stood between me and the CO's wrath many times, being my stout and loyal champion against all comers. I can never repay old Ben for what he has done for me, but he has my wholehearted admiration and love and I would do anything on God's earth for him.

The result of my trial has been that, though hard, it has made me confident, self-reliant, quick to think and as quick to act, it has given me a determination, resolution, a fixity of purpose and singleness of aim that otherwise I might never have known. Even as the CO says, if ever I return, my own mother won't know me and that some day I will thank him for the pitiless gruelling he has given me. I am now only sixth in the regiment mother. There are above me the CO, Ben, Major Imlay, and three Captains so that I have become a senior officer very rapidly. If my life has been hard, the net results have been entirely satisfactory and for one who was a Sergeant nine short months ago, I have little to growl over and I am a proud man to be able to give my mummy three stars. It was my ambition to gain you your commission, but I never in my wildest dreams credited myself with being a Captain and sixth senior officer in such a regiment as 'The Joan of Arcs'.[103]

As a captain, Allan was second in command of his Uncle Ben's platoon and, in November, wrote to his father of his happiness at being a part of 'a jolly fine company'. The onset of what was to be one of the worst winters ever experienced in France drew comment from Allan, who described the paralysing cold and the mud to his father who would have been all too familiar with the conditions. He wrote of the men in his command and delighted in the esteem in which they held him. Later that month, in a letter to his mother, he detailed the rigours of the training course to which he had been sent. Allan knew full well the importance of this opportunity, for good marks would ensure that a return to the battalion would see him assume command of his own company. In spite of the weather and personal hardships, both letters reflected a new-found confidence in his endurance and resilience. The only blot on the Leanes' record is evident in his concluding lines to his mother when he remarks, 'All of us are fit except one of Ern's boys, who has been wounded and missing since some time ago. Poor chap, it's 100% he's gone.'[104]

By January 1917 Allan had made good his promise to propose to 'Dutch' and recounted to his mother that he had:

> ... received a letter from the Dad telling me of a letter from you which informed him that Dutch had accepted me. I could not believe my eyes and read the letter over and over again and at last came to the conclusion that I had read alright. I am the luckiest man alive and the news was through the Leane section of the Joan of Arcs like smoke. I was the subject of all sorts of compliments and everyone seemed as giddy as I was. They have all been anxiously waiting with me. The Dad in his letter was most enthusiastic about it and reckons also that I have gained the pick of the Sydney girls, there is only one thing that is lacking and that is Dutch's letter herself. I am afraid to believe it and oh Lord, I feel like a bottle of fizz that badly wants the cork out. Look at me! Can't go wrong so far, from Sergeant to Captain, and now only three places removed from a majority. The dearest people in the world and the sweetest girl alive, something has turned my star into a lucky one. I hope that it will continue to the finish and enable me to return to you and make up for the rotten time I gave you when I was home, marry Dutch, settle down to try and forget this grisly business if possible. God being willing all these things may yet come to pass.
>
> As you doubtless know by now, the Dad leaves for home at the end of this month. I would wish for no other thing and please God when you get him, you will keep him. He has done the work of about ten men and has now been mentioned in Haig's Despatches and obtained six months medical leave. It won't be anything like as homely as it was when the dear Dad was in Blighty, but you at home have the claim on him. We've had a long loan and are

jolly glad that he is going home to be mothered, see to it that you keep him. By this time you have heard of Allan's death.[105] It came as a fearful shock to us all, but as you can guess it hit Ben and the CO fearfully hard. The CO had the body brought down to where our Battalion was resting. There is a military cemetery there and he was buried with at any rate four of his own blood to see him go. The CO did not break up, but his face was a pitiful sight, the agony of an iron man. Ben bore it to the finish, then broke down. Clarrie and I bawled and the many other officers of Allan's own battalion just faded away. It was a matter of about twelve miles from his battalion, yet many of the privates took French Leave and footed it down to see him buried, a last tribute. Aunt Blanche returns to Australia by the same boat as she came over on.[106] It must have knocked those in London sky high, for he had been over there with them only a couple of days before. Thank God it was not our Dad is all I can say.[107]

By the time of his next letter home in March, Allan seems to have put the losses of two of the Leanes behind him, claiming that there was nothing to complain about at that time. He described in considerable detail an extensive underground bunker that the battalion had taken from the Germans, equipped with bunks and a labyrinth of chambers. Dry and snug, his description evoked a degree of reassurance as he added, 'here I sit writing to you at 9.45pm everything in the garden being lovely. It is the best HQ I have ever had and I am tickled to death with it. I reckon that it's just spiffing and hope we stay here some time. It's great to have a dugout where you can stand up and not dash your head against the roof. I can assure you that you can go to sleep with the comforting thought that nothing short of a 15" shell or a gas attack can get at you.'[108]

Back in Australia, this reassurance of Allan's sense of invincibility, must have heartened his parents, as together they could support each other and offer their prayers for his continued salvation. However the relief was to be short lived for, in April, the 48th Battalion was heavily committed in the battles of Bullecourt when family tragedy struck. On 10 April, Major Benjamin Bennett Leane was killed in action and, on 11 April 1917, Captain Allan Edwin Leane was declared missing after an offensive action. It is impossible to imagine the level of grief and despair that must have engulfed all members of the Leane family back in Australia, but particularly Edwin. As a father he must have felt that he had neglected his duty by returning home, for in being on the other side of the world, his protection had been absent. At least, had he been at his post and not accepted leave, he would have had sufficient authority to demand every detail concerning his son's demise. Access to official reports would have informed him exactly what had happened and precisely when Allan had been killed and he would have been privy to where his son was buried. Yet, in spite of his rank and military standing, back in Australia on the other side of the world, Edwin was to all intents and purposes impotent.

Information and consolation of a sort came in a letter from his son, Geoffrey, dated 25 April 1917. In it he tries to offer his father as much detail as possible about his brother Allan's death:

> Dear Old Dad,
>
> I daresay by this you have received the news from Uncle Ray's wife about Allan and Ben and I can imagine your grief as he was doing so splendidly and would have gone very much higher had he still been back with his unit.
>
> I dare say you will be surprised that I have not called home with the news, but when I tell you that I was turned down each time I went to send it, you will understand it. I then went to Uncle Ray and told him my trouble and he informed me that he had had just this same trouble himself, but finally managed to get it sent through Division to his wife asking her to pass on the news to mother.
>
> All cables were stopped early in February and I could get no one to accept my cable and damn near went mad with worry and I can tell you that it did not take me long to find Uncle Allan.
>
> My transfer to Allan never came through and on top of that I was transferred to another office and therefore missed seeing Allan before he went into the line the last time. I have seen Uncle Ray and he has promised to take me, in fact he put the papers through at once as an Officer and I am now waiting for word from him.

As usual I had my bad luck again as I rode on a bicycle from Bapaume to Millencourt if you know where that is, and missed him by half an hour as he had gone out on a route march. So my ride of something like 15 kilometres was for nothing.

You will notice Dad that I do not speak much of Allan but please understand that he is in my thoughts day and night and I have not had a night's rest since I got the news on 13 April. I am hanging onto myself for all I am worth to prevent myself breaking down. I have some terrible fits of the 'blues' but one hope still lives with me that is, to hear from him as a Prisoner of War as there are a hundred chances for him because I have spoken to men who were with him to the last. They swear that he was hit either in the leg or the thigh and NOT badly.

Oh Dad, it eased the pain a lot to hear how those boys spoke of him and poor old Allan wrote his reports right up to the last and the piece of work he did was marvellous and he would have received some recognition had he come out of it alive. I will try to describe the attack. Allan's instructions were to take over the second line with his company and Uncle Ray picked Allan as his strongest officer and on the right placed another officer, whom he could rely on, on the extreme left. Before they went over, Allan strafed Uncle Ray for not giving him a chance by putting him in the second wave. All the time our boys were enfiladed from the left and right by Fritz but they carried their objective till they reached the point marked ... Allan reached his lot, kicked Fritz out, held the line, the 46th battalion did not reach. Ammunition ran out and 46th cleared back. Fritz, at once surrounded Allan on front, back and sides. Allan rallied his men, held his objective and came back and kicked Fritz out of the trenches behind him and so again had clear ground to get back, a distance of 2.5 miles. Ammunition gave out and he had to clear out. He had reinforcements to back him up and plenty of ammunition. He would have held a most important part of the line but fate was against them and in getting back he was hit.

I have tried to describe the attack as well as possible, but I know I have failed as I can never describe it the way the boys did it or to tell you of Allan's beautiful work. I wish it had been me Dad and not Allan, as he is worth a dozen of me and I thank God that you are at home to buck them all up.

Please don't think of me and come back too early as they at home want you more than I do and if the mater is slow in recovering can

you not get a further leave? I come last in this Dad, so please help
them at home and not me.

Now Dad, I will close with the fondest love to you and mother and
all at home.

From yours lovingly

Geoff.[109]

A military enquiry was convened to investigate the circumstances
of Captain Allan Leane's death and a number of men in his platoon
later declared that they had seen him in a shell hole having been shot in
the head. No. 5839 Private H. Hewish reported at a further enquiry at
Hurdcott: 'On 11 April 1917 we had to evacuate a position and while
coming down a sap we met some of the enemy troops. Captain Leane
was leading and after travelling about a quarter of the distance, the
Germans we met immediately started bombing. It was with one of these
bombs that Captain Leane was wounded. There was only one thing
left for all hands to do and that was to get over the top in the best way
possible. I saw Captain Leane leave the trench but what happened to
him afterwards I am unable to state.'[110]

Meanwhile, in France, the members of the 48th Battalion were
devastated at Ben and Allan's deaths and it must have taken a steely
resolve from the CO to prevent the loss of such popular leaders deflating
the men's morale. However the Joan of Arc Battalion held other family
members who, in Colonel Edwin Leane's absence, wanted to leave no
stone unturned in determining Allan's fate. During World War I, the
Red Cross established a number of missing persons enquiry bureaux
to try to trace men who went missing and others for whom no remains
could be found. They liaised with the Swiss Red Cross and the German
Red Cross and exchanged information accordingly. The London Branch
was headed by Miss Vera Deakin, the daughter of former Prime Minister
Alfred Deakin, and it was to her that Lieutenant Clarrie Fairley, Allan's
adopted cousin, made enquiries. Her reply, dated 23 July 1917 stated:

Dear Sir

In answer to your inquiry for Captain A.E. Leane 48th Battalion AIF, we beg to inform you of official evidence given by one of his men when at No.1 Command Depot Perham Downs. He reported that he was with Captain Leane during the attack and retreat at Bullecourt on April 11 during which he and 20 men were cut off and engaged by the Germans. They took refuge for a time in a shell hole and then he told them to make for our own lines, he being the last to leave the shelter. Just as he was getting into our trenches he was shot through the head and they were all certain that he was killed. The ground was lost so there was no chance of bringing in his body.

Informant adds that Captain Leane did not consider himself at all, but thought only of his men.[111]

A later letter dated 2 October 1917 from the London Branch of the Red Cross to Lieutenant Fairley promoted the findings that Captain Allan Edwin Leane had been captured and subsequently died in an advanced German dressing station as a prisoner of war on 2 May 1917. No further reports were promulgated.

The loss of his son and such a fine officer must have been a tremendous blow to Edwin. He may however have drawn some comfort from the recommendation that his brother Lieutenant Colonel Raymond Leane submitted for a Military Cross (MC) to be awarded posthumously to his son. The citation reads: 'At Bullecourt on 11 April 1917 for conspicuous gallantry and devotion to duty during the attack on the Hindenburg line. This officer was the only Company Commander who succeeded in reaching the second objective and it was due to his resourcefulness and fearless leadership that the objective was gained and held for over six hours despite several heavy enemy counter attacks.'[112]

When Colonel Edwin Leane returned to Europe he resumed his correspondence with Vera Deakin. He was at pains to request that any belongings of Allan's be returned to him rather than his wife. Oddly enough, one of the few possessions to be returned to his mother, as next of kin, was Colonel Edwin Leane's identity disc. Apparently Allan had secured one of his father's discs and carried it as kind of talisman. Having been brought up in awe of his father and imbued with a love of all things military, Captain Allan Edwin Leane was haunted by the possibility that he would never live up to his father's expectations. Hopefully, by the end of his brief life, Allan realised that he had successfully made the journey 'from a boy with the heart of a man' and was without question worthy of being a Leane.[113] What more could he have done but sacrificed his life? With no known grave, Captain Allan Edwin Leane's sacrifice is remembered on the memorial wall at the Australian National Memorial, Villers-Bretonneux.

Edwin Leane's second son, Geoffrey Paul, enlisted at Liverpool on 2 March 1915. He too was aged just 18 on enlistment with three years' military experience in the senior cadets behind him. He was described as a 'smooth faced lad, vivacity beaming from his countenance and pluck characterising his actions.'[114] Initially he was allocated to the 18th Battalion, embarking at Sydney on HMAT A40 *Ceramic* on 25 June 1915. On arrival in Egypt he was seconded to the Australian Army Service Corps as a postal clerk. He held this position for almost 12 months during which time he would have met family members in Egypt and heard of their exploits at Gallipoli. No doubt his father, Edwin, felt some relief that he had orchestrated Geoffrey Paul's role as a non-combatant, but that is not to say that his son felt the same way. Hearing of the exploits of the 48th Battalion and knowing that his Uncle Ray was the CO, it seemed inevitable that Geoffrey Paul would apply for a transfer. This was finally effected on 6 May 1917 following the deaths of his brother and Uncle Ben.

Geoffrey Paul Leane had a great deal to live up to and it is certain that his Uncle Ray cut him no slack. By October that year, the heavy casualties suffered by the battalion in critical battles saw him promoted to lieutenant. During the battle of Polygon Wood, young Lieutenant Geoffrey Leane assumed a great deal of responsibility. He was also confronted by the terrible loss of life in the aftermath of the battle. He wrote of the brutal death of No. 2452 Private J.T. Martin in a Red Cross report, his description plainly revealing his despair at leaving a comrade unburied. 'The lad was killed by a shell just outside my dugout at about 8.15 this morning. This position afterwards became untenable and had to be evacuated. Martin, with others, was left behind and to my knowledge no burying party stayed behind or went up to that position after we had evacuated it. So I am afraid that the lad was left there. I knew Martin well and recognised him when I turned him over that night. He had been terribly blown about and there was barely a stitch of clothing left on him.'[115]

In the same month, news came through that Lieutenant Geoffrey Paul Leane had been awarded the MC. The citation read: 'For conspicuous gallantry and devotion to duty when in charge of a party carrying rations to the front line. His party came under a heavy barrage and eight of them were wounded. He got his men to cover, despatched the wounded to the aid post, reorganised his party and delivered the rations to the front lines.'[116] His father would have been proud. Geoffrey Paul continued his service with the 48th Battalion and, on 23 June 1918, was appointed assistant adjutant, a position he retained until the Armistice. On 8 December he was attached to the 12th AIF Brigade as a staff trainer before being granted leave in February 1919.

As thousands of young servicemen had committed themselves to the war at the expense of any personal career, training opportunities were offered to those awaiting repatriation in England. Edwin's influence appears to have been behind Geoffrey Paul's secondment to the Guardian Mutual Insurance Company in London and then Cardiff. From February to August 1919 he worked with the firm as a clerk before returning to Sydney in December 1919 aboard *Nestor*.

Like so many returned servicemen, Geoffrey Paul Leane was a very different man to the blithe lad who left Sydney aged 18. To expect otherwise would be naïve. At only 22 years of age, he had participated in some of the nation's most horrific and seminal battles as a member of the famous 48th Battalion. He had served under the legendary Brigadier

General Sir Raymond Lionel Leane. In winning the MC he had fulfilled family expectations of both service and gallantry. However, he had suffered deeply with the loss of his beloved brother Allan Edwin, his cousin Arnold Harry and his revered uncles Allan William and Benjamin Bennett. The excitement of battle, the camaraderie of men and the prestige of military honours left Geoffrey dreading a commitment to 'the round eternal of the cashbook and the journal' that a civilian clerkship offered.[117]

With his sons' interests and welfare always at the forefront, Edwin realised that his boys had little interest in and few prospects for civilian life after the war. While waiting for repatriation to Australia, Rueben had also undertaken some basic experience working for a poultry farmer in Kent. Based on this limited experience, Edwin decided to help his sons by providing sufficient capital for Geoffrey and Rueben to purchase and run a poultry farm on their return to Australia. He had not factored into the plan that neither of his sons had a practical bone in his body or that food costs for poultry would outstrip production. Of greater significance was the fact that large-scale poultry farming lacked the modern preventative measures for disease which would soon see the flock decimated. Consequently, the business failed and Geoffrey and Rueben lost every penny of Edwin's money. All parties were devastated by the failure and this additional blow was to be the catalyst for much of the bitterness that Geoffrey Paul harboured for the rest of his life.

With few other options, Geoffrey obtained a position as a clerk for the British Phosphate Commission which saw him sent to Nauru. Previously a German colony, the island had become a League of Nations Mandate after World War I, administered by Australia, New Zealand and the United Kingdom. It was on Nauru that he married Beryl Pryde in 1925. It was also the place where his son, Peter Douglas Leane, was born in 1929—possibly the first white person born on the island. Life on Nauru proved claustrophobic for Geoffrey, and in 1932 the family moved to Auckland where he obtained a position as a clerk with the Apple and Pear Marketing Board.

A further two children, Edwin and Margaret, were born there. Edwin recalls a wasted childhood with a remote and unloving father. In an attempt to win his father's interest and favour, Edwin invited his parents to watch him play football. The little boy played his heart out, only to have his father say to him at the end of the game, 'Well, you didn't do much did you!'[118]

His father's bitterness continued to undermine the development of a warm and loving relationship with his youngest children. In spite of entreaties to learn of their father's World War I experiences and the story behind his MC, Geoffrey refused to be drawn. Having grown up in such a rigid and repressive environment, Edwin sought to leave home as soon as possible. He lamented that his father could not even rejoice in news of Edwin's first appointment as a journalist, as he was consumed with envy that Edwin was earning more than he was.[119]

Reuben Ernest, the third of Edwin's sons, was 18 when he enlisted on 28 December 1916. Inspired by his father's military example, he had become a career soldier and registered at the Royal Garrison Artillery at South Head, NSW. Gunner Reuben Leane embarked from Melbourne on HMAT *Ascanius* on 11 May 1917 and marched into Parkhouse, England, on 21 July 1917. After musketry training he was deployed to France in November to join the 55th Battalion. Sickness saw him hospitalised from December to February, by which time he had obviously heard from his father and brothers and was no doubt encouraged to apply for a transfer to the family battalion, the 48th. This was duly accomplished by March 1918. By April his initiative, and perhaps his name, had seen him promoted to corporal. Yet his continued participation in the 48th Battalion was limited to just a few weeks. Later that month he was sent to Administrative Headquarters in London and was transferred to an officer cadet training battalion at Cambridge. Having lost his eldest son, it is not difficult to imagine that Edwin had pulled strings to have Reuben removed from the action in France. Edwin was no doubt grateful that, by the time Reuben had completed his officer training course, the war was over. The transfer had kept him safe. Following the Armistice,

Reuben was employed by a poultry farmer before his return to Australia in November 1919 and subsequent demobilisation on 18 December of that year.

Edwin Leane's youngest son, Maxwell, eschewed the army altogether. Instead, he chose to enlist in the navy at Williamstown in Melbourne. He served with the 'senior service' from 1918 until 1924 when he was demobilised. He rose to the rank of lieutenant and offered his services again at the outbreak of the Second World War, albeit in a shore-based capacity. He married Eileen Rose Hay and moved to Boston in the United States where he lived until his death in 1979.

Colonel Edwin Leane must have counted his blessings when his youngest son, Maxwell, completed his service with the Royal Australian Navy in April 1919. Three of his four sons had survived the carnage of the war and all had honoured the family tradition with meritorious service. Evident in the correspondence cited is the aura of reverence in which Edwin was held by his sons. He was enshrined as a kind of demigod whose approval was paramount and whose standards had to be met. Even in the post-war period when his surviving sons were adults, Edwin's heavy-handed intervention continued as he endeavoured to direct and shape his sons' futures. While Allan Edwin displayed qualities of initiative, resilience and unbridled courage, he and his brothers hardly epitomised Bean's larrikin digger. Father and sons were all extremely conservative. They were modest Methodists who, in many ways, were the antithesis of the traditional myth that influences much of the Anzac legend.

7. Paradise Lost

Edwin Leane was described as a 'big man both physically and mentally.'[120] However, his lifetime involvement with the military must have left him feeling adrift after his demobilisation at the age of just 52. Success, status and prestige had been bestowed on him. After a career characterised by action and adventure, civilian life must have appeared almost mundane. He was not alone, and both the Hughes and Bruce governments were supportive of the notion of rewarding returned servicemen with positions of power for the career sacrifices they had made in service to the nation. Like other returned men, Edwin needed to find employment, and in pursuit of this he wrote to Senator Edward Millen as Minister for Repatriation on 11 November 1919. In his letter he emphasised his service record and his insurance expertise, while also assuring the Senator of his 'ability as an organiser and controller of men.'[121]

In the short term, nothing of significance presented itself and he returned to the National Mutual Life Insurance Company in Sydney. However, in 1924, the Administrator of Norfolk Island, John William Parnell, who had held the office for four years, announced his retirement, and the Australian government began the search for his successor. Norfolk Island is a small, isolated, outcrop of land in the Pacific Ocean some 1700 kilometres east-north-east of Sydney, 100 kilometres north-west of Auckland and 800 kilometres south of Noumea. The island was initially settled by Polynesian seafarers in the 15th century and later abandoned, before the British colonisers of NSW in 1788 recognised the commercial benefits of exploiting the island using convict labour. Subsequent convict settlements proved unsuccessful. Yet the Pitcairn survivors of the infamous *Bounty* mutiny found a haven there—a semi-tropical island with palm-fringed shores, fertile soil and green-capped hills. The islanders lived under the auspices of the NSW colonial government until Federation. In 1913 the island became an external territory to be administered by a government-appointed administrator. Until this time, the islanders had lived a fairly *laissez faire* existence based on barter and other measures that ensured they remained self-sufficient.

While ostensibly idyllic, the society of Norfolk Island was divided, with political tensions over government administration at variance with the island's peaceful image. A government appointee had to be a man of astute business acumen as well as an efficient and sensitive organiser of people. By 1924 the island's economy had significant potential for development with overseas markets, although most of the local buildings were in need of refurbishment. Someone with drive and initiative was needed to address internal and external development. Over 115 applications were received for what promised to be an idyllic sinecure that amounted to a mini fiefdom. A personal reference from the National Mutual Life Association declaring Colonel Edwin Leane as a man of 'the highest principles, [who is] genial and large hearted, tactful, diplomatic and able to handle other men to the best advantage' proved irresistible.[122] This opinion was reinforced by a letter from a former respected Administrator, Michael Vincent Murphy, to Mr F.J. Quinlan as the Secretary for the Department of Home and Territories. He declared that Colonel Leane was 'a very fine fellow and with his splendid war service, he should be an authority to which the residents would bow complacently. His wife too, I am sure will in any social matters, with the assistance of her winsome daughters be a great acquisition.'[123]

Given Colonel Edwin Leane's previous submission to Senator Millen, the Senate agreed that there could be no better man. How wrong they were!

To Colonel Edwin Leane and his family, the position of Administrator of Norfolk Island must have appeared tailor-made for his abilities and expertise. A population devoid of public transport and the accoutrements of civilisation, the island must have seemed a kind of *tabula rasa* for Leane, a society to mould to his business principles and where he could assert his authority. Following his appointment, Colonel Leane, his wife Katie and two daughters, Marjorie and Hatherley, moved into the palatial Government House on 1 July 1924. The official residence was a commodious Georgian building that clearly set the Administrator apart from the island residents. His salary was to be £700 per year with an allowance of £100.[124]

As well as occupying Government House and acting as President of the Executive Council and Chief Magistrate, Edwin was to be the arbiter of all issues on the island. From all appearances the appointment seemed totally autocratic in nature; yet it was not in the nature of the islanders to 'bow complacently' to anyone. Unrest was evident from the outset of Edwin's tenure as his military mien and temperament struck a discordant note within the social and general atmosphere of the island community. This was a remote community where the inhabitants generally lived by independent negotiation. Yet a man of Colonel Edwin Leane's aristocratic stature, both physically and socially, did not readily lend himself to consensus and mutual decision-making.

From the outset, Edwin tried to actively engage in all aspects of community life. As Administrator, he saw himself as 'the father of the people', but his paternalistic instincts were far from appreciated by his community which, after all, was living in the 20th century.[125] Edwin embraced the position with a kind of missionary zeal in an endeavour to establish a harmonious community that could engage in trade and commercial activity with the wider world. Initially, he made numerous proposals to improve the farming and agriculture of the island. As the cattle were largely inbred and in very poor condition, he imported a stud bull to the island. Inexplicably, it disappeared. He cultivated a fine vegetable garden in the grounds of Government House to demonstrate to the islanders the potential largesse of careful horticulture. He even introduced artificial manures to the islanders to encourage similar cultivation, but they showed little interest. From the early days of his tenure as Administrator, Edwin took an interest in public works such as road building. These works were completed by the islanders themselves as a community duty, working 24 days a year. Each islander was paid 4/- per day for his labour. However, a visit to a work party saw Edwin declare in frustration that the party was 'hopeless', and that the work of 55 men, 9 carts and 18 horses over three days, which amounted to 120 yards of road eight feet wide, was 'ludicrous'. Asserting that 'he knew what represented a fair day's work as well as any man', he drew the ire of the men when he claimed that 'two self respecting roadmen in Australia would have made a better showing in three days.'[126]

Colonel Leane's critical view of the islanders was made public in February 1925. He had been seconded from the island for three months as Acting Administrator of the Northern Territory as the incumbent was ill. In Adelaide he told the *Northern Standard* that 'it was difficult to awake any energy or enterprise among the people ... They did not need to work to live, like other people and thus did not have incentive for effort that prevailed elsewhere.'[127] Yet, in spite of the islanders' perceived reluctance to work and change, they did submit a proposal to their Administrator to introduce a junior secondary curriculum. Edwin opposed the idea and virtually impugned the integrity and intelligence of the islanders by denying the need for higher education in their remote community. In his view, the island had no place for such advanced skills and it would be impossible to employ anyone of worth to deliver higher education. Yet, in contradiction to that, and with implicit criticism, he postulated that teachers from Victorian private schools with greater educational qualifications would be cheaper, with the added benefit of giving the children 'the gentle breeding which they now lack'.[128]

The island's main governing body was the Executive Council, of which Edwin was President. It consisted of six members elected by the islanders and six chosen by Edwin himself. Immediate tension developed within the group as it was perceived that Edwin's appointments were fundamentally government men and that they were easily intimidated by his forceful personality and stern demeanour. In some instances, when voting within the council reached a deadlock, Edwin was heard to declare, 'Whether you like it or not, it will become law.'[129] Yet he underestimated the power and influence of the old families on the island. Such a force was Mr Charles Chase Ray Nobbs, who angered Colonel Leane from the early days. The island's influential grocer, Nobbs continued to communicate directly with the Department of Home and Territories over a grievance, rather than follow due process and lodge his concerns with the Administrator. In order to assert his authority, Leane wrote to the Minister stating, 'In my opinion there is one way only to deal with this type. Send his letters back to him in a cover without any comment. He has been informed so many times, what is the correct channel to communicate that he simply takes no notice of it.'[130]

Of greater concern however, were numerous occasions when Edwin's role as both Administrator and Chief Justice caused personal and community conflict. Altogether, Edwin had too much power and he exerted it rigorously and often insensitively. While his knowledge of military law had been clear, and servicemen were controlled by orders, civilian life proved far more complex. By 1925 the islanders had begun to express their dissatisfaction with their new Administrator to the Australian government and, as a consequence, a Royal Commission was established. Mr Frances Whysall was appointed Commissioner and spent three months on the island in the early part of 1926. During this period he met with the islanders and compiled a body of evidence to explain their discontent. This decision was regarded as totally justified by Northern Territorians who had had a brief taste of the Colonel's rule. In the *Northern Standard* of October 1925 the headline 'HOW POOH BAH LEANE RULES NORFOLK ISLAND' crucified

Leane's administrative style.[131] From that point on, a number of specific complaints were directed at Edwin's ruthless and often unjust application of his authority.

General discontent was expressed over alcohol restrictions and boating ordinances which involved everyone on the island. The Administrator had been directed to close down illegal alcohol supplies and it was understood that the grocer, Mr Nobbs, would sell a bottle of 'vinegar for 12/6' to anyone who asked. Edwin's intervention in this procurement immediately alienated Nobbs and many of the islanders. One of the first of a series of personal complaints was that lodged by Robert McPhail in relation to criminal proceedings instituted by the Administrator against his wife, foster daughter and two sons. The proceedings stemmed from the loss of a thanksgiving basket of fruit and vegetables offered at St John's Church on 26 November 1924. The gift had come from the Leanes and the basket bore the label 'Government House, Norfolk Island'. The next day, George Quintal, as caretaker of the church, noted that the vegetables had not been disposed of and, as he saw no name on the basket, told Charlotte McPhail to feel free to take the produce. He allegedly told her not to take the basket itself, but she apparently did not hear that instruction. When informed that the produce was available, Mrs McPhail asked her sons, John and Thomas, to collect the basket and its contents, as she believed the basket belonged to her sister, who she knew had made an offering in a basket. Although Mrs McPhail made it known that she had the basket, it was not immediately connected to the missing basket from Government House.

The missing basket caused the Leanes considerable consternation. Accordingly, the Administrator directed the island's sole policeman, Constable Werner, to locate the item. Given the small size of the island, this was not difficult. The constable was then instructed to issue a summons charging Charlotte McPhail (aged 18 years), John and Thomas McPhail (12 and 10 years respectively) with the theft of one clothes basket, the property of His Majesty the King, and Mary Ann McPhail with receiving property, well knowing it to have been stolen. The cases were heard in the Norfolk Island Court on 5 December 1924 with the plaintiff, the Administrator, presiding as Chief Magistrate. Under these circumstances it is not surprising that the Administrator delivered a 'guilty' verdict and imposed a deferred sentence of an indefinite period. This effectively gave the alleged perpetrators a criminal record. In 1925, when Charlotte McPhail wished to leave the island to assume a position on the mainland, she was informed that she would require the Administrator's permission. Subsequently, a pompous and humiliating letter was composed by Edwin and signed by the Registrar of the Court, Mr E. Stephenson, stating:

> The Chief Magistrate has granted permission for Charlotte McPhail to leave Norfolk Island, by steamer leaving the 10th day of January, 1925, on the following conditions:- That upon arrival at her destination she reports at the nearest police station and leaves her address, and notifies any subsequent change of residence.[132]

Outraged and humiliated by a virtual ticket of leave for Charlotte, Mr McPhail lodged a formal complaint declaring that the proceedings were harsh and unjust and that there had been a gross miscarriage of justice. He further postulated that 'the Administrator's adjudication of the case was contrary to the ethics of justice, inasmuch as nominal owner of the property alleged to have been stolen, he directed the prosecution and as Magistrate disclosed a biased mind in the conduct of court proceedings.'[133]

Under oath at the Royal Commission, the Administrator admitted that, 'being the first case of this kind, while I was forced from the evidence brought before me, the demeanour of the witnesses, to find a verdict of guilty I felt that every necessary purpose would be served if I inflicted no penalty, but took the opportunity publicly, in the Court House, in the presence of a large concourse of people, to make this a starting point of a new era.'[134] It may have been an admirable aim for Leane to start as he meant to finish, but an unjust finding was not the means to achieve this. Furthermore, in deferring the sentences without a time limit, the Administrator was in breach of the Crimes Act, as there was no provision for deferment in a case of petty larceny. After a thorough investigation, the Commission 'decided that the convictions in all cases were against the evidence, inasmuch as intent is not disclosed, and the actions of the persons were, throughout, consistent with innocence. It is suggested that a pardon be granted to Mary, John and Thomas McPhail and that the convictions be expunged from the court records of Norfolk Island.'[135]

Naturally Edwin opposed the pardons, declaring, 'If an alteration is made to my ruling I fear that this element will feel they have won a victory, and in every future case which occurs on the island, similar petitions will be forwarded, therefore for the sake of law and order, even though there might possibly be an injustice done to any one of the defendants, I feel it is not wise to give them any excuse to repeat this.'[136] Yet Colonel Leane's impulsive and autocratic rule had broken down the *esprit de corps* that must exist in any isolated community. Word had begun to spread about his inflated view of his own importance.

Leane's treatment of the McPhails had obviously disturbed his relationship with the Rector, the Reverend Martin and, in his usual combative style, Edwin let the elderly gentleman learn of his displeasure in a letter. In the missive, Leane accused the Reverend of:

> ... boorishness ... and gross deliberate disrespect to me in my capacity as Administrator of Norfolk Island. The rudeness shown by you to the Administrator during the last few weeks, culminated today, when in the presence of other government officials, you were guilty of not making the customary acknowledgement which is expected from a gentleman to those in authority, but which is the imperative duty of an official when the Administrator enters a government office. I have been very patient with you, but will not overlook this impertinence any longer. I have decided to abolish the position which you occupy with regard to the government of this island and to cease paying you the emolument attached to it.[137]

On another occasion, he wrote to the secretary of the vestry:

> On Saturday last my daughter, in company with Mr Cameron Buffett, met Rev. Martin at the foot of Longridge Hill. She made the usual salutation of a lady who wishes to be recognised by a gentleman, and

she said, 'Good Afternoon Mr Martin.' Mr Martin did not give any indication that my daughter was on earth, but pointedly looked at and spoke to Mr Buffett. In consequence, no members of my family were at church yesterday, and will not be while this rude old man is the priest. His action would have been despicable to anyone, more than that when offered to the daughter of your Administrator.[138]

Taken out of context, both letters could have been written by a member of the aristocracy or landed gentry in 18th-century England. Edwin Leane appears to have regarded himself and his family as clearly beyond the station of the other residents of the island.

Another complaint submitted to the Royal Commission was lodged by Mr Ernest Stephenson. As Registrar of the Courts of Norfolk Island, he had served under three different administrators since 1913. On 31 July 1925 he was suspended from his position by Edwin Leane. It was alleged that Stephenson was guilty of neglect of duty, the excessive use of intoxicating liquors, and discourtesy to the public. Two previous administrators and a number of residents testified to Mr Stephenson's good character, his ability as an officer and his courtesy to the public. Mr Stephenson admitted to occasions of intemperance and made a commitment to modify his behaviour. Accordingly, pressure was placed on the Administrator to reinstate Mr Stephenson as Registrar of Courts and Associated Offices from 1 April 1926.

In any small community, gossip is common currency, and the Leanes fell prey to this, eliciting further complaint to the Royal Commission concerning the Administrator and his wife. Evidence tendered revealed that, in November 1925, Mrs Leane had informed a number of women that Mrs Warner, the wife of the Officer in Charge of the Pacific Cable Station, was a woman of immoral character. She further claimed that Mrs Warner had lived with another man for 12 months and that the Cable Board had notified Mr Warner that he must 'put his house in order' or leave the service.[139] Mrs Leane denied having made these accusations and her husband endeavoured to deflect the blame by declaring that he had heard rumours early in his tenure but only made mention of the information to the women in the presence of their husbands. Further enquiry proved the falsity of the rumours, as the General Superintendent of the Pacific Cable Company revealed that no such advice had been given to Mr Warner. The Commissioner's summation of the issue was damning:

> The evidence is against the Administrator and his wife, and it fails to disclose any foundation for the very serious statements made against the complainant's honour. Whilst no legal liability rests with the Commonwealth, it is suggested that the moral obligation of the Government call for suitable acknowledgement to Mrs Warner as compensation for the pain of mind and body suffered in consequence of the defamatory statements publicly made against her.[140]

The Administrator's wife was central to yet another complaint submitted for enquiry by the Commission. Mrs Leane was a regular visitor to the school where she spoke to the children about religious and moral issues. It must be said that the Leanes were generally horrified by the deceit, loose morals and sexual promiscuity of the islanders. However, she overstepped her position when she arrived during school hours to tackle the teacher, Mrs Evans, over comments made at a public meeting. The discussion became very heated and very public and most unbecoming of the position held by both ladies on the island. As a consequence, Mrs Evans felt her position to be untenable and withdrew from the island's service.

Investigation by the Commissioner disclosed the fact that the Administrator had instructed his wife to interview Mrs Evans, 'to pin down the scandal before it got any further.'[141] The Commissioner was at a loss to explain why the Administrator would instruct his wife to investigate an allegation of impropriety against a public officer, particularly when the result of such an enquiry may have rendered disciplinary action necessary. The Commissioner was convinced 'that had the Administrator attended officially to the complaint, the cause of Mrs Evans' grievance would not have arisen.'[142]

The Administrator's wife, Katie Leane, did little to endear herself to the islanders. Apart from her imperious demeanour, she was determined to have her own way on many matters even if the issues were sensitive. According to family lore, she angered the islanders with an order to have a stately Norfolk Pine felled in order to improve the sea vistas from Government House.[143]

A further grievance against the prejudice and injustice of the Administrator was lodged with the Commissioner by Mr Francis Yeaman. He had been charged by criminal summons of having misappropriated £20 and with unlawful detention of property—a sheet of paper on which it is alleged the Administrator had written detailed information to serve the plaintiff's cause. Mr Yeaman was Secretary of the Norfolk Island Agricultural and Horticultural Society and the plaintiff was Parkin Carty Christian, who was Secretary of the Norfolk Island Whaling Company. At a horticultural fundraiser initiated by Mrs Leane, in which the Leanes were enthusiastic participants, Mrs Leane declared that she would donate £20 to the whalers, who had lost a boat, if £50 was raised that evening. The proceeds amounted to £50 gross with the net profit for the evening of £47 11s. On 10 October, Mrs Leane presented two cheques to Mr Yeaman, one to the Norfolk Island Agricultural and Horticultural Society for £27 11s and one to the Norfolk Island Whaling Company for £20. When Mr Christian requested his cheque, it was refused and he was advised by the whalers to institute proceedings. Mrs Leane was involved to the extent that she issued the disputed order and her evidence was material to the issue.

As the Report of the Royal Commission describes: 'A further objection in writing lodged with the Registrar of Courts at Norfolk Island and an objection raised by Mr Yeaman when the case was called for hearing, were overruled by the Administrator acting as Chief Magistrate who proceeded to hear and determine the plaint. During the course of the proceedings such remarks as 'You have been badly advised by your bush lawyers', 'You are reading it off like a parrot', were made by the Magistrate who entered a verdict for the full amount with costs and witnesses' expenses.'[144]

In his assessment of the situation, the Commissioner determined that Christian was influenced, if not instructed, by the Administrator. Given

Mrs Leane's involvement in the affair, the Commissioner was 'convinced that the proceedings against Mr Yeaman were actuated by a spirit of vindictiveness, and suggest, in the light of the evidence, that a pardon be granted and the criminal conviction expunged from the records of Norfolk Island.'[145]

Having heard numerous complaints and considered countless items of evidence and witness testimony, the Commissioner's findings on Colonel Leane's tenure as Administrator were devastating for the Leanes and supportive of the residents. Commissioner Whysall specifically cited problems of social unrest, triggered by broken promises, the recognition of hearsay and gossip without foundation or fact by the Administrator, unauthorised intervention by Mrs Leane and the couple's 'treatment of the people generally as base and unworthy of respect', all of which undermined community harmony.[146]

Furthermore, the Commissioner added that, 'It is freely admitted, that the Islanders look to the Administrator for the maintenance of dignity appropriate to his office, but it is contended that an attitude autocratic and superior in its character, associated with elaborate formal arrangements for attendance of an administrative party at public functions, is alien to the conditions of the Territory and the lives of its people.'[147] He added even more damning evidence as he continued:

> It is, however most unfortunate that the temperament of the present Administrator is not in harmony with the social and general atmosphere of an isolated community. The evidence reveals that his tendency is to usurp the powers vested in him for the protection of the people, and disregard the need of encouraging sympathetic understanding and cooperation. It is manifest that in the exercise of his judicial functions his conduct was distinctly combatant and quite inconsistent with the principles of justice. Apart from the strictly judicial duties of his office, it is regrettable that he acted upon uncorroborated statements, derogatory to the inhabitants, statements, which simple enquiry would have made clear to him were without bases in fact.
>
> It is patent that the view of the Administrator and those of the residents are so widely divergent that healthy cooperation is

not possible and after full consideration of the evidence, your Commissioner is forced to the conclusion that the interests of the Commonwealth and of Norfolk Island would best be served by the immediate withdrawal of the present Administrator in favour of one possessed of proved temperamental suitability and a knowledge of community oversight and management.[148]

This report was submitted to the House of Representatives on 12 August 1926 and Edwin was given two months' notice. Colonel Edwin Leane and his wife were outraged and the publicity concerning his termination must have been humiliating. Edwin was determined to vindicate his position in an action before the courts. His fury was vigorously supported by his old military contemporary, Senator Harold 'Pompey' Elliott, who acted as his lawyer. Colonel Leane declared that:

> My appointment as Administrator is from July 1924 to July 1927. The reason assigned for termination is temperamental disability. There is no charge suggesting misconduct of any description. I assert publicly that the Royal Commission was a farce from its inception, because when I alleged that perjury was being committed, and wrote to the Department, stating my intention of taking action under the Royal Commissions Act of 1902-12, I was informed by the Department that the Act did not apply to Norfolk Island and that the Commissioner had no power, therefore to call witnesses to take evidence on oath. In an action before the courts I shall disclose evidences which have already been placed before the Minister, of bias on the part of the Commissioner, of witnesses asked for but not called and of portions of my own evidence used apart from the context to support a finding, which had the context been used, could not have been made.[149]

In his defence, Edwin further contended that Commissioner Whysall had been unduly influenced by Mr Nobbs, who had curried favour with the Commissioner, and that Mr Whysall, as a former Deputy of the Postmaster General's Department of NSW, was ill equipped for his undertaking. He then threw out a challenge to the Minister for Home Territories, Sir William Gladstone, to visit the island himself to make a truly informed decision.

While the Commissioner's report acknowledged the excellent work that the Administrator had initiated to stimulate trade and agriculture and to rehabilitate public buildings on the island, the criticisms were the focus of the report tabled in parliament. The publicity surrounding the case took its toll on Edwin and his wife and they were outraged and bitter at what they felt to be an unjust investigation. The stain of the dismissal must have galled Edwin and weighed heavily on him. He must have felt that his life's contribution to the nation and the family name had been sullied by false and petty grievances.

As the eldest son, no doubt much had been expected of Edwin and life had presented him with every opportunity to shine. His extensive military service had certainly seen him achieve a degree of fame and an exalted status which was, of course, reinforced by his immediate family. Yet, ironically, it was the principles of his military life which undermined his transition to an unusual civilian appointment. As a senior officer he was accustomed to a disciplined lifestyle and instantaneous obedience to his law. Such precepts were anathema on Norfolk Island where the population had long adjusted to a very *laissez faire* lifestyle. Sensitivity, patience and tact would seem essential qualities for any administrator, but Edwin's stubborn and autocratic style failed to recognise that military efficiency could not be imposed on an isolated community in the middle of the Pacific Ocean.

Notwithstanding these deficiencies, the irony of Edwin's appointment cannot be overlooked and, in many ways, it contained the seeds of his failure. Norfolk Island had initially been settled by the British as a convict colony, brutally ruled by an autocratic governor. Having outlived that purpose, the island had been resettled by the descendants of the mutinous Pitcairn Islanders who adapted and adopted a unique lifestyle. In those post-war years the island's inhabitants had every reason to hope that a new order, which promised men fit to run a new democracy, would apply to them. Instead the government of the day made a regressive decision that perpetuated an entrenched British class system in contradiction of

20th-century democratic values. It failed to acknowledge the constitutional separation of powers and, in establishing Edwin and family in the historic Georgian mansion, set him apart from the population and affirmed his pre-existing delusions of grandeur. From the islanders' perspective it would not be drawing a long bow to view his tenure as reminiscent of Captain Bligh, whose tyranny and intransigent rule had forced the islanders' forebears to cast him adrift in 1789.

It is evident that Colonel Edwin Leane was a member of a military family initially characterised by its number. His Boer War and World War I experiences in the military had, until 1924, been the defining points of his life. Yet he could not graft his wartime experiences onto civilian life and, because of this, he failed. Thus, his enduring legacy is negative, which in many ways undermines Bean's promotion of the Anzac legend as Bean understood it.

Following his departure from the island, Edwin Leane and his wife retired to Melbourne where he virtually removed himself from public life. In choosing to retire to Melbourne, Edwin, Katie and their family were geographically isolated from family and friends in Sydney and Adelaide, thus removing themselves from obvious censure. Although his fall from grace was not widely discussed within the family, the perception of subsequent generations was that he had blundered badly in misjudging the tenor of island mores. In fairness and perhaps a limited defence of Colonel Leane, history has shown that the Nobbs family continued to prove a constant thorn in the side of subsequent administrators.

The island remained self-governing for 40 years until Canberra dissolved its parliament in 2015 and set up a new regional council to administer it, subject to NSW law. Obviously the move by Australia is unpopular with the locals. As recently as 2016, a descendant, Dr Chris Nobbs, vigorously opposed the Australian government's proposal for limited self-government for Norfolk Island. He has been the driving force alongside Geoffrey Robertson QC to lodge a petition with the United Nations to have Norfolk Island listed as a self-governing territory with its own parliament and government. Clearly the islanders continue to rail against the restrictions imposed by what they perceive as an undemocratic colonial form of administration. Another relative, Andre Nobbs, a former Chief Minister of the disbanded Norfolk Island government, asserts that he is open to the island becoming a territory of New Zealand. Unlike Australia, New Zealand generally allows its territories to govern themselves rather than acting as an overbearing host. He argues that New Zealand is geographically closer and has a track record of making its territories productive. However, the hapless Colonel Edwin Leane went to his grave lamenting an ignominious failure that still lacks resolution a century later. He died of cancer at his home in Athelstone Street, Camberwell, Victoria, at the age of 61 on 27 August 1928 and was buried at the local Box Hill cemetery.

8. WARRANT OFFICER ERNEST ALBERT LEANE AND FAMILY

The second of Thomas John and Alice's sons, Ernest Albert Leane, enlisted on 25 January 1915. He was born in Nailsworth on 1 October 1869 and was therefore, at 45 years of age, another older Leane enlistee. He had married Martha May Boswell on 23 June 1894 and the couple had 11 children between that year and 1911. Again, the call to arms seemed to appear more attractive to one of the Leanes than staying in Australia to support his wife and young family. He had already abandoned his wife and children before the war and, for him, perhaps the war provided an opportunity for a justifiable escape. In spite of what most likely were strained feelings between father and sons, Ernest Albert Leane and his son, William Ernest Raymond, both enlisted in South Australia on 25 January 1915 and were Nos. 373 and 374 respectively. Ernest Albert's oldest son, Arnold Harry, later enlisted on 21 May 1915 and joined his father and brother as a member of the 27th Battalion as No. 1055. Perhaps because of his previous three years' service in the militia, Arnold appears to have avoided an Australian training camp and so joined his father and brother on 31 May to embark on HMAT A2 *Geelong*, bound for Egypt.

All three family members trained in Egypt before being deployed to Gallipoli where they landed on 11 September 1915. From the outset, the battalion suffered from the relentless and accurate shrapnel and rifle fire and, by the end of the month, both William and Ernest had been evacuated to Malta. Ernest was hospitalised with a septic thumb and William with contusions to the head, after which he developed Enteric Fever. Arnold Harry remained with the battalion until the withdrawal, but his service on the peninsula also undermined his health. Following the battalion's return to Egypt he was hospitalised at Tel el Kebir in February 1916 with pharyngitis.

The rigours of his experience at Gallipoli had severely compromised Ernest's health and, on his return to Cairo, his much older body quickly succumbed to influenza and rheumatism. This resulted in his hospitalisation at No. 2 AGH at Gezirah from December 1915 through to February 1916 and his subsequent transfer to a convalescent hospital at Helouan. Clearly Ernest's age and previous sedentary occupation as a clerk were not conducive to active service. After his recuperation, it is highly likely that Edwin, in his senior position, orchestrated a transfer for Ernest from the 27th Battalion to the Australian Army Pay Corps (AAPC) in Egypt. Ernest remained in his AAPC appointment from 10 March 1916 until he was transferred to the London office on 1 September 1916. Here he was promoted to corporal. Similarly, William Ernest's protracted illness had also left him weakened and it is likely that Edwin's influence saw him likewise transferred to the AAPC on the same date as his father. Both men were then moved to AIF Headquarters in Horseferry Road, London, when Edwin's duties demanded his presence there.

Ernest's eldest son, Arnold Harry, was also redeployed in March 1916. Like all the Australian troops, he was fed up with the frustration of inaction and the desolation of Egypt and he longed to rejoin his battalion. The 27th Battalion embarked from Alexandria and landed in Marseilles on 1 March 1916. However Arnold's health had also been compromised by his early service at Gallipoli. After a brief period in France he reported sick to the 6th Field Ambulance on 11 March and did not rejoin his battalion until 17 March at Armentières. From April through to November, the 27th Battalion moved through the trenches of northern France, relieving other battalions in the firing lines close to Amiens, Pozières, Bapaume and Mouquet Farm, or working on improving trenches and communications. However a failed offensive at Dernancourt on 5 November 1916 would cost Arnold Harry his life. No. 1790 Sergeant Solly, of the 27th Battalion, witnessed the young man's death and reported on the cruel sequence of events that finally killed him:

> This man was wounded in the attack at Flers at about 6.20 am. on November 5 1916. After 9 am. he was taken away by the stretcher bearers. As they were taking him to the dressing station, a fragment of shell hit him and he died on the stretcher. I saw him lying dead on the stretcher but have no knowledge of his burial. I was wounded later on in the day and was taken to the dressing post. He was about 6 feet, well built, dark, 20 years. Was a Railway Porter in Adelaide South Australia.[150]

Another report was offered by No. 3140 Private Harding, also of the 27th Battalion. He stated that he knew Corporal Arnold Harry. 'He was in my platoon. He was a big strapping fellow. He was wounded on 5 November at Flers and went to England. Several fellows in the battalion had letters from him in hospital in England. He died in England. This was given out on parade. I heard the announcement. I did not see him wounded.'[151]

These conflicting reports must have caused Mrs Martha Leane, as next of kin, and Arnold Harry's siblings at home enormous and sustained anguish. Given her estrangement from her husband, we can be justified in presuming that she received no news or solace from him. Battling on alone, she requested further details on her son's demise from Base Records in Melbourne and from the Red Cross in London. Martha's despair must have been exacerbated by her continued penury and the fact that she did not receive confirmation of Arnold's death until April 1917. Ultimately, her enquiries not only confirmed the death of her son, but suggested that he had been buried 'In the vicinity of the Maze and Blue Cat. Map location Gueudecourt 1/10 000M10C. Somme valley. Effects for 3rd Echelon including watch and kit store military testament and three military books forwarded to Mrs Leane. Package 807.'[152] In spite of this information,

Corporal Arnold Harry Leane's remains were never located after the war. With no known grave, Arnold Leane's sacrifice is commemorated among the missing at Dernancourt Communal Cemetery. A tribute to his memory was published in the daily papers by his family on learning of his death:

> Leane. Killed in action in France on November 5 1916. No. 1055 Corporal A.H. Leane 27th Battalion.
>
> *Renew my will from day to day*
> *Bind it with thine and take away*
> *All that now makes it hard to say*
> *Thy will be done.*
>
> Inserted by his loving mother, sisters and brothers.[153]

A further tribute was inserted by 'his loving friend, Violet,' who wrote,

> *He lived a man, he died a hero*
> *One less for earth, one more for heaven.*[154]

Corporal Arnold Harry Leane.
Australian War Memorial H12530

Both tributes speak of a faithful acceptance of God's will, from which no doubt family and friends drew some comfort. Most likely, Arnold Harry's father, Ernest Albert, at AIF Headquarters in Horseferry Road, would have received the news of his son's death first. Yet there is no record of any initiative undertaken by him to ascertain further information to offer solace to himself or his family.

Grief and loneliness must have consumed Ernest Albert and William Ernest while stationed in London as members of the AAPC. In many ways it must have proven a boring and frustrating appointment, far removed from the real action of war. During 1916, William's poor health had seen him hospitalised for significant periods with severe bronchitis, laryngitis and the dreaded venereal disease (VD). News of Arnold Harry's death no doubt compounded William's misery and his father's despair. Perhaps his brother's death inspired William to seize the day for, in early 1917, his service record began to document blemishes. As a formerly responsible, if not always moral young adult, his behaviour was incongruous and appears cavalier and defiant. London offered all sorts of temptations to a young man and it is obvious that William readily succumbed to them. In February of that year he absented himself for a fortnight without leave. For this offence, he forfeited 31 days' pay and was sentenced to 12 days in detention. Unsurprisingly, in March 1917, he was admitted to Bulford Hospital with VD for 23 days, after which he was promptly transferred to the 70th Battalion. Clearly this did not appeal either for, on 7 May 1917, William faced a District Court Martial for yet another incidence of Absence Without Leave. It was alleged that he absented himself from 14 April through to 29 May 1917. The court hoped that the forfeiture of 158 days' pay and detention at Woking for 54 days would curb his disobedience.

William served just over a month in detention before he was deployed to France on 17 October 1917. He would again be reunited with his father for, by August 1917, Edwin, as DADOS, had orchestrated Ernest Albert's transfer to Ordnance Corps. On this basis, it is highly likely that his father Ernest and

Uncle Edwin may have conspired to keep the young man on the straight and narrow for, by 4 December, William had also been seconded to Ordnance Corps. Under the watchful eye of his father and Uncle Edwin, William continued in his appointment until the end of 1918 when he was promoted to corporal and posted back to London as an army records clerk. However, this too must have been tedious and devoid of the glamour that had come to surround the Leanes. On 14 August 1919, William met and quickly married a 25-year-old widow, Lillian Musselwhite.[155] His father, Ernest, also remained stationed in London throughout 1919. During this period, Ernest was commended by the Secretary of State for War for valuable services rendered. As Colonel Edwin Leane was also based at Horseferry Road at that time, it is not difficult to suspect his imprimatur in promoting his brother's service. Consequently, Ernest was immediately promoted to Warrant Officer Class 1, thus ensuring that all of Edwin's brothers had achieved significant rank. The honour of the Leane name was assured. On 13 March 1920, Ernest boarded *Ceramic* for his passage to Adelaide and inevitable demobilisation, effected on 5 April 1920. William and his young bride, Lillian, boarded *Megantic* on 9 January 1920, also bound for Adelaide where he was demobilised in late April. Free of military constraint and exercising his new-found freedom, William and Lillian Leane immediately relocated to Kalgoorlie. For Lillian, a second marriage and relocation to what must have been an alien and uncivilised environment, would have represented an enormous culture shock. For William, domestic fidelity proved an impossible expectation after his varied amorous encounters abroad. Unsurprisingly, the union was not an enduring one. In 1926 the *Western Argus* reported that Lillian had filed for divorce:

> At a sitting of the Divorce Court in Kalgoorlie, Mrs Lillian Leane stated in evidence that she was married to the respondent in London in August 1919 and that they had come to South Australia in the same year. After a few months in Adelaide, they came to Kalgoorlie and lived there together until 1925. While on a holiday at Easter 1924, the petitioner heard rumours of her husband's misconduct with a nurse but could get no proof. About the same time, she found in his pocket a letter to him in a woman's handwriting in very

affectionate terms. In October 1925 she heard of his misconduct with a certain woman and accused him of it. They had a 'row' over the matter and Leane left her, since which time they have not lived together. ... The respondent went to live in a hotel in Boulder and about a month later, left his employment and went to Adelaide. ... Leane on being served with divorce papers in Adelaide admitted misconduct with different women.[156]

Undaunted by shame or scruples, William was quick to marry Vera Mary Davies in 1928. Although the couple had a son, David John, William remained unsettled. His drafting business failed and, by 1938, Vera Leane had also successfully filed for divorce on the grounds of desertion. William then married for a third time, to Eleanor Blanch Wadham, who he met on the train between Peterhead and Adelaide.

Eleanor had come from a very respectable Adelaide family and was an intelligent woman of feisty independence. Educated at the Wilderness School, she was inclined to snobbery and regarded the Leanes as beneath her. She regularly criticised her mother-in-law, Martha, whose post-war penury often saw her shopping in an old coat secured by a safety pin. In spite of the birth of the couple's daughter, Glenda Rae, in 1942, there was no joy in the family relationships for father, mother or daughter. The marriage was a volatile battlefield, and Glenda recalls endless bitter arguments between her parents. William's war service resulted in ongoing sickness as he suffered recurring bouts of pleurisy and bronchitis. This no doubt added to the strain on the marriage, which was exacerbated by William's excessive drinking and womanising. His contempt for domestic life was again obvious when he walked out of the family home when Glenda was 13. On that occasion Eleanor decided that she and Glenda would follow William to find out where he was going. They followed him to Klemzig, where he took up residence with a woman who became known only to mother and daughter as 'Ma Bellman'. William lived with 'Ma Bellman' until he died in 1964. He was buried in the AIF section of West Terrace Cemetery. Glenda recalls feeling no sorrow at his burial, as he had never shown her one iota of affection in her whole life. Her childhood memories are painful, devoid of love from an unfeeling mother and a derelict father.[157]

Clearly William suffered from the common dislocation experienced by First World War veterans. His father Ernest encountered the same problems. Having been absent from his wife and family responsibilities for five years, Ernest also could not, and did not wish to pick up the threads of his former life. His long-suffering wife, Martha, had struggled to keep the family together in Ernest's absence and the death of her son, Arnold Harry, must have exacerbated her pain. No longer able to afford to live in O'Connell Street, Adelaide, the family had moved to more modest accommodation at Mile End. Knowing that her husband had returned, Martha Leane was angry that her straitened circumstances had not ended with his demobilisation. Her husband had disappeared. In desperation she wrote to Major James Lean, Officer in Charge of Base Records in Melbourne, on 7 December 1920, seeking some avenue of supplementary income:

> Dear Sir
>
> In the Advertiser of December 3 I have noticed a paragraph re Federal Allowance. I receive an allowance of 10/- a week as a result of my deceased son Corporal 1055 A.H Leane 27 Battalion KIA Nov. 5 1916. With that allowance and the help of my two sons' board money of one pound each per week I keep them in food. Out of the one pound a week I work to pay my rent of one pound five shillings a week and have to keep three children ages 13, 11, 10 years old. Their father is alive and left my house in 1915 for the front. He returned in April 1920 but has deserted his home and children. I have had no money from him since the end of September 1920. He has had all his defence pay—every penny himself. Also his great bond too. [This refers to the gratuity of 1/- a day retained for servicemen to tide them over after the war until they could secure employment.] He has made over his half of my dead son's grant to me and said it must keep me and the children, but up to now I have not received it from the military.
>
> I think you will find I am in need of the increase [in the Federal Allowance].

Hoping you will testify to find my statement correct and consider this case. Please it is awful. I have capital but what I have stated is true.

Thanking you
Yours respectfully
M.M. Leane

P.S. I know my husband went to Western Australia but whereabouts in the state I do not know.[158]

Warrant Officer Ernest Albert Leane.
Image courtesy of: Kingsley Leane.

In reply, Major Lean directed Mrs Leane to contact the Deputy Comptroller of the Repatriation Department in Adelaide concerning an increase in the weekly allowance and Keswick Barracks in relation to the gratuity. Nonetheless, her letter must have struck a chord with Major Lean for, in distributing Corporal Arnold Harry Leane's service medals and mementos, he directed them to her, avoiding the search for and prescribed distribution under the Deceased Servicemen's Estates Act of 1918, to Ernest as the father. Martha Leane filed for divorce on the grounds of adultery in 1933 and successfully secured costs and allowances for herself and her children. Ernest Albert Leane subsequently married Alice Jones (née Garrett) on 6 September 1934. The union was short lived as he died on 15 October 1936. His own service medals remained unclaimed as, after his death, Base Records declared that no next of kin could be traced. Given Martha Leane's previous correspondence, this is somewhat surprising, although different times and different personnel may offer some explanation. Ernest Albert Leane was buried at Walkerville Wesleyan Cemetery, in the grave next to his parents. Yet one might be correct in presuming that the ceremony was no family affair.

As in so many cases of soldiers failing to adapt to a return to civilian life after demobilisation, Ernest and his son, William, appear to have suffered similar degrees of dislocation. Removed from the civilising and responsible influences of family and familiarity, they appear to have lost their way. As an older enlistee, Ernest must have found the transition to army life gruelling and highly regimented. Having made that transition, the emotional energy and the physical adjustment required for a return to civilian life were obviously beyond both will and desire. Monogamy and its associated responsibilities had no doubt lost their allure. While this imposed enormous hardship on his wife and children, it is not difficult to understand that perhaps an all-consuming ennui had engulfed him after such a herculean and sustained commitment. The loss of his son and the hardships he had personally endured must have demanded some sort of processing and re-evaluation before he felt able to pick up the threads of a normal existence.

Like so many others, William, as a young man, had sown his wild oats over the years away, and perhaps, in the euphoria of peace, had married in haste. Without ever shouldering marital responsibility, and having tasted carnal delights, he must have found the return to civilian life totally restrictive. William returned to Australia totally uninhibited in terms of his relationships with women. Pleasure and instant gratification replaced rectitude and responsibility. For him, the traditional Wesleyan beliefs were lost, as new and fleeting moral codes papered over the old.

9. LIEUTENANT COLONEL ALLAN WILLIAM LEANE

The third of Thomas John and Alice's sons to enlist was Allan William Leane. He was born on 11 May 1872 in Mount Gambier where his parents had relocated to be closer to Felix and his family. After a few hard years however, Thomas John and Alice moved their growing family to Rose Street in Prospect, where Allan, like his brothers, was educated at the North Adelaide Public School. Following in the footsteps of his eldest brother Edwin, Allan first joined the militia as a member of the 3rd Battalion, South Australian Infantry, in 1890 aged 18. He transferred to the South Australian Lancers as a trooper in 1891, and then returned to his former regiment and was gazetted as a lieutenant in 1893. He later joined his older brother, Edwin, in the 4th Contingent of Imperial Bushmen and sailed with him to South Africa to fight in the Boer War. There, his service was rewarded with a Mention in Despatches. In his civilian life, Allan served an apprenticeship as a commercial traveller with Goode, Durrant and Co. in Adelaide.

On 16 August 1895, Allan married Fanny Blanche Scutt at St Paul's Church in Adelaide. She had been born in 1870 in Bere Regis, Dorset, and, like the Leanes, her family had generational connections with the southern English counties. In 1896 Allan was transferred to Coolgardie in Western Australia by his long-term employer to become Departmental Manager of Goode, Durrant and Co. He remained with the firm for many years and was a valued staff member and a popular comrade. Later that year Allan and Blanche, as she was best known, moved to the cooler climate of Esperance for the birth of their first child. On 29 March 1896 the couple's only son, Eric Allan Leane, was born.[159] Sometime later a large fire wiped out a major part of the town, including the shop managed by Allan. He was then sent to Albany to act as joint manager of Economic Store alongside his brother Raymond. Economic Store was another branch of Goode, Durrant and Co. Allan was then posted to the company's Western Australian Head Office where he was a senior manager and traveller for a section. In 1908 he resigned to establish his own agency, Economic Limited, in High Street, Fremantle.[160]

Following his arrival in the west, Allan's military interests were temporarily suspended and he initially remained on the unattached list. When a vacancy occurred however, he accepted an appointment as a lieutenant in the 11th Australian Infantry Regiment with alacrity. Business interests soon saw him transferred to Kalgoorlie with his brother Raymond. Keen to maintain his military pursuits, Allan transferred to the Goldfields Infantry Unit, with which he remained for two years. With the establishment of his own business agency near Perth in 1908, he transferred back to the Perth-based 11th Australian Infantry Regiment. He assumed command of D Company and was promoted to captain in 1912.

When war was declared in 1914, Allan was aged 42, and had a wealth of military and managerial experience behind him. With one child, and despite his wife's entreaties, he enlisted in the AIF as a major on 28 April 1915. To cater for the spontaneous surge of enlistments in Western Australia, a hastily assembled and primitive training facility was established at Blackboy Camp near Midland. Allan was promptly appointed CO of the 28th Battalion and embarked with his battalion on *Ascanius* at Fremantle on 9 June 1915.

After training and garrison duty at Abbassia, Major Allan William Leane and the 28th Battalion boarded *Ivernia* on 4 September 1915 bound for Gallipoli. The battalion arrived in Lemnos two days later and embarked for Gallipoli on 10 September. While the battalion remained on the peninsula until the evacuation, Major Leane soon developed pharyngitis and was admitted to the field hospital at Gallipoli. He did not regain his previous good health and a further period of hospitalisation was necessary at No.1 Stationary Hospital in Egypt. By that time he had also developed influenza.

Following his discharge from hospital on 4 March 1916, Major Allan Leane returned to the 28th Battalion as second in command and sailed for Marseilles later that month. On 29 July 1916 the battalion commander, Lieutenant Colonel Herbert Bayley Collett CMG, DSO, VD, was severely wounded at Pozières and had to be evacuated to hospital. Major Allan William Leane assumed command of the battalion and was promoted to temporary lieutenant colonel, his promotion and appointment as CO of the 28th Battalion confirmed on 29 November 1916. Within 18 months of his enlistment, Allan William's meteoric promotion through the ranks was both acknowledgement of and reward for his courage and leadership. These qualities were clearly demonstrated at the Battle of Pozières. This small village was situated on a ridge in the Somme Valley between Albert and Bapaume. The 2nd Division, to which the 28th Battalion belonged, was charged with following the 1st Division to attack the village, rout the German stronghold and gain command of the strategic position. With German artillery on three sides and the Australian artillery behind the attacking troops, the offensive at Pozières was said to be the most concentrated artillery barrage of all time. Allied casualties between 23 July and 3 September amounted to some 23,000 men. During his period of service in France, with his battalion decimated at Pozières, Lieutenant Colonel Allan William Leane provided inspired leadership.

Following its exposure to such a horrendous onslaught, the 28th Battalion was rotated out of the line to regroup. During this time, Lieutenant Colonel Allan William Leane learned that his wife and son were planning to visit London for the festive season. With Christmas approaching, he was granted leave to visit London from 14 to 30 December 1916. It would be the last celebration the family enjoyed together. On Lieutenant Colonel Allan William Leane's return to his battalion, he was engaged in action at Waterlot Farm on the Somme on 4 January 1917. Here he was struck by a high explosive shell which hit him on the back and head. He died of his wounds later that day and was buried at Dernancourt Communal Cemetery.

In an article in the Adelaide *Observer* in February 1919, the journalist wrote fulsomely of the commitment and gallantry of the 'Fighting Leanes of Prospect'. Of Lieutenant Colonel Allan William Leane, he wrote 'that he was second in command of the 28th on the peninsula and in that capacity was regarded as an outstanding officer there. He possessed a genial manner of conversation with the most junior of ranks and without depreciation to their previous Commanding Officer, all ranks hailed with delight his appointment to the command of the unit. After the Gallipoli campaign, when the battalion was stationed in the canal zone, Colonel Leane's care for the men of the unit earned it the name of the 'lucky 28th'. He died in an heroic feat that would have certainly brought him the MC had he not been fatally hit.'[161] Charles Bean also lamented the loss of Colonel Allan William Leane. In his diary entry at Heilly on 11 January 1917, he penned a sad epitaph. 'Poor Leane's death – a splendid fellow. The fine colonel of a fine regiment.[162]

After the war, with the establishment of the Commonwealth War Cemeteries, families of deceased Australian servicemen were given the opportunity to compose a personal epitaph for their loved one's headstones. The epitaph could not exceed 66 letters including spaces, with each letter to cost $3^1/_2$ pence Fanny Blanche Leane chose the Latin 'Aspera ad Astra'—'Through hardship to the stars'—for her beloved husband, believing that it epitomised his service. To the men of the 28th Battalion, Lieutenant Colonel Allan William Leane was a star. Adelaide newspaper *The Chronicle* describing his early years in the war, observed,

Colonel Allan William Leane.
Image courtesy of : Moya Sharp. Outback Family History Society

There is no need to emphasise the magnificent work Lieutenant Colonel Leane has accomplished since the memorable landing. Many soldiers have testified to his great gallantry in the face of extreme danger and if only half of what we are told is correct, he has proved a most worthy soldier of the Commonwealth. Among the men, he has made a great reputation and often times we have heard that the rank and file would follow him anywhere. He would never send his men where he was not prepared to go himself, and on every available occasion he has exhibited all the true qualities of a real leader of men.[163]

There is very little information available on the specifics of Lieutenant Colonel Allan William Leane's service, apart from the suggestion of merit ascribed to his rank and the reported laudatory comments. He was obviously a valued leader, but his claim to fame remains sparsely documented. Schooled in the legends of the famous 'Fighting Leanes of Prospect', Lieutenant Colonel Allan William Leane's son, Eric Allan Leane, enlisted in the 2nd AIF in July 1940. He rose to the rank of sergeant in the

4th Motor Transport Company, which was deployed to Singapore in April 1941. He became a prisoner of war of the Japanese in Changi until the cessation of hostilities on 15 August 1945.

10. Brigadier General Sir Raymond Lionel Leane and Family

Raymond Lionel Leane was the fourth of Thomas John and Alice Leane's sons to etch the family name indelibly into the annals of Australian military history. He too was born in the Adelaide suburb of Prospect, on 12 July 1878. Like his siblings, he was educated at the North Adelaide Public School, but left at 12 years of age to work for a wholesale and retail business. The firm was the prestigious Martin Brothers Drapers of Burlington House in Rundle Street, Adelaide. Over a period of five years, Raymond gained experience in all departments before the firm transferred him to work in its store in Albany, Western Australia. [164] The personable and gregarious Raymond Lionel Leane was a man of great physical strength and stature and, in keeping with the family's military bent, was soon engaged actively in the part-time militia. By 1898 he had enlisted in the Albany Garrison Artillery as a gunner. While in Albany he met Edith Louise Laybourne Smith, the 20-year-old daughter of chemist and dentist Joseph Laybourne Smith and his wife Annie Rosalie. Their family of two sons and two daughters were well educated, all attending private schools, with their elder son, Louis Edward, later establishing a notable career for himself as an architect in South Australia. Raymond's love for Edith and his lowly status pitted his intentions against the grandiose expectations of her father. Joseph was not supportive of Edith's marriage to Raymond Leane, as he felt that she had married beneath her status and that her husband had limited prospects.

Edith was just as intelligent as her siblings and was an outstanding musician who had intended to train as a concert pianist. Born in an affluent environment with household servants, she was in many ways ill-equipped to raise a large family with a restless and ambitious husband. However, she adored her handsome husband and was quick to understand the need for adaptability in mastering the steep learning curve of the domestic arts. Raymond married Edith on 14 June 1902 at Christ Church, Claremont. In 1905, now based in Perth, he transferred to the 11th Infantry Regiment and, in 1906, joined the firm of D&W Murray Ltd. Raymond became manager of the Millinery and Lace Department in Fremantle, which seems rather incongruous for a man of such military mien.[165] He was commissioned as a 2nd lieutenant and, by 1908, had been promoted to full lieutenant. His enthusiasm and energy also saw him serving on the local council.

In 1908, Raymond and his brother Allan became joint managers of the Kalgoorlie and Boulder Branch of the New Economic Ltd and Raymond later purchased the Boulder Branch of what had formerly been J.H. Pellow and Co. The company had been, and continued to be considered a 'high class establishment'.[166] With his business interests in the goldfields, Raymond transferred his military pursuits to the Goldfields Infantry Regiment where he was promoted to captain in 1910. He passed his major's examination and the General Staff Course in Tactical Fitness to Command in 1911, and became a member of the 84th Infantry Regiment in 1912. At this stage, Raymond and Edith had four children and, between family, work and military interests, Raymond Lionel Leane must have possessed prodigious energy to maintain such a busy and demanding life. As a parent, he also adhered to a policy of strict family discipline. Like his brother Edwin, Raymond quickly established himself as the family patriarch but, one suspects, while intrusive, Edwin's role was more benign than Raymond's. His rule was law. The third of his sons, Geoffrey Malcolm, no doubt like his other brothers, grew up in awe of his father. In his biography he recorded that 'he was a martinet of the top order.'[167]

On the outbreak of World War I, Raymond Lionel Leane was a volunteer captain in the 84th Infantry Regiment at Kalgoorlie. However, he was quick to see the opportunity that the war presented for him to apply his increasing military expertise, and enlisted in the AIF on 17 August 1914. While Geoffrey felt relief at his father's enlistment, he 'got the impression that his mother was not overjoyed with the prospect of caring for four children and running a business in Kalgoorlie.'[168] It was perhaps fortunate that between 1899 and 1905, Western Australia had also witnessed the marriages of three of Raymond's siblings. His sister Ethel had married William Taylor in 1899, his sister Hilda had married Arthur Hunter in 1902, and his brother Norman had married Calla Caldwell in 1905. With the outbreak of war, the adult children of Thomas and Alice had successfully established a close family circle on the edge of the continent. This exposed them, and in particular Raymond Lionel, to a much more diverse demographic than the close-knit religious community of Adelaide.

Following the frenzied days of enlistment after the declaration of war, it is not surprising that Raymond Lionel's military experience and qualifications quickly established his potential and promise. Accordingly, he was appointed company commander of F Company, 11th Battalion, AIF. The 11th Battalion was the first battalion raised in Western Australia. The recruits had come from all over this vast state and were resourceful and resilient men. Consequently, the battalion consisted of tough gold miners, station outriders, railway gangers and men accustomed to hardship and deprivation. In a sense they were seasoned men who, after only two weeks' training, boarded *Ascanius*, bound for disciplined military training in the desert sands of Egypt. Little did anyone know at their departure that the men of the 11th Battalion would join their comrades of the 9th, 10th and 12th battalions to form the 3rd Brigade. Their unenviable, but legendary task was to land at the foot of Ari Burnu at 4.30 am as a part of the strategic plan to land at Gallipoli on 25 April 1915.

In a letter to the *Kalgoorlie Miner*, Captain Leane described the landing. 'The water was white with bullets. The defences were impossible to storm. They had barb wire enough in front of the trenches to fence in Kalgoorlie. It does one good to see our fellows taking their gruel. Fight. I never wish to lead anything else. ... I shall be a proud man if I do return safe, for I have been through all that is possible in modern warfare, including landing under fire from the sea, which does not come often to a soldier.'[169]

Volumes have been written about the Gallipoli campaign and the futile deaths of 8709 members of the AIF, but for the men of the Leane family it proved a springboard to fame. With the decimation of senior officers, promotion was speedy for those who demonstrated initiative and had the luck to survive. Captain Raymond Lionel Leane was just such a man. On 4 May 1915, Captain Leane was charged with the hazardous task of capturing the Turkish fort at Gaba Tepe. Leane was ordered to 'land at Gaba Tepe, from boats, attack the fort, capture or kill the garrison, destroy guns and material, and obtain papers, records and information of value.'[170] Like the landing, it was a delusional expectation. Nonetheless, Captain Leane and Lieutenant W.H. Rockliff formed a party of 98 rank and file infantry, four signallers, one medical officer, one Army Medical Corps sergeant and five stretcher-bearers, all of whom had volunteered for the raid.[171]

Once again the volunteers boarded their small boats in the early hours of the morning to be towed by the navy to land on the fortified beach. As dawn broke, the men began their assault, facing the anticipated barrage of fire. Many were killed in the boats, the deep water, or the furious scamper across the sand to cover. 'All who had made it, threw themselves behind the cover of a 12-foot bank lining the beach. Without its shelter, the landing party would undoubtedly have been wiped out in the open, but even here, they were enfiladed by the guns on the point to their right.'[172] Leane, surveying the prone forms of his dead and the entrenched position of the Turks behind barbed wire and the heavily fortified walls, knew immediately that an attack across the beach would be suicidal. He ordered a withdrawal.

But this was easier said than done. An evacuation had to be made by sea. Yet again, the navy was called on to provide protective fire cover and small boats to assist the withdrawal. Miraculously, and out of respect for the Red Cross flag, the Turks held their fire and the majority of men were rowed back to the safety of the destroyer *Colne*. In all, Leane estimated that five men had been killed in the landing, two were missing and 19 were wounded. Although the raid was a failure, Leane's courage and leadership earned him an MC. Other than that, all that could be salvaged from the perilous mission was Leane's belief that 'Western Australia can be justly proud, for it [the raid] was carried out by men from one of the finest battalions which served in the war—11th Battalion AIF.'[173]

Stranded on the narrow strip of beach at Anzac Cove and with mounting numbers of casualties due to illness and enemy action, the ANZACs—the men of the Australian and New Zealand Army Corps—were forced into a bold offensive to capture the peaks and ridges to the north in an effort to break out of the beachhead. In preparation for an attack on Lone Pine scheduled for 6 August, the CO of the 12th Battalion, Lieutenant Colonel Hilmer-Smith, requested that a trench named 'the Turkish Despair Works', which lay just in front of the Australian trenches, be captured and incorporated into the Australian lines in time for the opening of the offensive. The commander of the 3rd Brigade, Colonel Ewen Sinclair-MacLagan, agreed and devised a plan utilising the men of Leane's 11th Battalion to mount the attack. By the night of 31 July, the strategy had been mapped out and preparations made. The men, all volunteers, were prepared. In spite of the failure of two pre-laid mines to explode, Captain Leane made the decision to attack. The single, delayed explosion added to the mayhem of the assault, which met fierce resistance from the Turks and resulted in brutal hand-to-hand fighting. By dawn, the weary and thirsty troops had secured the position, although relief was not possible until noon.

This assault saw the capture of the first Turkish trench at Gallipoli, and was vital to preparations for the combined offensive at Lone Pine on

6 August. Casualties were heavy, with Captain Leane receiving wounds to the face and arm. However, the mission was described as 'a brilliant operation by a tired and weary battalion ... which was carried out with great dash and coolness and led in a brilliant manner by Captain Leane.'[174] Fittingly, the new acquisition was named Leane's Trench. In spite of his wounds, Raymond's tenacity and daring did not go unnoticed by the men or senior officers. When his brother Benjamin returned to Gallipoli on 15 August, one of the first details he noted in his diary was that 'Ray is an absolute hero. Everyone talks of the wonderful work he has done. They say he is bound to get a DSO [Distinguished Service Order].'

Brigadier General Raymond Lionel Leane.
State Library of South Australia B-5943.

Raymond's initiative and leadership established his reputation as an outstanding soldier. On 5 August he was promoted to temporary major and on 11 September his promotion became substantive and he was appointed to command the 11th Battalion. By 8 October he was a temporary lieutenant colonel and was twice Mentioned in Despatches before the December withdrawal. His rapid promotion was wholeheartedly endorsed by all of his men who, due to his size and strength, nicknamed him 'the Bull'.

Nonetheless, he was human and, by November, the weather and the burdens of leadership had undermined his health to the point that he was ordered to Mudros to rest. When his brother Benjamin was also invalided to Mudros, he was alarmed at the state of his older brother. In his diary, he recorded on 27 November, 'Poor old Ray is not at all well. You know I said before, that I reckoned he would go to pieces when he got away from the trenches and relaxed, and that is just what has happened.'[175] Worse was to follow. By 30 November, Raymond had been ordered to hospital. Benjamin, perhaps in an endeavour to reassure both himself and Phyllis, his wife, wrote, 'Ray is not seriously ill – just run down and a good spell of rest and nursing will pick him up. It is tough luck, as his rank of Lieutenant Colonel is only temporary and he reverts to a substantive major in hospital.'[176] Yet, by 5 December, Raymond had developed pleurisy and pneumonia. Benjamin recorded that 'Poor old Ray is right down to it. He's not talking now of getting back to duty soon. When I got there, a nurse was supporting him while he took a drink from a feeding cup. Afterwards he was so exhausted that he could not speak for some time. He stuck it too long and is positively broken down.'[177] Nonetheless, Temporary Lieutenant Colonel Leane's service and leadership had set a fine example of initiative and resilience. For his service at Gallipoli he was awarded the DSO.

With his prolonged illness and the withdrawal from Gallipoli, Raymond never returned to the battlefield on which he had established himself as a legendary fighting figure. Instead, he proceeded to Egypt for further medical treatment while the rest of the Australians recovered, regrouped and reorganised. Remnants of the depleted battalions which had fought at Gallipoli were merged with fresh reinforcements from Australia. On 3 March 1916, the remainder of the 11th Battalion under Major Raymond Leane were joined by members of the 16th Battalion to form the 48th Battalion. In an inspired promotion, Raymond was appointed CO, his rank of lieutenant colonel confirmed. The battalion was immediately charged with defending the Suez Canal against potential Turkish attacks, while rigorous training was implemented. Route marches across the burning desert, infantry attacks in formation and rifle exercises became daily routine. The troops loathed this period of time in Egypt. It was hot, dusty and boring. They wanted to join the real action.

Much to the joy and relief of the men of the 48th Battalion, their anticipated deployment to France was realised on 1 June when they embarked on *Caledonia* for Marseilles. There they entrained at 5.00 pm on Friday evening, finally arriving at Bailleul in northern France on Monday morning to be marched to their billets in the village of Merris. Rigorous training resumed immediately, designed to equip the men for the very different conditions of the Western Front. After a week at Fleurbaix—the week before the fatal attack by the 15th Brigade at nearby Fromelles—the battalion moved to Pozières and, on 7 August, repulsed a heavy German counter-attack.

Volumes have been written about each of the battles in which the 48th Battalion participated and I do not intend to repeat them here. Suffice to say, the 48th Battalion's outstanding courage and resilience in battles at Mouquet Farm and Gueudecourt in 1916, and Bullecourt, Messines, Wytschaete and Passchendaele in 1917, established the men of the 48th as fearless and highly disciplined fighters. In these conflicts, the battalion suffered horrific casualties, and even Lieutenant Colonel Leane was severely wounded at Passchendaele. He suffered nine wounds, the worst of which was in the thigh and prompted a lengthy stay in hospital. He was absent from the battalion for four months, during which the pride and morale of the men never wavered. Undoubtedly, this stemmed from the outstanding personal courage and leadership of their CO, the larger-than-life Lieutenant Colonel Raymond Leane, affectionately referred to as 'the big fellow'. Certainly Raymond Leane was a physically imposing presence, athletic, broad shouldered and over 6ft 2ins tall. 'He stood straight as a gun barrel, all wire and whip cord. Stern and unrelenting in his sense of duty, a man who if he knew the meaning of fear, kept his knowledge well hidden under an iron will, his very demeanour an inspiration to those who had the honour of serving with him.'[178] Charles Bean, in his *Official History*, described Raymond Leane as a 'man of somewhat difficult temperament' with a 'jaw as square as his great shoulders and a cheek muscle that seemed to be always clenched, with a sense of duty which constantly involved his battalion in the most dangerous tasks and a sense of honour which always ensured that he, or one of his family bore the brunt, he was creating a magnificent unit.'[179] As master and virtual father to the battalion, Colonel Leane 'set himself the task of persuading the world to the desirability and necessity of his creed and conduct.'[180]

Lieutenant Colonel Leane was a participant in all that he commanded his battalion to do, and his willingness to lead by example saw him awarded a Bar to his DSO for his courage and leadership at Passchendaele. His citation reads:

> For conspicuous gallantry and devotion to duty. Although suffering from extreme agony from an acute attack of neuritis, he insisted against his Medical Officer's advice, on commanding his battalion in the attack. After his battalion had been forced to retire, owing to enemy attack on his battalion's flank, which was consequently left unprotected, he went forward under a very heavy artillery barrage and collected stragglers and parties of men who were retiring past their original line and organised them and sent them forward again to assist in repulsing the enemy.
>
> His rapid grasp of the situation and his capable disposition personally ensured the retention of the front against the advancing enemy.
>
> He continued to handle his battalion under a massive barrage and remained at his post though badly wounded until the enemy were checked and the defence assured.[181]

Apart from his own herculean presence, the battalion contained many members of the Colonel's family. His brother, Major Benjamin Leane, was second in command while his nephew, Allan Edwin, was a captain and a company commander. His other nephews, also Edwin's sons, Lieutenant Geoffrey Paul and Corporal Reuben Ernest, were all members of the battalion at some stage. Likewise, his sister Ethel's adopted son,

Lieutenant Clarence Fairley, was also a member of the battalion. In fact the family connections were so conspicuous that the battalion wags developed a particular sobriquet for their unit, calling it 'the Joan of Arcs' (a play on the title 'the maid of Orleans') because the battalion was 'made of all Leanes'.

On the home front, Raymond's wife Edith was no less committed to the service of her country. She became a foundation member of the Sailors, Soldiers and Nurses' Relatives' Association (SSNRA) and was a keen worker for the welfare of the troops. She was an excellent pianist and gave numerous charity concerts to raise money for the Comforts Fund. In addition, she and other members of the SSNRA regularly met at her home, knitting hundreds of garments and organising other fundraising activities to provide comforts for the fighting forces. She continued this level of engagement all throughout World War I and then again in World War II. As a consequence of her devoted and untiring efforts, Edith received the Long Service Medal from the Red Cross in 1952, followed by the First and Second Bar in 1953 and 1956 respectively, to acknowledge 40 years of effective service to the Australian Red Cross Society.[182]

Although surrounded by immediate family, the bond that developed between the battalion chaplain, Father Devine, and Lieutenant Colonel Leane, cemented the former's place as 'extended family'. So close was the relationship between the chaplain and his CO that his astute summation of the man has become accepted as fact. Father Devine viewed Colonel Leane as a totally self-made man, and attributed his strength of character to 'the atmosphere of puritan ethics and non conformist theology' of his formative years as the foundation on which all else developed.[183] He recorded that, as a man of many moods, Colonel Leane delighted in the sports and concerts of the unit. 'He was not only with them but of them; gay and boyish as themselves, in fact a big boisterous digger.'[184] In anger, he was 'a stern, hard man and in the conception and performance of his personal duty, he had little sympathy for those who culpably fell short of his standard.'[185]

Raymond's compassion and his sense of duty were sorely tested with the deaths of his brother Benjamin and his nephew Allan Edwin, who were both killed at Bullecourt:

> Bullecourt to him was a tragedy. There on that unforgettable morning, he saw his battalion slaughtered and could do nothing to prevent it. Thinking back over the years to the conference held in the sunken road near Noreuil on the eve of the battle, I realise that he had his doubts as to the efficiency of the arrangements made for the support of the infantry. I know now that he was by no means content, but he realised the necessity for putting a bold face on it.
>
> And he was right. He, who loved his men, and who had been a father to them, saw them stricken down, and the memory of it will live with him forever. But there was also a loss, a personal loss too, enough to break down the strength of any man. There, as he went forth to his battle headquarters, was the body of his brother Ben, a loveable character combining the gallantry symbolical of the family, with a gentleness of nature which made him all the more delightful as a comrade. It was a bitter blow, yet he never flinched, going forward to his duty like the soldier that he was.[186]

Benjamin's death was horrific, resulting from a direct hit on an ammunition dump which blew him to pieces. The next day Raymond scoured the battlefield looking for the remains of his much-loved youngest brother. He identified the head, and gathered the remains of his brother's shattered body and placed a cross over the grave he had dug himself. A fellow officer, Captain Norman Imlay MC, spoke in awe of Raymond's composure during this dreadful ordeal. 'Ray Leane was made of case hardened steel. To be with him that morning after the discovery of Ben and see him concentrate on his job, without an outward sign of mental distress was but to verify that statement. But what he suffered inwardly no-one ever knew. Ben, no less brave or capable a soldier than Ray, had a gentler disposition that endeared him to all and sundry, and made officers and men alike go to him for advice and help. His loss cast a heavy gloom over the whole battalion.'[187] Raymond knew firsthand the cost of war, but it never hardened him or caused him to waver from his duty. 'His officers and men gave him a loyalty almost religious in its intensity' because they respected him and the principles he espoused.[188] His courage, judgement and will all contributed to unerring leadership in the field which inspired both loyalty and affection.

Worse was to follow. 'As though that were not enough [Ben's death], Fate in the most vicious mood, had yet another arrow to send into his quivering soul, for as the battalion, or what was left of it came back, Allan, his nephew and one of the same invincible breed was stricken down. Therefore, when I think of Bullecourt, I think at once of the Colonel, and I wonder if he ever realised the measure of sympathy which his battalion felt for him that day. I'm sure that he did, for he was a man of wonderful vision, who could scarcely fail to understand the unspoken words of friendship of devotion, forged in that hell which was Bullecourt.'[189] Allan's remains were never located and it was believed that he died as a prisoner of war.

Colonel Leane's leadership in the sustained fighting at Bullecourt and Messines during the harrowing year of 1917 saw him appointed a Companion of the Order of St Michael and St George (CMG) on New Year's Day 1918. His citation lauded his:

> Indefatigable energy and zeal as a leader during the period 26 February to 20 September 1917. This officer displayed extreme courage when in command of his battalion during the attack at Bullecourt on 10 April 1917 and in the Messines battle on 7 June 1917, he handled his men with great skill and success.
>
> During the trying times after heavy casualties he has displayed great initiative and has succeeded in quickly reorganising his command and rendering it fit for further action. Lieutenant Colonel Leane is an officer of great courage, and the success that has always attended the efforts of his battalion are due to his strong personality and example.[190]

After a sustained period of hospitalisation following Bullecourt, Lieutenant Colonel Raymond Leane returned to the battalion in February 1918. He continued to command the 48th Battalion until the end of May 1918, when he was promoted to command of the 12th Brigade with the rank of brigadier general. In this capacity he was able to witness the success of the Australians as they pushed back the German Spring Offensive, with the

48th Battalion playing a significant role in halting the German advance on Amiens on 5 April. Brigadier General Leane described this period of the conflict as the most important in which he had served, writing:

> Since we were drawn from the north in 1918 to stop the Hun in his advance on Amiens, when my battalion arrived at Millencourt on the morning of March 27, after a night march of about 25 miles, things were in a very bad way. The English had no idea of the situation and the only orders received were that 'the gunners are in front of you, you have rifles and bayonets at them'. I made depositions and moved to the attack at 12.30 pm, for being under full view from Albert, we were heavily shelled and suffered casualties from our own air force who thought we were Boche and flying low fired into us. We passed through the few English who remained and held the railway embankment at Albert and Dernancourt. My battalion held this position on a frontage of 2500 yards, despite heavy attacks until April 5. ... At no period from that time we arrived in the north, were we on the defensive for any length of time, but kept at him day and night. Capturing trenches, strong points and prisoners, keeping him jumpy. The advance on Proyart on August 8, proved how superior the Australian soldiers are as an individual fighter to the Hun. This again was the case on September 18. Positions well selected and ideal for defence and strongly held, were captured with few casualties. I enquired from a German Battery Commander how it was we succeeded against each position and numbers and he replied, 'Your men are so brave and so quick, it is impossible to stop them.' The Australian has proved himself a fine soldier. He may have his equal but certainly not his superior.[191]

Leane also organised successful resistance against German attacks at Villers-Bretonneux and Monument Wood, which facilitated the final assault on the Hindenburg Line in September 1918. This effectively helped draw the war to a close. In January 1919, Brigadier General Leane was honoured with the French Croix de Guerre and the Companion of the Order of the Bath (CB).

The citation for this final award is an apt summary of the service that Brigadier General Raymond Lionel Leane offered, specifically during 1918 and in the previous four years of war:

> This officer has commanded the 12th Australian Infantry Brigade during the operations of 1 June to 17 September 1918 and the period 18 September 1918 to 11 November 1918. In the latter period his brigade made a brilliant advance and captured the Hindenburg outpost line north of St Quentin with over 1200 prisoners and many guns and although enfiladed from the south, held this important position in spite of very considerable hostile opposition and counter measure.
>
> This officer is a most gallant and able officer and has commanded his brigade with great skill, gallantry and resource during the whole of the operation since 4 July 1918. He is recommended for high distinction.[192]

Brigadier General Raymond Lionel Leane returned to Adelaide aboard *Euripides* in June 1919. He had been overseas for four years. Having left as a company commander, he returned as a brigade commander. After the Armistice he was appointed to command of the 4th Division. His exalted rank was distinguished by the fact that he had been Mentioned in Despatches eight times and wore the insignia of the CB, CMG, DSO and Bar, the MC and Croix de Guerre.

Following his return to Australia, the Leanes relocated from the hills of Adelaide. Brigadier General Raymond Leane had been highly impressed with the men in his battalion who had attended St Peter's College, Adelaide, and he subsequently enrolled his sons in the prestigious and expensive school. For his son, Geoffrey, the experience smacked of his father's expectation which proved both intimidating and daunting. He felt that, 'even as a schoolboy, the fear that I would fail never left me and I think I swore then that I would either equal or beat his record in the years to come and it remained a burning ambition throughout my life. Little did I know that there could never be another like him or even be an equal.'[193]

This excruciating sense of inferiority was inevitably exacerbated by the press coverage his father's activities received. Brigadier General Raymond Lionel Leane was widely feted and became a much-sought-after public speaker. At these gatherings he rarely spoke about himself, but instead praised the work and courage of the Australian soldier. He highlighted the enormity of what the troops had done, regaling his audience with the remarkable details of the last months of 1918. 'From March 27 to October 6, the Australians captured 24,144 prisoners, and large numbers of guns and mortars. They advanced over 40 miles, releasing 120 villages and freeing many French inhabitants. There were only five Australian divisions, but they engaged during the period mentioned, 39 enemy divisions and defeated them. It was a noble achievement and the Australian, drawn from all walks of life and with comparatively little training, was the equal of the best soldiers in the world.'[194] At a gathering of the Commonwealth Club, Brigadier General Leane also alluded to those seeking to jeopardise the Australian way of life, such as the Sinn Feiners and the Bolsheviks. Although he had been engaged in a war against Germany, he was sufficiently well read to recognise the threats that an altered world posed to established democracies. He was to harbour this antagonism for the rest of his life.

11. A MAN FOR ALL SEASONS

Having spent four long and harrowing years away from his family, Brigadier General Raymond Leane probably envisaged a return to civilian life devoid of public responsibility. Accordingly, when demobilised, he purchased a property and began to establish a small orchard at Longwood in the Adelaide Hills. Here, he perhaps thought he could indulge his love of horses and dogs, and remove himself from public scrutiny. However, when a young nation has few heroes on the global stage, those who shine can be assured that their personal life can never regain its former anonymity. Such was indeed the case for Sir Raymond Lionel Leane.

In May 1920, the Premier of South Australia, the Hon. A.H. Peake, offered Brigadier General Leane the position of Commissioner of Police on the retirement of Mr Thomas Edwards. Edwards, at 66, was well over retirement age and showing signs of tiring. At only 42 years of age, Raymond Leane had the youthful energy, drive and commitment that such a position demanded. As a famous South Australian resident, the Brigadier General was deemed 'a man of exceptional personality, with all the attributes that go to make a successful leader and organiser.'[195] The appointment was to commence on 1 July 1920, with a commencement salary of £750 per annum, plus a uniform allowance of £20. Leane was also appointed aide-de-camp to the Governor-General, Lord Henry Forster.

Although a celebrated appointment, overwhelmingly received with considerable enthusiasm by most sections of society, Brigadier General Leane's new role was met with a measure of disquiet among police ranks. A possible internal candidate, Duncan Fraser, had been overlooked, and the 'outside appointment' was resented in police circles. Leane, however, was undaunted and sought to justify his appointment with fresh vision and dynamic reform. The hardship of the war years had taken its toll on the South Australian Police Force. Young, vibrant men had joined the army and, as a consequence, the existing members of the force had grown older and become tardy in their duties. Morale was low and the conditions of service had not been reviewed for many years. Unsurprisingly, the force was under strength and the rumblings of industrial unrest were ever present within the police union, the South Australian Police Association. Raymond Leane was determined to change all of that and the South Australian community had enormous faith in his determination and ability. In remarking on the announcement of his appointment, the Adelaide *Advertiser* wrote: 'As he has proved himself to be a leader of men in the more serious business of war, so he should be fitted to grasp the problems which will confront him in the administration of such an important public utility, as the body of men who are always at war under standards of peace and honour. To him the men look with hope ... With an unbiased mind, Brigadier General Leane is expected to put new life and vigour into the department.'[196]

Commissioner Leane's military service had taught him a great deal about managing a body of men and, as for vigour, he had plenty of that. The Commissioner was a believer in firm discipline, high standards, honour and integrity—the very same qualities he had demanded of his men in the AIF. His fundamental management premise was that slackness in police administration was the greatest incentive to crime. Commissioner Leane instilled into the force the belief that the police were the servants of the public and must at all times remain accountable for their actions.

He also demanded that they take pride in their own appearance and performance. Having taken his oath of office, Raymond Leane quickly set about rebuilding the force. In his first three years in office he implemented a raft of initiatives and innovations.

Prior to his appointment, there had been no night supervision in South Australia. In response to this perceived deficiency, the new Commissioner quickly introduced reform that saw a service that was on duty 24 hours a day, seven days a week. In acknowledgement of this increased expectation, a daily increment in wages of 1/6 was approved. Furthermore, and much to the chagrin of some of the long-serving members of the force, the Commissioner established promotion by merit rather than seniority. He realised that 'the existing system was painfully slow and did little to encourage or reward ability. He promptly abolished the rank of senior constable and introduced three grades of sergeant.'[197]

With the South Australian Police Force in a virtually moribund state, Leane firmly believed that 'the time has passed when seniority alone should ensure promotion in any walk of life. Such a system side tracks the efficient. Seniority has its claims to consideration, but must also carry with it efficiency and suitability before a more competent officer is passed over. The *esprit de corps* and efficiency in any service depends largely upon the officers for its supervision. I am more than satisfied with the results of promotion by merit, and I am certain that the Police Service will improve as a result of it.'[198] In order to ensure the integrity of the process, the Commissioner established a Promotions Board which was responsible for conducting all examinations for non-commissioned rank. This board consisted of Inspector Birt of the Mounted Police, Inspector Whittle of the Criminal Investigation Branch and Inspector Horseman from the Plain Clothes Branch.[199] Each man knew intimately the personalities and merits of the men in his department, and the Commissioner empowered them with his faith in their good judgement.

In his first Annual Report to the Chief Secretary, Commissioner Leane informed the government of the changes he had implemented.

He felt that, 'To ensure efficient detection and prevention of crime, it is essential that only those constables are appointed who have shown keenness and aptitude for this work. Slackness in administering the law, want of zeal and intelligence on the part of the officers responsible, are the greatest factors contributing to an increase in crime in the community. The best police work is prevention.'[200]

Obviously such a proposal demanded intelligent and well-trained recruits. To this end a Police School was established in the city watch house. Prior to this, recruits had completed just six weeks of basic training. Under Commissioner Leane, the South Australian Police Force implemented a more rigorous and diverse program that took three months to complete. Recruits now undertook a formal course of instruction which included lectures in law by highly qualified legal practitioners. In a further bold initiative, Commissioner Leane set to work to revise the Police Regulations which governed the force. These were approved and gazetted in April 1921, and 'were the first revisions of the Regulations since Peterswald's Manual of Instruction of 1883. Everything relative to police administration, powers and duties, was included. Disciplinary action would be taken against any officer who did not keep this new 'Bible' up to date. The format he laid down would not change for almost 60 years.'[201]

Further initiatives saw the establishment of another three-member board, this time to conduct examinations for members eligible for commissioned rank. This was again chaired by Inspector Birt, with the other members the acting Crown Solicitor, A.J. Hannon, and the Police Department Secretary, Archibald Oakley. In a continuing program to boost police morale, Commissioner Leane sought to improve the men's working and recreational facilities. The subtext of this was, of course, to improve health and fitness, and the initiatives were adopted with alacrity by members of the force. His drive saw the establishment of the Police Amateur Athletic Club, police cricket, football and rifle teams, with an annual sports carnival held from 1923 under the Commissioner's patronage.[202] During his years of command in the 48th Battalion, Raymond Leane had given his men every opportunity to seek recreation in sport and, often as an active participant himself, he fully understood the value of sport in reducing stress and cementing camaraderie.

In pursuit of better working conditions, Commissioner Leane authorised 'a second storey to be added to the city watch house, where recreation rooms with a dry canteen, pianos, billiard tables, gramophones and a library were established. At the Thebarton Barracks, similar facilities were provided for the Mounted Police with the additional bonus of a tennis court.'[203] During these early years, female police also gained greater acceptance, although a doubling in number from five to ten did not exactly endorse this as a strong female career path. Nonetheless, it was a step in the right direction.

However, the times were changing and Commissioner Leane was quick to perceive the logistical deficiencies of the South Australian Police Force. He realised that the war had caused a stagnation in policing, which had allowed an undercurrent of criminal networks to permeate the country. Accordingly, he organised meetings with commissioners from the other states in an effort to establish links to assist in the suppression of crime. Through these exchanges, he became acutely aware that other states had cars and motorbikes in their service, while the South Australian Police Force was still hamstrung by the use of bicycles and horses, with many of their patrols conducted on foot. This meant access to criminal activity was slow and often delayed. The Commissioner himself did not even have access to a car, and his only available means of transport was a cab and a pair of horses. Not one to accept second best, Leane submitted a proposal to the government to upgrade police transport. The request was eventually accepted and two Harley Davidson motorcycles were purchased, at the cost of £325 10s each. While Leane acknowledged minor progress, he insisted that a car was essential for greater police efficiency and, of course, his own personal dignity.

The story behind the eventual purchase of a car in a tight-fisted economy demonstrates not only Leane's justification of its merit, but his remarkable skill as a negotiator and master manipulator. In August 1922, the arrest and imprisonment of a bankrupt from Western Australia involved the seizure of an expensive Hudson Super Six. The Western Australian Public Trustee asked Leane to secure 'the best offer' and sell it locally, rather than undergoing the costly exercise of shipping it back to Perth. Leane saw his chance. Although he was aware that a new Hudson cost well over £900, he replied that the best offer he could find was just £200.[204] At the same time, he presented a submission to the Chief Secretary, detailing the deficiencies of a police force without a car at its disposal, and the indignity of being the only Police Commissioner in the country without access to one. He also hinted to the Chief Secretary that he had the opportunity to purchase a suitable car at about the cost of a Ford. In the interim he had written to the Perth Receiver, suggesting that the car was not in good condition and would take around £50 to repair. For good measure, he highlighted the difficulty of selling such a car in cash-strapped Adelaide.

With little response from the Receiver, Leane contacted the Western Australian Police Commissioner. During the conversation he quite deliberately suggested that the car's condition was deteriorating and that he doubted it would fetch even £150. Commissioner Leane knew full well that this assessment would eventually filter back to the Receiver. Totally flustered and intimidated by Leane's bluff, the Receiver came to the conclusion that shipping costs for a dubious asset made the repossession untenable. Believing that he was striking a hard bargain, the Receiver finally acquiesced, and sold the car to the South Australian Police Force for £200. Through such machinations, Commissioner Leane had obtained his car and the South Australian Police Force was literally on the road to mechanisation. While the Commissioner claimed the car for himself, his grandson, Bruce Leane, recalled that his grandfather was a terrible driver, inclined to speed and unable to brake quickly. In such circumstances his equine experience caused him to yell 'Whoa!' before he realised that he had to jam his left foot on the pedal.[205] Given Bruce's perspective, it was not surprising that his grandfather hit a young cyclist in 1946—it was possibly more remarkable that it did not occur sooner.

As a proud South Australian, Commissioner Leane was acutely mindful and often envious of policing developments in other states. Word of radio telephones in Victorian cars, which enabled communication between police cars and headquarters up to a radius of 15 miles, could not be ignored. With such a facility, police attendance at a crime scene could be significantly expedited. However, the South Australian Police Force had only one car, which was most often in the Commissioner's possession. Still, the importance of speedy communication was a burning issue, with the police whistle the only recourse for the man on the beat. Ever innovative, Leane established a system of street telephones, located at strategic intersections, which connected directly to police headquarters. Each of these telephones was housed in a metal box to which all members of the force had a key. Leane's enthusiasm for the new system was frustrated when surveys indicated that the call boxes were rarely used between 8.00 pm and 8.00 am. Undaunted, the Commissioner, a truly lateral thinker, decided that the potential of the system would be best realised if members on the beat were required to ring in at stated intervals. As a consequence, all suburban stations were linked by this method to headquarters, thus ensuring comprehensive communication and a more effective deployment of personnel.

Raymond Leane was not only a big man physically, he was also a man of broad vision. As the Commissioner for South Australia, he appreciated that he had to understand how country stations fared and how communication with them could be improved. On investigation, Leane was concerned to find appalling levels of discontent and flagging morale in country areas. Some stations had not been visited by a divisional inspector for decades, with stations at Inaminka, Eliston and Port Lincoln last visited in 1904. Worse still, stations such as Cleve, Cummins, Murat Bay and Tumby Bay, had never been inspected at all.[206] Alarmed at this revelation, Leane demanded that divisional inspectors visit and submit a report on the efficiency of every station within their jurisdiction, at least once a year. Clearly laziness was not to be tolerated. Constant supervision and accountability would ensure that the South Australian Police Force was a body of which the state could be well proud.

Commissioner Leane's concern for the welfare of the members of his force was—surprisingly—also extended to the police union, the South Australian Police Association. While he despised unions, communists and any organisation opposed to the status quo, he knew full well that, in order to gain ground, you sometimes had to give a little. Accordingly, he agreed that the Police Association should have the right to publish a police journal which, by virtue of advertising, was free to all members. There were contributions from a diverse membership and, in some cases, the material was critical of the Commissioner. While content of this nature may not have sat well with him, the journal allowed him to monitor potential grievances and to anticipate a necessary response.

All of Commissioner Leane's initial revisions and innovations revitalised the South Australian Police Force while, in the process, he established himself as a decisive and visionary commander. It was just as well that he had established firm foundations for his new force, as the optimism of the early twenties was to unravel into a maelstrom of turmoil and social unrest as the decade drew to a close. The increasing power of the unions, social unrest and economic depression would test his strength of mind and diplomacy to the limits.

While serving as Commissioner of Police, Raymond Leane also continued to pursue his military interests. He retained his command of the 3rd Infantry Brigade, Australian Military Forces, at the rank of lieutenant colonel from 1921 to 1926. In this role he was keen to ensure that Australia maintained a fighting force of suitably trained young men, equipped to cope with the rigours and expectations of army life and its inherent discipline.

As a consequence of his continued military involvement, he was a prime mover behind the proposal to establish a training camp at Wingfield for members of the militia. Such camps were seen as vital inclusions in the military calendar to ensure that young men had the opportunity to improve their drills and firearm skills, and enable them to become more familiar with the discipline of military life.

The first camp was held between 19 and 24 March 1923 and recruits came from as far as Broken Hill and were accommodated in a tent city at Wingfield, on the outskirts of Adelaide. In total there were 1820 recruits and 66 officers under the command of Lieutenant Colonel Raymond Lionel Leane. Given his outstanding war service and his reputation as an exemplary commander, the whole affair must have seemed a mere formality to the experienced leader. However, nothing could have been further from the truth. The men under his command were not at war and, in fact, for many, the camp was regarded as an all-expenses-paid holiday. The trainees arrived with the expectation of good food, fresh air, a meeting of mates and a little military training. This was far from Lieutenant Colonel Leane's expectations, and well short of the plans that had been put in place for the camp.

Some military activity did indeed take place, but by and large the feedback from the camp was negative, from both the trainees and civilians who were residents of the surrounding area. News of an undisciplined disaster broke in *The Daily Herald* on 27 March 1923, under the headline 'THE WINGFIELD CAMP: BREEDING GROUND FOR OUTLAWRY'. The editor, Henry Kneebone, had sanctioned a lengthy diatribe that depicted the camp as an unruly shambles. *The Herald* asserted that money from the defence budget of over £4 million was wasted on 'the Wingfield festival', and that it was a breeding ground for 'outlawry' through its lack of discipline. The location was remote and constantly shrouded in dust, and 'the men were simply caked in it'. There were insufficient bathing facilities which compromised hygiene. Substandard bedding consisting of straw-filled sacks and the issue of two blankets per man was inadequate. Colds and coughs were rampant as a result. The trainees learned nothing from the camp because the young officers were afraid to enforce their orders, with the natural result that the men took advantage of them and did practically what they wanted. Ill-discipline prevailed, with 'counting out, answering back and generally holding superiors in disregard common'. The camp was a farce as, without discipline, there was confusion. The food was insufficient and of such poor quality that, in a united act of complaint, General Leane himself was 'counted out'. And, as the article noted, 'It speaks little for discipline when the commandant of a military camp can be counted out.' There were unhygienic food preparation areas and limited washing-up facilities. While the men were refused leave at night, the officers took it upon themselves to leave. 'The result was that at night, the camp was a "veritable bedlam".' In spite of piquets posted to see that the men did not break bounds, hundreds were seen in Adelaide at night, ostensibly in search of a decent meal. Vandalism was allegedly rife, with trainees cutting guy ropes, shredding blankets, smashing lamps and showers. Every light on the way from Alberton Station to the camp was broken, while stones were thrown at cars and people. On the day of departure, straw from the bedding was supposed to be bagged, but was instead piled into a great bonfire.

The article concluded with the comment, 'No doubt much of what has been related, has been the result of boys' wild spirits, and the discipline could not be expected to be up to the standard of a war time encampment. That it could have been on a much higher scale, and that the comfort and the well being of the men could have been looked after in a much more organised and much better manner, is undoubted.'[207]

Unaccustomed to criticism, let alone accusations of incompetence, Lieutenant Colonel Leane was outraged at what he perceived as an erroneous and defamatory criticism of his command. Having read the article the next day, he immediately contacted his superior, the 4th Division Commander, Sir

William Glasgow, who advised Lieutenant Colonel Leane that he was within his rights to lodge a libel suit against the editor of *The Daily Herald*, Mr Henry Kneebone. The charges alleged 'That the defendant contrived unlawfully, wickedly and maliciously to injure, vilify and prejudice the informant and other officers of the Commonwealth Military Forces in charge of the camp, and to deprive him and them of their good name, fame, credit and reputation and to bring him and the military into public contempt.'[208]

A lengthy trial ensued over the months of June to October 1923. While the defendants claimed that the public had a right to be informed about the excessive cost and waste of a military budget and the wanton vandalism of the trainees, Lieutenant Colonel Leane denied every criticism levelled at both him and the officers in charge of the camp. His answers to almost all questions were a defiant and somewhat contemptuous 'yes' or 'no'. Such responses gave the prosecuting attorney little room to move in terms of verifying the claims made in the article.

The court of public opinion was divided over the integrity of Raymond Leane as Commandant of the Wingfield Camp. As it transpired, the jury felt the same way. 'After a long trial in the Police Court, which was repeated in the Criminal Court, the jury was unable to reach a verdict and the case was made a remnant for next sessions.'[209] Given that order on 9 November 1923, the Crown decided not to carry the prosecution further and the costs and reputations of both men retired in an unhappy stalemate. One can imagine that the Commissioner of Police found such widely publicised scrutiny both irksome and a waste of valuable time. It is highly likely that the Government of South Australia would not have enjoyed its esteemed Commissioner's reputation remaining in the hands of the press. This concern was compounded in August 1923 with a report by *The Daily Herald* stating that Lieutenant Colonel Leane in his role as Commissioner of Police had 'given preference to one type of officer to the detriment of another ... as certain men had been deprived of plain clothes duties and sent back to uniform duties.'[210]

There was indeed truth in the report, which stemmed from the Commissioner's continued confrontations with the Police Association. His autocratic and high-handed manner and his revision of the police 'Bible' had led to tempestuous relations with the union from the beginning of his tenure. Leane himself felt that the working conditions of the South Australian Police Force had been vastly improved under his administration and that no-one had cause for complaint. However his refusal to discuss issues with the union executive resulted in proposals for a mass resignation which the Commissioner viewed as insubordination. From his perspective, union activity was designed to undermine the discipline of the force and frustrate the reforms he had initiated. He responded in true military style, parading the members of the executive before him, and making it quite clear to them that they had five days in which to agree to his leadership style.

After seeking legal advice, each member replied in a standard and non-committal manner, hardly the unequivocal support Leane had sought. However, he was determined to assert his authority and refused to be intimidated. In a somewhat dictatorial show of power, the Commissioner 'transferred the president of the Police Association, Sergeant Joseph Naylon, from his position as Officer in Charge at Unley Station, to headquarters, where he was closely supervised. The Secretary, Constable Norman Trestrail, was transferred from a position as a clerk in the Police Enquiry Office, to uniform beat duty.'[211]

The reputation and integrity of the Commissioner and the South Australia Police Force came under further public scrutiny in 1925, when four Royal Commissions were convened. The first, convened at Port Pirie, investigated complaints that a police arrest on New Year's Eve was effected by drunken police who exerted undue violence. Just as damning was the charge that four colleagues had suppressed information at the preliminary enquiry. The Royal Commission found the defendants guilty and their supporters guilty of perjury. A protest from the Police Association saw another sitting of the Royal Commission, which resulted in the men being exonerated with back pay reimbursed. Commissioner Leane was incandescent with rage at the outcome and promptly transferred the men to Adelaide.

A third Royal Commission developed from a simple illegal bookmaking case at the Cheltenham Races on Boxing Day 1925. It was a case unlikely to attract much attention until one Samuel Lampard, a part-time bookmaker, gave two days of evidence which disclosed the widespread bribery and corruption that had been rife within the police force and the racing fraternity for years. The presiding Commissioner, Judge Halcombe, described the case as 'most extraordinary', handing down his verdict with the comment that, 'It began by being just an ordinary betting case, but developed into investigations of charges of wholesale corruption against the police.'[212]

Consequently, a fourth Royal Commission was ordered, which convened on 3 May 1926. It trawled a wide net of bank accounts, mortgages and the business affairs of police suspects who were clearly living beyond the limits of a police salary. It was a sensational trial that dragged on through the death of Commissioner Mitchell, heard from more than 90 witnesses and cost over £3000. By 27 July 1927 the new Commissioner, Judge Paine, had been unable to document conclusive findings against the 21 officers who had been named and the 12 who were strongly suspected of taking bribes. For Commissioner Leane, the findings were devastating. Such nefarious dealings under his command were intolerable and smacked of insubordination and ill-discipline. In a move to restore public confidence and his own authority, he immediately demanded the resignation of officers who had been named at the Royal Commission and transferred the other miscreants. In order to ensure that members of the force would not be subjected to the temptations of bribery and corruption, he replaced the Plain Clothes Branch with a Licensing Staff, whose tenure was for one year only.

In line with his intimidating and militaristic management style, Commissioner Leane spared no-one his wrath if he felt it was deserved. Brutal but fair justice was even meted out to his sons, Raymond Lionel and Geoffrey Malcolm, who also joined the police force under his watch.

Geoffrey had initially intended to join the police force at Broken Hill, only to receive a letter from his father stating, 'If you must join a police force, you must join mine.'[213] Having experienced his father's unyielding discipline as a child, Geoffrey 'knew from the outset he would receive a tough deal from his father, nepotism being something he would not tolerate' and if he was to succeed it would be 'despite my father'.[214] His resolve was tested quickly when he decided to become a mounted policeman. Unlike other candidates, Geoffrey was forced to pass the test over hurdles that had been specially planned for him. He knew that it was a '*try on*' influenced by his father', and was delighted that, in this instance, his father actually failed.[215] Nonetheless, attempts to best the Commissioner were generally unsuccessful. On one noted occasion, Geoffrey was paraded before his father by Superintendent Wylie Nelson. Constable Leane had suffered a dislocated shoulder and a broken thumb when arresting a criminal. With no health scheme or workers' compensation in place, his son begged permission to be reimbursed for the three guineas that the injuries had cost him in medical fees. In spite of the costs being more than half his weekly wage, the Commissioner put his son through the third degree.

'Did you have your baton with you?' he asked.

'No Sir,' replied Constable Leane.

'Why not?'

'It was Sunday, you remember Sir.'

'I remember,' said the Commissioner. 'I also remember that a Police Officer is on duty 24 hours a day, seven days a week, 52 weeks of the year.' Then he added. 'Surely you had your twitchers [handcuffs] with you?'

Constable Leane, stiffly at attention, replied, 'No Sir.'

'It's obvious,' the Commissioner rapped back, 'that you were put on the street ill equipped. You can pay the bill yourself. Application dismissed. Take him away, Superintendent.'[216]

Not only was the Commissioner totally scrupulous in his administration, he embraced his own mantra of being on duty 24 hours a day, seven days a week. Yet again, Mounted Constable Geoffrey Leane bore the consequences of his father's vigilance. On one balmy morning he was on duty at the docks. 'All was quiet and so he thought to buy a newspaper and enjoy a cigarette. His horse was dozing off, so he removed his feet from the irons, hooked them over the pommel and lit up. Suitably relaxed, he did not hear a car stop, but he heard the voice and recognised it immediately. "What the hell do you think you are doing constable?" At that both he and the horse leapt into the air nearly unseating him.'[217] Caught out again, Constable Geoffrey Leane was confined to barracks for 14 days for breaches of discipline. Such a punishment was possible for members of the Mounted Police, as they had to live in at the barracks at Thebarton to care for their horses.

In a later parade before his father, by which time Geoffrey was a detective, the Commissioner was equally uncompromising. Detective Leane and Detective Gully had arrested a long-time criminal, whose capture attracted advertised rewards of up to £10,000 from various insurance companies. In parading before his father, Detective Geoffrey Leane made application for the reward for himself and Detective Gully. History does not relate the actual words of the Commissioner's excoriation, but he made it quite clear that there would be no reward, as both men were being paid to catch criminals.[218] In his command of the 48th Battalion, Raymond Leane had granted no favours to family members, and as Commissioner he was not about to start. With the police force ever under public scrutiny, he was determined that integrity would be exemplary from the top down.

In spite of his vision and innovation, Commissioner Leane found the initial transition from unquestioned military leadership to the public scrutiny of civilian leadership difficult and at times galling. In the military, his leadership had been regarded as courageous and bold. In civilian life his leadership was rapidly perceived as dictatorial. In military life, his 'office' was a fortress where he issued orders; as Commissioner, it was described as a 'Star Chamber'. Somehow Commissioner Raymond Lionel Leane had to find a way to promote his vision for the best police force in Australia without riding roughshod over civil liberties and public scrutiny. His early years at the helm indeed tested his resolve, but greater trials were in store that would test his indomitable will to the limits. Towards the latter part of the 1920s, he was perceptive enough to realise that the moral laxity within the police force was in many ways a reflection of the wider society. Union power was on the rise and growing unemployment and social unrest led to constant protests. As an arch conservative, Raymond Leane loathed unions and the increasing sway of the communists who threatened the status quo. Believing that prevention was better than response, he drew up a series of contingency plans to maintain essential services in case of civil unrest. 'Squads of Special Constables were recruited under police and military control, preferably ex-servicemen and retired officers. They were to be armed with rifles, bayonets and ammunition by agreement with the Commonwealth Government.'[219] It was a pre-emptive move that proved its worth when the waterside workers began their nationwide strikes in 1928. Then, the Commissioner was again on familiar territory.

The communists had provided the catalyst for the strikes, harnessing the despair of the unemployed and poorly paid to promote their doctrine. The waterside workers, with a long-standing tradition of militancy, were the principal respondents to this propaganda. Prior to this, in 1914, Mr Justice Higgins had endeavoured to 'greatly improve the working conditions of wharf labourers and give them an industrial status never before enjoyed.'[220] Their rates of casual pay were higher in Australia than any other casual occupation in the Commonwealth. Yet, in September 1928, Mr Justice George Beeby brought down a revised labour award in the Industrial Court of Conciliation and Arbitration. Under the new Arbitration Act, laws had to be obeyed, with refusal to comply amounting to contempt of court. The union maintained its belief that it had the right to determine its own behaviour. The new Act also established a series of provisions, including that all waterside workers had to be licensed, not by their own union, but by the government. The right of employees to choose their own labour was also enshrined as was the abolition of compulsory 'smokos' unless the men had worked for two hours. It was recommended that the 'Bull' pick-up system would occur only once a day, rather than two. This was a system which saw wharf labourers assemble at a set point to await selection for work. Ironically, this amendment stood to significantly benefit the workers.

The waterside workers rejected the award and the nation's wharves ground to a standstill. The strike meant that ships sat idle in all Australian ports, unable to load or unload. In desperation, unemployed workers were encouraged to offer their services, to ensure that the nation did not grind to a halt with the resultant economic burden. These non-union labourers were vilified as 'scabs' by the waterside workers who used mass violence in an attempt to prevent them working. The first of these confrontations occurred at a timber yard at Port Adelaide, where police protection of the yard against unionists attempting to intimidate the 'scabs' provoked rioting. *The Register* reported the events of the day that would shock the city of churches to the core:

SERIOUS RIOT ON THE WATERFRONT.

A DISGRACEFUL SCENE WAS WITNESSED AT Port Adelaide on Thursday morning when about 4000 wharf labourers and others swarmed Robinson's Bridge with the object of compelling volunteer labourers to leave the vessels on which they were working. The volunteers were not given time to leave the vessels peacefully, and although a number were escorted off safely by benign wharf labourers, others were roughly handled. The police soon intervened and dispersed the unionists after considerable trouble.

During the afternoon, an estimated 2000 men marched six miles from Port Adelaide to Outer Harbour, the alternative port for ships too large to negotiate the Port River, and rushed the police lines, which had been strengthened by calling all available officers including traffic and water police. A potentially ugly situation was resolved by strikers being frustrated so far. This number of determined marchers was significant and caused widespread public alarm considering Adelaide's metropolitan population was approximately 300 000.

It was the beginning of many desperate confrontations between Mounted and Foot Police at Port Adelaide Outer Harbour. The 4000 wharf labourers mentioned earlier went through the Port Adelaide docks like wildfire looking for 'scabs' with weapons comprising iron piping bars and bale hooks. Men who fell while trying to escape were savagely kicked. Serious injuries were inflicted. Volunteers on a German liner jumped overboard and swam to safety.

The 2000 strong body of wharf labourers who marched on Outer Harbour were met by a force of 150 police under the personal direction of the Police Commissioner, Brigadier General R.L. Leane. When the vanguard of the close packed marchers reached the southern end of the harbour, they were met by the Commissioner in plain clothes, accompanied by Inspector Horseman. The Commissioner's attempt to dissuade the men from attacking the volunteer labourers at the harbour failed, and the mob ran through the wharf shed shouting threats.

But General Leane had laid his plans well. The stone throwing mob was first met by a body of Mounted Police who soon had to use batons. When the horses were hit by stones, they reared up and kicked up clouds of dust. The mob was deflected off course and predictably rushed towards an area behind a railway station. Here they were attacked by large numbers of plainclothes police using batons, and they ran back towards the wharves between two blocks of buildings.

Before the mob could cross the road to reach the wharves, they were confronted and attacked by General Leane's second line of defence, a cordon of foot police. The mounted police had re-formed and with more foot police, blocked escape to the rear and closed in on the flanks of the mob. The ships' crews had been ordered earlier to haul up all gangways, and so passengers, crews, and volunteer labourers were able to witness, in safety, the neat coup at the closing stages of a situation probably without parallel in the industrial history of South Australia. The mob gave up and stood around in dejected groups.[221]

However the outburst of violence and dissent was far from over and, accordingly, three battalions of the Citizen's Defence Brigade were stationed at Fort Largs. Only a man with the Commissioner's military expertise could have organised so much so quickly. Accommodation, albeit in tents, catering facilities and stabling for horses were quickly established in spite of foul weather. A tribute to General Leane was published in the *Adelaide News*. 'The commissioner stated that the organisation of the special constabulary force occupied only 36 hours, during which time a fully equipped camp was brought into existence at Fort Largs. This was a wonderful tribute to the asset Australia possessed in her former leaders and members of the Australian Imperial Force.'[222]

Further riots broke out on 17 and 19 January 1929. On the latter occasion, over 800 wives of unemployed waterside workers marched in support of their husbands. This proved a dilemma for crowd control, as obviously the women were unarmed and many carried children and babies. The problem was compounded when men joined the march, and it rapidly spiralled out of control as the marchers rushed to Queen's Wharf. A steamer, *Van Spilbergen*, was being loaded with wheat by non-union labour. Chaos ensued as the mob hurled rocks and an assortment of missiles at the workers, the foot and mounted police. Complaints were made about the use of mounted police to break up the crowd, but in his report to the Chief Secretary, Commissioner Leane declared, 'I am more than pleased with the restraint and efficiency shown by police on duty and any fair minded onlooker must be of the same opinion.'[223]

Of course worse was to come as the Great Depression of the 1930s began to bite. Higher levels of unemployment and destitution were rife and, although police duties increased, their wages were cut and their numbers reduced. By 1931 the police force was 40 men under strength, with no money available to recruit the large numbers on the recruiting list. Nonetheless, the discipline and integrity that Commissioner Leane had instilled into the South Australian Police Force ensured that his 'army' was respected and that it held the full confidence and support of the government. The force's efficiency was evident once again in the 'Beef Riot' of 1931. This arose in response to the removal of beef from the dole ration issue by the Federal Government. Outraged citizens and their families, determined to take the matter to the Premier, marched from Port Adelaide to the

Treasury Building in Victoria Square. The police anticipated the protest and were there in numbers. Their presence angered the crowd and, after a tense stand-off, rocks and bricks were hurled at the police, who had no option but to initiate a baton charge. Much blood was shed, people fled in all directions, but yet again, a disciplined and organised police force minimised a potential monumental loss of life.

Respect and support for Commissioner Leane's police force was reflected in the press. 'Remove the police and there would be downright anarchy ... an effective disciplinary force is needed if society is to be protected against the evils of mob rule. An overwhelming majority of the people of South Australia feel that they are under a debt of gratitude to the police officers, who by courage and resolution, dispersed truculent and threatening mobs yesterday.'[224]

During this period, the community teetered on the brink of civil war, and violence would continue on the waterfront and in protest marches for many years. However, Commissioner Leane's military-style preparations and disciplined force pre-empted many problems and minimised the harm, both personal and physical, to South Australians. His consistent philosophy of 'stand, resist, prevail, then talk' echoed his military strategies which had established his legendary status in the Great War.

After his participation in a global war and a virtual civil war on his home territory, one would think that Commissioner Leane would have been physically and emotionally exhausted by conflict. A lesser man would have called it a day. Not 'the Bull'. He had much more to do and, during the difficult years of the 1930s he worked even harder to ensure that the South Australian Police Force became highly respected in the community. He encouraged cultural pursuits among members of the force. He revitalised the Police Band and ensured that it performed publicly. He organised a police ball, formed debating teams and held sports competitions across a range of activities. He also ensured that his members paraded at public events such as Empire Day and at memorial services for police who had been killed on active duty. In such instances his men were immaculately turned out and looked the epitome of professionalism.

On Empire Day 1939, with the threat of another war imminent, the parade was led by a corps of Police Cadets. The Cadet Force had been another of the Commissioner's initiatives. It was no doubt planned to ensure continuity in the force, but also perhaps evolved from the Commissioner's very real understanding of the needs and energy of impressionable young men. Initiated in 1932, the scheme offered a comprehensive syllabus in subjects as diverse as musketry and oratory. 'The boys aged between 15 and 17, would serve a five year cadetship before being sworn in aged 21. This innovative approach heralded a new era in police recruitment and training. It was one of the first in the Commonwealth and was soon emulated by other police forces.'[225]

Comparison of his cadet system, and the establishment of his Junior Constable Program in 1934 and its adoption in an English Police Training College, left no doubt about the superiority of the South Australian Police Force training system. Leane's innovations and initiatives enhanced the quality of the South Australian Police Force beyond anyone's wildest dreams. Leane believed that 'The object of the many and varied subjects of instruction is to eventually pass into the service young, ambitious men, who have been taught that the Force demands dauntless devotion, iron endurance, inflexible loyalty and a knowledge of work well done. In the spirit of these high ideals, the young man is guided, encouraged and trained to uphold the traditions of the South Australian Police Force.'[226]

The vision that Commissioner Leane had demonstrated in his plans of 1927/28 for a 'National Emergency', prepared him for the outbreak of war in 1939. Discussions between the police commissioners from all states and the Defence Department revealed the need for a revision of internal security. Arising from this, Leane formed a Special Branch. This was to act as an intelligence unit, collecting and collating information on people suspected of subversive activities, from Leane's perspective, all communists.

In 1941 the branch was absorbed into the Commonwealth Security Service, which merged with the Commonwealth Investigation Branch.

With the declaration of war however, Commissioner Leane's force was immediately decimated by the loss of large numbers of young men eager to enlist. Leane understood all too well the call to arms and so ensured that those who enlisted from the South Australian Police Force would not have to resign as it was an exempted service. However, after Japan entered the war in December 1941, he had to withdraw the exemption as even more police flocked to the colours. His priority as Commissioner had to remain internal security, and this demanded additional support from a Home Security Guard. As an esteemed citizen and soldier, Raymond Leane was instrumental in rallying support for a Returned and Services League (RSL) Defence Corps, of which he was unanimously appointed commander. He recognised the fragility of Australia's geographic position and understood that ex-AIF men would make valuable instructors to the new young army, as well as acting as second-liners themselves.

In order to generate support for this proposal, he travelled throughout South Australia to speak at numerous RSL functions. The *Border Chronicle* reported on one such function in July 1940. 'Addressing 60 members of Tatiara, Wolseley, Keith and Kaniva at Fox's Hotel, Bordertown on Friday night last, the State Commissioner of Police (Brigadier General R.L. Leane) urged diggers to link up with the Volunteer Defence Corps, which has been formed by the RSL as a second line of defence for Australia. Details of the scheme, which it is hoped will embrace all returned men in Australia to the number of about 100 000, were explained by the Brigadier, who later left for Naracoorte, Kingston and Mt Gambier.'[227]

Such was his passion that the corps was inundated with requests from thousands of civilians seeking to join up. Brigadier General Leane had to refuse many of these applications as permission had been given only for the recruiting of ex-servicemen. In spite of his commitment to home security, in this war, the shoe was on the other foot for the General. All of his five sons had sought to enlist, with three accepted. In addition, 14 nephews were now members of the 2nd AIF, so the threat of bad news was always in the wind. Sir Raymond knew all too well the carnage of war, but with his own sons, Kenneth Morton, Geoffrey Malcolm and Benjamin David Devine deployed, as well as his son-in-law, Aubrey Clutterbuck, he had to remain steady at the helm.

On his enlistment, Geoffrey Moreton was told by his father not to return unless he was a colonel. He subsequently joined the 2/48th Battalion which was sent to Tobruk. Prior to his departure, his youngest brother, Benjamin David, approached Geoffrey, who was in charge of a company training at Keswick Barracks, with a request to join the battalion if he was made a sergeant. Like his father, Geoffrey was not inclined to nepotism and rejected Benjamin's request. As events transpired, Geoffrey's battalion was deployed to the Middle East and the lengthy and gruelling siege at Tobruk. After his return to Australia, he was on piquet duty on board a ship at 7.30 am one morning when a familiar shape strode up the gangplank. 'He stopped the man coming aboard and said "State your business Sir!"' His father replied, 'I did not know you were here. I came to see your brother and I suppose you know that it is your fault that your younger brother Ben is a Prisoner of War with the Japanese.' Geoffrey replied that he had not heard this news and then added, 'But why is that my fault?' His father replied that, had he accepted Benjamin as a member of his unit, he would have been in the Middle East rather than the Far East. Geoffrey's reply was controlled and pragmatic. 'That is possible, but by the same token, I lost more than half of my men in Tobruk and he could have been one of them. At least he is still alive, that is as far as you know.' His father left without another word and Geoffrey received the distinct impression that he was not number one son and was never likely to be.[228]

In spite of his gruff façade and bravado, it was essential that the Commissioner's personal anxieties were kept at bay by constant activity. It is little wonder that, during this period of World War II, the Leane household greeted every mail delivery with some trepidation. Perhaps Raymond could draw some solace from the events of the late 1920s which had ensured that the South Australian Police Force had its own auxiliary. This, of course, comprised the 3500 citizens who had been sworn in as special constables. With the outbreak of yet another war, these men were detailed to guard vulnerable points in an honorary capacity.

As if these multiple commitments, as a parent, Commissioner of Police and commander of the RSL Corps, did not demand huge reserves of energy and effort, on 14 April 1942, at the age of 64, Raymond Lionel Leane formally re-enlisted. He was appointed Commander of the Volunteer Defence Brigade of South Australia and given the rank of colonel. This brigade was formed to include civilians who had wished to serve in a home capacity. Needless to say, all of these diverse groups needed organising and training and, for the duration of the war, General Leane was a highly visible presence at any military parade or function. 'The Bull' was back!

By 1944 Commissioner Leane had reached the retirement age of 65. As was the custom, his appointment was terminated on 30 June. Celebrations to mark his record 24 years of service as Police Commissioner were widely held in his honour. In his acknowledgement of such occasions, he expressed his pride in a job well done and a police force that was second to none in the entire Commonwealth. One of the most touching ceremonies for their retiring chief was a surprise parade, conducted by the junior constables at the Police Training College. The junior constables presented Commissioner Leane with a gold dress watch and ink stand. In shaking each man's hand and thanking the group, the Commissioner reminded them all that, from the Commissioner down, they were all servants of the public.

His final good wishes to all members of the force were added as a supplement to the *Police Gazette*:

To Members of the Police Force

South Australia.

Upon the eve of my retirement as Commissioner of Police for the State of South Australia, I desire to express to all Commissioned Officers and other ranks who have faithfully performed their duty to the department and the community, my sincere thanks.

The South Australian Police Force is second to none in its efficiency. I have been extremely proud of the excellent service that has been rendered by Police Officials in every part of the State, sometimes under very difficult and dangerous conditions.

The welfare of the community to a great extent is dependent upon the zeal and efficiency of members of the Police Force. Since my appointment as Commissioner of Police many occasions have arisen where this was amply demonstrated. Upon every such occasion members of the Police Force met the situation with tact, zeal and efficiency. The success of the Police Force is largely dependent upon the confidence and goodwill of the community; therefore continue to perform your duty in such a way as to merit that confidence.

The Empire is passing through dangerous and difficult times. To emerge victorious will require the united effort of all citizens, including members of the Police Force. I shall watch the activities of the Police Force with great interest. I know you will continue in the future as you have in the past, to secure the safety of the public in regard to both life and property. Be always loyal to the oath you took upon your entry to the Police Service. You will then be able to look back upon a life well spent in the service of the people.

I convey to you my sincere good wishes for the future health and happiness of yourself and those you love.

Goodbye and good luck.

Raymond L. Leane, Commissioner of Police

28 June 1944.[229]

In the same month he relinquished his civil appointment as Commissioner of Police, Raymond Leane also relinquished command of the Volunteer Defence Corps. From his early years in the militia until

Brigadier-General Sir Raymond L. Leane, CB, CMG, DSO, MC.

Commissioner of Police, South Australia

1920 - 1944

Order of the Bath.   Order of St. Michael & St George.

Distinguished Service Order with bar.
Military Cross
Order of St. John
1914-15 Star
British War Medal 1914 – 1918
Victory Medal with Oak Leaf for Mentioned in dispatches
War Medal 1939 –1945
Australian Service Medal 1939 –1945
King George V Silver Jubilee 1935
King George VI Coronation medal 1937
Colonial Officers' Auxiliary Forces Decoration
French Croix de Guerre with star for Mentioned in despatches

Framed Photograph of Medals Awarded to
Brigadier General Sir Raymond Lionel Leane.
Image: South Australian Police Museum, Thebarton

the formal conclusion of his working life, Raymond Lionel Leane had served his country in both war and peace. The next year, in June 1945, his service was again recognised in the King's Birthday Honours List, when he was made a Knight Bachelor of the British Empire. Such an award acknowledged his substantial contribution to the nation. The title carried no postnominals, but the member is addressed as 'Sir'. His title was now Sir Raymond Lionel Leane CB, CMG, DSO and Bar, MC, VD. Finally, with Japan's defeat and the end of the war, Sir Raymond Leane was again blessed with the safe return of his sons. Geoffrey Malcolm returned as a lieutenant colonel after gallant service in the Middle East and New Guinea, and Kenneth Morton returned as a lieutenant after service at Tobruk. His youngest serving son, Benjamin David Devine, the family namesake of a loved brother and a respected priest, was returned to the family after three years as a prisoner of war in Changi. However, the incarceration had taken its toll and, although he married Zita Joy Boehm in 1946 at the Pirie Street Methodist Church, there was no issue from that marriage. Benjamin died in May 1968 at the age of 48.

Relieved of the mammoth responsibilities that had governed his entire working life, Sir Raymond Lionel Leane was finally able to indulge in his own pleasures. He and his wife, Lady Edith, engaged in a vibrant social life in support of many charities and reputable causes. They were guests of honour at myriad military commemorations such as Anzac Day and Violet Day, with Sir Raymond Chairman of the Committee. He was also the first President of the Legacy Club of Adelaide, the first President of the South Australian Regional Group of the Institute of Public Administration and the first Principal of the United Services Institution. He also became President of the Commonwealth Club of Adelaide. While he was accustomed to a public life, he claimed to dislike it and was at his most content at home in the spacious acreage of his property at Plympton. Here he kept cows (which he loved to milk), calves, poultry, horses and his great passion, dogs. This interest saw him become a patron of the South Australian Kennel Association and the 'Tailwaggers Club'. He later became Chairman of the Committee of the Dog's Rescue Home in Mitcham. Sir Raymond was not averse to physical labour either, and worked a vegetable garden that grew sufficient produce for him and his wife and their extended family.

Post-war austerity concerns soon raised the issue of the future of the militia. There was criticism of the government in Canberra where Mr H. Gullett MHR ventilated the vexed issue of Australia's defence. He argued that the threat of atomic warfare and the increasing influence of communism should see Australia maintain an army of specialised, highly trained troops. He felt strongly that a voluntary militia was inadequate. He proposed that an army of 70,000 to 80,000 men should be trained continuously in lots of 20,000 for approximately four months, after which they would join an army reserve. With military issues to the fore, it did not take Sir Raymond Leane long to offer his point of view, which was, of course, reported by the press. Sir Raymond asserted that he 'was a great believer in universal military training, not only from a defence standpoint, but because of its benefit to a young man. Every young man between the ages of 16 and 21 should serve in the militia forces. Far from being a failure, militia forces in peacetime had supplied the backbone of officers and NCO's in two wars.'[230]

While enjoying a busy and fulfilling retirement, Sir Raymond Leane was savouring the reflected glory of his successful children. His firstborn, Raymond Lionel Laybourne Leane, who had been rejected for service with the AIF, was making a name for himself in the South Australian Police Force as a detective sergeant. Geoffrey Malcolm, aged 42 in 1949, was appointed the youngest inspector ever in South Australian Police history. A decade later, in 1959, Geoffrey, exhibiting much of his father's drive and intelligence, was appointed Deputy Commissioner of the South Australian Police Force. It was a position he would hold until 1972, during which time he would head the search following the tragic disappearance of the Beaumont children. Over this period, Benjamin's twin brother, another namesake, Allan William, was making a unique contribution to the family as an accomplished pianist and composer.

With the passing of the decades and the emergence of the 'swinging sixties', Sir Raymond Lionel Leane became increasingly contemptuous of all that the new age espoused. The permissive society, characterised by the 'dropout' and the long-haired heroes of pop culture, were the antithesis of all he had valued. The emerging drug culture and the rise of anti-authoritarianism, which saw the police as protectors of moral and civil order reviled and abused by demonstrators, appalled him. Decency, honour and respect had been usurped by rudderless youths who opposed everything, and stood for nothing. As a man who was a product of an age that upheld the male virtues as a breadwinner, a worker and protector, this apparent abrogation of responsibility was akin to anarchy and the total destruction of the civic values he had worked so hard to preserve. Against this backdrop, Sir Raymond Lionel Leane declared that he was glad that his time was nearing its end.[231]

Sir Raymond Lionel Leane passed away on 25 June 1962 aged 83, but not before he had made his final assertion of will. During his last illness, his fighting qualities prevailed, as he refused to die until after 14 June, which was his diamond wedding anniversary. Before he finally succumbed, he spoke lovingly to his wife, entreating her 'to not make me wait too long Edie.'[232] The man of iron knew that, without Edith's love and support, his earthly achievements, titles and success would never have been realised. His passing generated a huge funeral, as members of both the military and the police force turned out in considerable numbers to honour his contribution to the nation and the state of South Australia. At the service in the chapel of the Repatriation General Hospital, Springbank, the Commissioner of Police, Mr J.G. McKinna, offered a tribute to the life of a 'grand man and an excellent soldier'. He added that the former General and Commissioner 'was really the father of the present day police force, as during his term as commissioner he reorganised the whole service. The force was now receiving the benefits of his reorganisation and the many new systems and improvements he introduced. He was always a strict disciplinarian, but was scrupulously fair in all of his dealings. Sir Raymond Leane had been held in the highest esteem by all members of the force, to all of whom his death was an occasion of great sadness.'[233] Sir Raymond Lionel Leane was survived by his loved and loving wife of 60 years, Lady Edith, and their children, Raymond Lionel Laybourne, Kenneth Moreton, Geoffrey Malcolm, Betty Gir Clutterbuck, Allan William Henderson and Benjamin David Devine Leane. His grandchildren, who numbered just three, Robert, Peggy and Bruce, were to remain the custodians of his legacy well into the 21st century.

Sir Raymond Lionel's post-war career is a story of success, the antithesis of his brother Edwin. Like Edwin, he was authoritarian and ruled his family and his police force in a paternalistic way. However, the challanges he faced were quite different to those confronting Edwin and, initially, far more compatible with his military experience. A police force, with a clear hierarchy and established rules, was not totally removed from the discipline required in military circumstances and undoubtedly his firm and decisive discipline underpinned the development of an outstanding police force. Yet the duration of his tenure, encompassing the Wingfield crisis, the Waterside Strikes, the Great Depression, the Beef Strikes and the general depression of the 1930s, suggests a mellowing of his early intractability. In these situations he had to deal with the civilian population which, in many cases, harboured justifiable grievances. Although he was appointed by a conservative government, during the 1920s he served three Labor governments, whose policies were often at odds with his personal beliefs and values. As was evident in his car acquisition, Sir Raymond was capable of manipulation and negotiation. As he aged and established the confidence and command of his position, he tempered his authoritarianism. In the context of his public life, it was essential that he overcome the temptation to fly into an instant rage. These qualities of self-control and self-belief were paramount given the stormy nature of his tenure.

12. Major Benjamin Bennett Leane

Thomas and Alice's youngest son, Benjamin Bennett Leane, was actually the sixth of the Leane sons to enlist and the fifth to serve overseas. He was born in Prospect on 3 June 1889 and, like his brothers, attended the local school. As the youngest of the boys, he was profoundly influenced by the family's religious values and the military interests of his brothers and cousins. Consequently, in 1910, as soon as he was eligible, he enlisted in the South Australian militia, as a member of the 10th Infantry Regiment, and rose to the rank of lieutenant. The esteem in which he was held saw him attached to Lord Kitchener's staff during his visit to Adelaide. He was also a keen student and studied to be an engineer while employed as a clerk and warehouseman.

On 17 July 1912, Benjamin married Phyllis Gwendolyn Hall and, in 1913, the first of their daughters, Gwenyth, was born. Marjory arrived in 1915, after her father had embarked for Egypt. Notwithstanding his loving family life and the impending birth of a new child, Benjamin was quick to enlist at Morphetville on 19 August 1914. He was allotted No. 3 in the 10th Battalion which was formed in South Australia. Benjamin was aged 26 and, on the basis of his previous military experience, was immediately appointed Quartermaster Sergeant of the 10th Infantry Battalion. By 20 October, Benjamin's decision to put duty before family saw him embark on

HMTS *Ascanius* bound for the rigours of desert training in Egypt. After the tedious months of desert training and conditioning, Sergeant Benjamin Leane and the 10th Battalion embarked from Alexandria aboard *Ionian* on 2 March 1915 to join the Mediterranean Expeditionary Force for the assault on Gallipoli.

From the day he departed Australia, Benjamin resolved to write a diary for his wife Phyllis, as so much that he wanted to tell her would not pass censorship. He hoped that, after the war, they would be able to share his exploits together. His early entries from Egypt reflect his commitment to the AIF and his fear that he might be excluded from the first assault. He wrote, 'Every fibre of my being is against the thought of inaction, and I'll guarantee I would suffer a nervous breakdown if I was left at Base.'[234] In the days before the landing, his diary reveals the conflict between his dual loyalties. His love of the military life is evident in his desire to pursue it as a career path. 'If I come through this war dear, I intend to be a soldier for the remainder of my active years and I shall study assiduously with this end in view.'[235] Yet the depth of his love for Phyllis and his young family is indelibly etched in an anticipated farewell before the Gallipoli landing:

> Dearest, we have just received orders to embark on the destroyer at 10.45 tomorrow. ... In case the worst happens and I am unable to make any more entries, I will take this opportunity to bid you goodbye dear girl. I trust that I will come through alright, but it is impossible to say, and I must do my duty whatever it is. But if I am to die, know that I died loving you with my whole heart and soul, dearest wife that ever a man had. Kiss little Gwen and our new baby, who perhaps I may never see and never let them forget daddy. And you dear girl, I would love to write you a long letter, but I must do my work and there is no time. But I love you dearly my own dear Phyllis, and I trust that you will always love me. But remember dear, that if I am killed, I wish you to do absolutely as you think advisable for your future.[236]

Benjamin was fortunate that his brief career did not end at the landing as he sustained a severe gunshot wound to the arm and elbow. Undaunted, he courageously fought on with only one arm functioning, dragging a supply of ammunition boxes uphill to the depleted forces, a deed which earned him a justifiable Mention in Despatches. The citation read: 'Although wounded through the right arm and unable to use a rifle, Sergeant Leane carried ammunition up to the trenches on his left shoulder while under fire.'[237] However, his wound was serious and so debilitating that he was evacuated to Alexandria for treatment, after which he was transferred to England aboard *Ghoorka* to convalesce.

Hospitalised in Manchester, Benjamin's diary reveals a man who could make the best of every situation. Although longing for his wife and young family, these personal memoirs reveal a sensitive and sensual man who, amid personal adversity, could find delight in the world around him. He enthusiastically describes fresh food and wine, conversation with curious children, the beauty of the English countryside and the warmth of hospitality so generously offered by local families. Just as significant are Benjamin's religious sensibilities. His diary entries reflect his abiding faith, documenting his attendance at numerous church parades, the joyous singing of hymns and the peace that followed communion.

By August 1915 Sergeant Leane had been declared fit for active service and embarked for Egypt and then Lemnos aboard *Alwick Castle*. On 15 August he returned to Gallipoli on *Braemar Castle*, virtually chaffing at the bit. Having been absent since the landing, he had missed the major offensives at Krithia and Lone Pine and was shocked to note the debilitated state of many of the troops and, of course, the absences. He was delighted though, to learn that he had been Mentioned in Despatches and promoted to lieutenant. More importantly, his return reunited him with his brothers, Edwin (Ted), Ray and Allan.

In this phase of his diary entries, Benjamin rejoices in the arrival of mail and parcels, makes light of hardships and positively recounts the minutiae of everyday life in a remarkable acceptance of the vicissitudes of battle. He writes with respect of the Turks and finds humour in their chance interactions. He recounts to Phyllis a plan that backfired due to the Australians' kindly treatment of Turkish prisoners. In so doing, and deliberately facilitating their escape, it was hoped that the favour would be returned for Australian prisoners of war. However, the food and comforts offered by the AIF were obviously too tempting for one pair of Turkish prisoners who, when sent out to collect wood, dutifully kept returning, laden with branches, irrespective of how far they were sent.

Benjamin reports the continued presence of Edwin and Ray Leane at Anzac and is delighted when Edwin's son, Arnold Harry, arrives with the 27th Battalion on 25 October, recording with pride his own appointment to adjutant on 26 October. The benefits of this promotion are evident in the description of his new quarters, a larger dugout in which he could actually stand. It is amazing what is merciful when one has so few comforts. However, life was harsh, and with limited and monotonous rations, Benjamin's health began to deteriorate and he developed jaundice. On 21 November he was transferred to hospital and the rest camp on West Mudros, where he observed the arrival of the cruel gales that would mark the onset of winter. By December, word of the proposed retreat from Anzac was being circulated and he was heartbroken as he came to terms with an expedition he describes as 'wasted utterly ... and above all the lives ... all thrown away in vain. Oh it seems too awful. And think of the blow to British prestige. I would rather a hundred times go back to ANZAC and die so that we might achieve our object and conquer the Turks and justify all that Gallipoli has cost.'[238] As the withdrawal continued, Benjamin watched with despair as the exhausted and skeletal troops disembarked at Mudros prior to their embarkation for Egypt. His view no doubt echoed the pain of the retreating troops as he remarked, 'After the money and the blood that has been spent on the project, and to think that it has all gone for nought. Oh! It's heartbreaking.'[239]

By the end of December the evacuation was complete, and the majority of the sick and wounded had been transferred from Mudros to hospitals in Cairo or England. For the AIF, the return to Egypt afforded a chance to regroup and rejuvenate the exhausted and depleted troops.

Fragments of some battalions merged with others, while new ones were formed, blending the seasoned troops with reinforcements from Australia. Benjamin's battalion was initially based at Tel el Kebir, and he was delighted that his brothers, Edwin, Allan, Ray and young Allan (Edwin's son) and Clarence Fairley (Ethel's adopted son) were all stationed at various bases in the region.[240]

Disillusioned at the evacuation from Gallipoli, Benjamin became increasingly frustrated with his second period of service in Egypt. In his diary entry for New Year's Day 1916, it is evident that his men felt an equal measure of disenchantment:

> It appears that quite a lot of the chaps went on the jog last night. They couldn't get any liquor in the camp and enjoy New Year in the good old fashioned style so they went to Zazazig (about 12 miles distant) to get it there. Unfortunately for them, they were nabbed by the piquet and brought back. Anyway, there were three sergeants. I had to have a little 'heart to heart' with them on the matter and then sent them to the lines with instructions to refrain from being—— fools and risk losing their stripes. I don't blame them a bit—— or rather, I do blame them, because an NCO [non-commissioned officer] ought to set a good example, but I don't wonder at their break. They can't even get enough food in camp, let alone liquor.
>
> I suggested to the CO to send into Zazazig and buy some provisions up out of Regimental Funds, but he wouldn't have any of it. He wanted to know who was going to recoup him. I was willing to put in a fiver myself and was sure all of the officers would do the same and chance whether we were recouped or not, rather than let things go on as they are. He got quite cross. I am fed up with the doddering old fool. Between ourselves so are the men and most of the officers. They have no respect for him.[241]

His CO was Lieutenant Colonel Miles Beevor, who Benjamin felt to be incompetent and indecisive. Yet, in spite of following military protocol, with the proverbial 'dressing down' of the miscreants, Benjamin's generosity and empathy for his men demonstrates why he was so beloved by his comrades. Unable to continue serving under Beevor and hearing his name as a universal butt of humour, Benjamin sought a transfer. When a call was made for volunteers to form a Camel Corps, Benjamin was one of the first to step forward, undaunted by the fact that he had just learned to ride a horse. He was duly made adjutant of the Camel Corps and was initially pleased with the new posting.

However, while the Camel Corps offered much promise, a limited supply of camels restricted the men's training and the development of a clear objective. By 20 February 1916, after weeks of drill and a dearth of camels, Benjamin's diary records, 'I am absolutely fed up with this life. It's a waste of money and a waste of time and the pleasure one gets out of it is a sort of dead sea fruit. I would rather a hundred times spend a quiet evening at home. I wish something would develop so that we could get into a scrap and do our job.'[242] As luck would have it, opportunity presented itself on 27 February 1916. 'I got a message from Allan asking me to ring him up. On doing so, I found that he went down to Ismailia yesterday and saw Ray who has been given command of the 48th Battalion and wants me to go with him as his adjutant. It has placed me in a quandary. On the one hand I have a job that suits me down to the ground, and in which I am more contented than ever before in my short military career, but in which there is not much opportunity for promotion and every chance of future promotion with Ray. I should be able to work very well with Ray. Everybody thinks I would be foolish to turn down the opportunity, so I think on the whole I had better apply for a transfer.'[243] By 2 March the transfer had been effected and, with rumours that the Australians were bound for France, Benjamin could barely contain his excitement. Edwin's son Allan was acting quartermaster in the battalion, while his sister Ethel's adopted son, Clarence Fairley, was also a member of the battalion. It amused Benjamin no end that the battalion was nicknamed 'the Joan of Arc Battalion' and that the standing joke was, 'What is the difference between the 48th Battalion and a strip of bacon?' Apparently a great deal, as bacon has some fat and the battalion is 'all Leane'!'[244]

By 25 March, Ray had been promoted to lieutenant colonel and, by 1 April, it was announced that Benjamin had been promoted to captain.

Working with members of his family, Benjamin thrived on his promotion and new appointment. Together, the family members worked hard to shape their new battalion which performed admirably in various encounters with the Turks along the Suez Canal. At an inspection, the battalion drew praise from the Brigadier and Benjamin's mood was exultant. 'Jove, my life as adjutant here is different to what it was in the 10th under Colonel Beevor. I work hard, even harder than I did in the tenth, but my heart's in the work, and I know it is appreciated.'[245] On 29 May orders were received for the battalion to entrain to Alexandria and there board *Caledonian* on 1 June, bound for Marseilles. Benjamin's excitement over the duration of the transfer and arrival in France is palpable. At last it seemed that this is where the action was, and that is exactly where he wanted to be.

Of course, as a captain and with his brother as CO, Benjamin's travel arrangements were a great deal more salubrious than those of the troops. While the latter were crowded on lower decks on the ship and shuttled by rail in horse boxes, Benjamin luxuriated in a comfortable cabin with a bed and clean sheets, a fine menu and a first class train carriage. It is little wonder that he and Ray were in raptures over the beauty of France on their long journey to Bailleul. Ever one to be easily stimulated by good company and new friends, Benjamin delighted in the journey, sharing it with the new Roman Catholic Padre and the new Medical Officer. As he recounts their diametrically opposed views and demeanours, one can almost visualise Ben soaking up the exchanges like the proverbial sponge:

> He is a fine fellow, Father Devine. None of your comfortable sleek priest about him, but a tall, gaunt sharp featured man ... with a voice that is manly, a keen sense of humour. A laugh that is hearty and a mind that is broad. He is the type of Catholic who makes you wonder why the Protestant Church is so bitter against his Roman Catholics. His particular friend, Captain Woollard, our Medical Officer, is an atheist with a propaganda, as he calls himself. So sure as the Padre makes up one line of argument, Doc will take the opposite. He is very clever and has a thoroughly developed humorous vein so you can guess that the discussions become both lively and personal ...

but always with good feeling and an entire absence of malice. He is a little fellow about 5ft 5ins, but he can strafe with the best. He is never lost for a word. He abuses the Padre most unmercifully, calls him 'Man of God', 'The Jesuit', 'The parasite of truth', and the Padre chuckles away until he is finished, and then opens out on him with equal force. But they are real good friends.[246]

By 14 June the battalion had reached Bailleul, where the troops were billeted in farms and barns while the men familiarised themselves with their new environment before being deployed to the front line. As senior officers, Benjamin and Ray made numerous exploratory trips to the front line to gain a working knowledge of tactics and the types of ammunition used by the enemy. For the enlisted men, there was much movement and drill at a series of billets and ranges to achieve maximum conditioning for the vastly different environment. Amid the uncertainty and enthusiasm to enter the fray, Benjamin's thoughts of his beloved Phyllis are constantly recorded in his diary. On 17 July, Benjamin's entry is both poetic and lyrical, as he acknowledges the importance of the date amid the beauty and the terror of his surroundings:

> Four years ago today sweetheart and what a happy day it was. The waking in the morning to realise that it was our day. The waiting in the manse and then your coming. The few words, your dear hand in mine, and the knowledge that you were my wife. The lunch at 'Arcadia', the train journey and Aldgate. And you, such a dear sweet happy girl. Oh chicken, I love you dearly, better now than even then, for I know you so much better now. And as to know you, was to love you, so to know you better is to love you better. Today, we have been on a route march. Beautiful country and oh the poppies, bright scarlet poppies. The wheat fields bright with poppies, corn flowers and poppies, poppies everywhere, a blaze of red, gay and flaunting.[247]

Descriptions of such vistas were soon to be destroyed though as the battalion joined the assault on the strategic position of Pozières. Benjamin had heard from his brother Allan of the 7000 casualties from the 10th and 11th battalions at Pozières. This was followed by later news from Allan that his battalion, the 28th, had been decimated, and that all of the company commanders had been killed. Allan had assumed temporary command of the battalion, 'or what was left of it.'

Benjamin's diary of 3 August records the horror and brutality of the 48th Battalion's baptism of fire. 'Oh child dear. I've been up to the first line today. All over the ground, recently taken by our splendid fellows and the English troops and it is hell. The dead are lying everywhere. Some of them several days old, others only today and yesterday. The stench is terrible, but that is nothing. It is the sight of the poor fellows huddled up there—gruesome—bloated—that makes you realise the full, the beastly side of war. The charges, the taking of little villages and ridges, all this is heroic and glorious to read of, but afterwards, the rotting dead, the unburied dead, the fine fellows who a few days ago were brave and handsome and full of life and health, now nothing but horrible putrid masses of flesh.'[248]

In spite of his sensitive accounts of war's barbarity, Benjamin never dwelt on it. He appeared able to move on and remain focused and professional throughout his service. As such, he was able to rejoice in whatever honours or surprises came his way. By 24 September, he was ecstatic over the news of Phyllis' plans to come to England for Christmas. On 2 October his jubilation knew no bounds when he recorded, 'The CO tells me today that the Brigadier has sent me for a decoration and he thinks I will get a Serbian decoration. Of course I shall be very pleased if I do get it. Anyhow, I think he could have found someone who deserves it more.'[249] In spite of his humility, Benjamin was awarded the Serbian Order of the White Eagle for 'Consistent good work as adjutant and constant attention to duty since his arrival in France. His painstaking work in the administration of the battalion has been of great assistance. This officer served on Gallipoli.' He also recorded with pride that 'Young Fairley, has been given a Military Cross for his work at Pozières. I am very glad for the boy, he thoroughly earned it. Dear old Ethel will be delighted too, to think that "her boy" as she calls Clarrie, has been so distinguished. Ray has also sent me on for my Majority. If I get it, I will go to a company, as an adjutant rarely holds higher rank than a captain.'[250]

Benjamin's joy was all too apparent when he recorded on 29 October confirmation that Phyllis was due to arrive in London on 10 December. 'I am wild with joy, darling, darling girl.' and that his promotion to major had been approved.[251] Although Benjamin was granted leave to London in early December, his wife's ship was delayed until the 19th. Nonetheless, the couple shared a week together over Christmas, until Benjamin had to report to Fliselles on 1 January 1917. His diary understandably lapsed during that period and, because Phyllis remained in England, the couple's correspondence was naturally more frequent, erasing the need for the diary. Meanwhile, in France, members of the 48th Battalion prepared for the mighty battles of Bullecourt. On the evening of the first battle, Major Benjamin Leane 'was sent out to make a dump on no man's land, in readiness for the big attack. He had 40 men with him and by all accounts, had completed the task. His brother, the CO, had just rung him up, and he had answered that all the work was complete. Then, he must have been struck by a shell that killed him instantly, as well as his nephew, Captain Leane and nearly all of the 40 men. His brother, (Ray) eventually located his scattered remains and he is buried at Quéant Road British Cemetery, but I think he was removed from there.'[252] Ben's death was not only the family's loss, but the whole battalion's. 'He was the best liked of the clan,'[253] and, according to Father Devine, Benjamin was 'A man with all the force of character of his truculent brother, but of a disposition as gentle as a woman.'[254]

Perhaps Ray and other members of the family withheld the gory details of Benjamin's tragic death from his adored wife Phyllis. No. 2749 Signaller Randolph Spargo of the 48th Battalion provided graphic evidence of Benjamin's loss for the official record. 'At about 3am at the village of Ecoust to the left of Bullecourt, close to the railway line, just over the first trench line of the 48th Battalion, I saw Major Leane blown to pieces. I saw his head and pieces of his shoulders. Colonel Leane recognised him from his head. His brother collected his remains and buried them. He was a popular officer and was well liked.'[255]

Major Benjamin Bennett Leane.
Image courtesy of: Moya Sharp. Outback Family History Society

Colonel Raymond Leane's actions were instrumental in securing a burial for his much-loved brother, and his initial interment took place at the Sunken Road, Noreuil, France. Later, his remains were exhumed and reinterred at Quéant Road Cemetery, Buissy, France. Prior to his death on 10 April 1917, Major Benjamin Bennett Leane was again Mentioned in Despatches. On 5 March, Major General William Holmes acknowledged that, 'This officer has rendered valuable and efficient service since the formation of the battalion as adjutant and company commander and during the last two tours of duty as senior major. His work has been consistent and good, always bright and cheerful, he sets a splendid example of soldierly bearing and devotion to duty to all he comes in contact with.'[256]

In reflecting on the life of Major Benjamin Bennett Leane, it may be difficult for the modern reader to understand how a man could reconcile the dichotomy between such passionate love for his wife and children and duty to God and Empire. Both were deeply felt by a man whose zest for life embraced every aspect of it, for better or worse. He truly honoured the tenets of his Wesleyan belief—faith, fidelity and family—until his death. Perhaps his courage is exemplified in his last letter home in which Major Benjamin Bennett Leane wrote, 'If anything should happen to me, mourn not for me, but for those who fear to come.'[257] His young wife, Phyllis, never remarried. In response to the Australian War Museum's request for details on her husband, Phyllis wrote, 'He had an almost perfect disposition, cheerful, happy smile, generous and he was in many ways soft hearted. In fact he had what is known as a "steel hand with a velvet grip," being a very strong soldier, yet having such a kind heart. In appearance he was very strong and sturdily built, not very tall, 5ft 10ins, but a picture of health and youth, plenty of colour and very handsome, dark.'[258]

Understandably, his beloved wife Phyllis was devastated by his death. But when her turn came to choose an epitaph for her husband's grave, she sought consolation in the bigger picture, just as Benjamin would have wished. 'He died for the greatest cause in history. Ever remembered.'[259]

13. WORTHY CONTENDERS

The previous chapters offer much support for the validity of Bean's assertion that the Leanes were the most famous family of soldiers in Australia's military history. However, the real test of this statement must be explored and evaluated by comparing their commitment and achievements with other families who may also justifiably lay claim to such fame. There appears to have been a 'domino effect' in terms of enlistment, in that when one family member enlisted, other relatives would follow, invariably joining the same battalion. It is therefore not surprising that many families suffered multiple fatalities with some losing all those who had entered the fray.

According to figures compiled by the Australian War Memorial (AWM), more than 2800 sets of brothers perished in World War I. More than 150 families lost three sons and at least five more lost four.[260] The contribution of the Single family from Castlereagh, NSW, for example, was extraordinary. Thirty-three of the descendants of pioneer grazier John Single, who opened up the north-western plains, enthusiastically flocked to the colours. Nine were killed, three of them on the same day. Craig Tibbits, as curator of official records at the AWM recorded: 'Of this extended family, nine did not return, either being killed in action or dying of disease. Their sacrifice plots a virtual map of the momentous battles of the AIF during the war: John Digby killed at Gallipoli in 1915; Percy Single at Pozières in 1916;

Gordon Yeoman, who died of disease in France in 1916; Alexander Fraser, killed at Passchendaele in 1917; Horace Thompson, killed at Hill 66, Belgium, and Francis Digby, killed at Mont St Quentin in 1918.'[261] This list excludes the three who died on that fateful day, 26 September 1917, at Polygon Wood: Captain Raymond Single of the 56th Battalion, Private Wilfred Single of the 29th Battalion and their cousin, Captain Hubert Thompson of the 56th Battalion. Service records reveal that the three men were buried in the field, but their remains were never relocated or identified. Their sacrifice is commemorated on the Menin Gate Memorial at Ypres in Belgium.

Within a nuclear family, the grief endured by Fred and Maggie Smith from Yongala, in losing five of their six sons, is unimaginable. The Keid family of Graceville, Brisbane, also paid a heavy price, losing four of their six sons who enlisted, much like the Williams family of tiny Dunkeld in Victoria, who lost four of their five sons. Four sons of George and Isabella Bartram of Richmond, Victoria, also enlisted. Arnold was 22 when he died at Bullecourt in May 1917. A month later Raymond, aged 23, was killed at Messines Ridge, and in October of that same year Reginald, the eldest at 37, was killed at Broodseinde Ridge near Passchendaele. The fourth brother, Cyril, suffered chronic influenza and was sent home, medically unfit, also in 1917.[262]

In each of these families, at least one son survived. The sons of William and Fanny Seabrook of Petersham, NSW, Theo, 25, George, 24 and William, 20, all enlisted as members of the 17th Battalion. Their first engagement was the Battle of Menin Road, fought near Ypres on 20 September 1917, in which all three were mortally wounded and died in the days that followed.[263] Privates Theo and George Seabrook's sacrifice is commemorated on the Menin Gate at Ypres, while 2nd Lieutenant William Seabrook's remains were interred at the Lijssenthoek Military Cemetery in Belgium. The records of the Commonwealth War Graves Commission describe each as the son of William George and Fanny Isabel Seabrook and notes that his brothers also fell on 20 September 1917. William's epitaph speaks for all three brothers and his parents' belief that their cherished sons' deaths were 'a willing sacrifice for the world's peace'. This can only be described as a courageous and remarkable acceptance of such grievous loss.

If one were to ascribe fame solely on the loss of life, then it would be difficult to overlook the contribution that each of these families made to Australia and its military history. The enormity of such sacrifice must have been almost unendurable for these bereaved families. Doubtless it would not have eased as these fathers and mothers entered the lonely years of old age, confronting what they must have regarded as the pointlessness of their lives as they battled through the Great Depression in the late 1920s and early 1930s.

It would seem then that additional qualifications are required to achieve an exalted status. Naturally, in a military context, the expected requirements would refer to rank and honour. Of the families previously mentioned, most men served as privates or NCOs. Only 2nd Lieutenant William Keith Seabrook, Lieutenant Leonard Keid, Captain Raymond Single and Captain Hubert Thompson were officers, while Private Clarence Leslie Smith was the only one to receive an honour, with the award of the Military Medal. Given the senior leadership positions that members of the Leane family held and the range of honours accorded them, it appears obvious that they possess a greater claim to Bean's title than any of these previously mentioned families.

However, I believe that one other family has a justifiable claim to Bean's accolade—the Howell-Price family. The Reverend John Howell-Price, of St Silas's Anglican Church in Waterloo, Sydney, and his wife Isobel, raised a family of six sons and four daughters. Their father was highly esteemed as a fearless preacher and a kindly minister. Of Welsh extraction, he came to Australia in his early youth and afterwards studied for the ministry before ordination in Bathurst in 1879. Over the intervening years he ministered in several remote rural parishes before becoming rector of St Silas's in 1915. Five of his six sons enlisted in the AIF at the outbreak of war, but only two returned home. The sixth and eldest son (of whom more later) served on the staff of 'Fighting Charlie Cox' as a lieutenant in the Boer War. The story of the minister whose five sons had enlisted obviously struck a chord with the press and public alike. Throughout 1916, before any were killed, the daily newspapers heralded the service and achievements of the brothers. Headlines such as, 'The Howell-Prices. A Fighting Family' and 'Warriors Born. Five Fighting Sons of Rev. J. Howell-Price', trumpeted their fame throughout Sydney before syndication to minor newspapers throughout NSW.

The Reverend John Howell-Price felt that, in spite of being a man of peace, his sons had inherited a strong fighting strain. When interviewed by the *Sunday Times* about his sons' gallantry, the Reverend claimed that 'It was in the blood', referring to his own lineage which was closely connected to the army, navy and mercantile marine of Great Britain.[264] His father had naval training, his grandfather fought in the Crimean War and, during the Burmese operations in the 19th century, one of his uncles earned a special tribute for carrying Rear Admiral Austin from the battlefield when he was wounded and in great danger. As testament to his uncle's courage, the family held an heirloom which 'was a cup given by the family of the Late Rear-Admiral. It bore the inscription 1862.'[265] The paternal line of the Reverend's wife, Isobel, traced its lineage to the famous 'Jack of Newbury', who raised, equipped at his own expense, and led 100 men to Flodden Field and also entertained Henry VIII and Catherine of Aragon in his own house.[266] The sons of whom he spoke with justifiable pride were: John Howell-Price, Frederick Phillimore, Phillip Llewellyn, Owen Glendower and Richmond Gordon Howell-Price.

Lieutenant Colonel Owen Glendower Howell-Price DSO MC was the fourth son, but the first to enlist after war had been declared by Great Britain. Having served with the militia, he quickly applied and was commissioned 2nd lieutenant on 18 October 1914. Following a training camp at Randwick Racecourse in Kensington, he embarked with the 3rd Battalion of the 1st Infantry Brigade. After strenuous training in Egypt he was promoted to full lieutenant. Soon after, his battalion left Alexandria for Lemnos and then Gallipoli where he landed on 25 April 1915. In the aftermath of the

Lieutenant Colonel Owen Glendower Howell-Price DSO MC.
Australian War Memorial, C 41639

landing, Captain Burns, then the Adjutant of the 3rd Battalion, was killed and Lieutenant Owen Howell-Price was recalled from the trenches and appointed Adjutant. On 4 August he was promoted to captain prior to the offensive at Lone Pine where the official record states that 'He showed the greatest bravery in leading the attack, frequently rallying his men under heavy artillery and restoring order at critical moments. He killed three men with his own hands.'[267] In that attack Owen was twice wounded, once on one of his hands and once on the neck. He was urged to retire, but refused to do so. The wound on the neck was very deep, but he bound it up and continued fighting, declaring that, 'The Turks will have to pay for it.'[268] His conspicuous gallantry and leadership in the attack saw Owen awarded the MC and later decorated personally by the King at Buckingham Palace. While on Gallipoli, Owen's courage did not escape Bean's scrutiny. He described 'Young Howell-Price [as the] greatest of men and conscientious to a fault.'[269]

On 1 December 1915, while secret preparations were under way for the evacuation of Anzac, Captain Owen Howell-Price was promoted to the rank of major. His rise in rank not only reflected the toll of officers on the Gallipoli Peninsula, but his intelligence and inspired leadership. Back in Egypt, where Bean had formerly not endeared himself to many members of the AIF, he again observed the Australians and the disciplined leadership of Major Owen Howell-Price. He recorded astutely that:

> It was also noticeable that a few officers of a certain type, who had fought their way to the front at Anzac, now, as soon as strong drink was obtainable, tended to break down and had gradually to be eliminated. There was emerging however, a particularly fine set of keen young regimental leaders, such as O.G. Howell-Price of the 3rd and Scott and Simpson of the 4th and these immediately and with fiery energy plunged the rusty and depleted units into the heavy toll of training and reorganization.[270]

Bean's assessment was incisive for, on deployment to the Western Front, Owen was immediately promoted, leading his troops as a lieutenant colonel. Aged only 26 years of age, he was the youngest Australian to achieve that rank at that time.

On the Western Front, Lieutenant Colonel Howell-Price continued to lead by example and demanded as much of his 3rd Battalion as Colonel Raymond Leane did of the 48th Battalion. On 1 June 1916, the Prime Minister of Australia, Billy Hughes, and former Prime Minister, Andrew Fisher, visited the troops at Sailly-sur-la-Leys near Armentières. Bean's diary entry for the day records his respect for Owen Howell-Price, and his admiration of the stature and discipline of his troops:

> It was the 1st Australian Infantry Brigade—the same that took Lone Pine and by heavens they looked splendid—I have never seen them look better—strapping straight bronzed men with their officers standing in front of them. Men who went through Lone Pine, little Howell-Price was there (why do I call him little—maybe because he was a junior subaltern when they left Kensington) in front of the 3rd Battalion as their colonel. Their drill was as good as you could wish to see.[271]

Like all great leaders Owen Howell-Price led from the front. Charles Bean reflects this in his diary entry on the Battle of Pozières:

> At 10 o'clock the 3rd Battalion, still south of the main road, was ordered to advance and connect the posts of the 8th along the northern edge of Pozières. Its Commander, Colonel Owen Howell-

Price gave instructions to Captain Middleton and Lieutenant Bartlett, then acting in command of the companies that were to move. On their returning to their men, both were killed. Price himself went up, having only four company officers left, re-allotted the commands and then, as the trenches south of the road were useless and indeed barely traceable, led the remains of all four companies forward through a barrage of terrible density. He himself was twice thrown down by the blasts of explosions.[272]

This willingness to brave all with his troops was a source of considerable admiration from his men. An interview published by the *Sydney Sun* with a returned soldier, Private Rogers, at Randwick Hospital, revealed the men's respect for their colonel:

He was brave. You know there are some officers that the men call "squibs." But the colonel was not one of them. He made us build him a dugout in the very front lines of the trenches, though the officer's headquarters are usually about two miles behind the lines. Whatever was coming to us the colonel took part in too, and no matter how pippy you felt in the trenches, to see him coming along smiling, made everything right again.[273]

On 4 November 1916, it was to be this brazen courage and initiative that would cost Colonel Owen Howell-Price his life. He died doing what he routinely did, leading from the front. During the Battle of Flers he was visiting one of the front trenches, in fact the forward line known by his name. Bean recorded that:

He had been out to a sap in no-man's land and was just back in Price Trench; there was some sniping—a machine gun had also been bothering the place. Price was directing the putting up of a machine gun to reply to it—one of our section was trying to get the gun up. Price turned to speak to Loveday when he fell forward on his face onto the parapet and then rolled over onto his back. They hurried him back in 20 minutes to the First Aid Post and he seemed pretty well himself.[274]

Bean's concern for Howell-Price and his belief that men like him 'make all the difference to the force he commands', is reflected in his diary entries following that fatal battle.[275] On 3 November he recorded, 'Little Howell-Price was hit through the cheek and neck the other day—looking over the parapet I'm sure. We saw him in hospital—unconscious.'[276] The next day Bean received news that 'Howell-Price conscious today; Jack [Bean's brother] spoke with him a bit. Jack tells me he has a slight squint which is the only bad sign.'[277] But Bean's hope and optimism were shattered on 5 November. 'It was a great shock when De Crespigny told me that Howell-Price died last night. I am sure that he was hit going around his line—he was a most faithful commanding officer—never missed this duty. I remember the time I saw him in Pozières when his battalion's position was uncertain. He placed it right enough himself.'[278]

The death of Lieutenant Colonel Owen Glendower Howell-Price was to be the first of three terrible losses that the Reverend and his wife were to face. From a military perspective, his death was a loss to the nation, and fulsome tributes reflecting both grief and the esteem in which he was held, were posted by senior officers at the front. General Birdwood wrote:

> My Dear Mr. Howell-Price,
>
> I feel I must send you a line to tell you how I sympathise with you and your wife in the very great loss which you have sustained in the death of your son who was commanding the 3rd Battalion yesterday. Since we started, nearly two years ago, I have seen a great deal and formed such a high opinion of him, while I had the greatest respect and affection for him. He was indeed a most excellent officer in every way, brave, conscientious, hard-working and completely self-sacrificing – a real example of what a commanding officer should be, and I deplore his death more than I can say, He came through all the hard fighting on the Peninsula so well, that I had always looked forward with full hope and confidence to his being saved to see this war through to the finish.
>
> As you will have probably heard, he was struck in the cheek by a bullet, which came out at the back of the neck. He was at once brought into hospital, when, I immediately went to see him. He was unconscious but I am thankful to say in no pain. The doctors up to a few hours before his death were full of hope that he would pull through. In fact when I left him at about 4.00pm yesterday, the medical officer in charge said he really did not feel any anxiety, his only fear being that the spinal cord might be affected; but if that were the case, he did not think he would have lived so long. I therefore left the hospital

perfectly contented in my mind about him, and indeed had every hope that we would be seeing him back commanding his battalion in due course. I fear there is nothing I can say which can be of any help to you in your loss, but it might be some comfort to know that others are feeling for you, and it will, I feel be a small consolation to realize that he fell fighting so gallantly for his King and country.

Yours very sincerely W.B. Birdwood.

Another letter, published on the same day and written by Major General Walker, Commander of the 1st Australian Division, also reflected the enormity of the AIF's loss with the Colonel's death:

It is with heavy heart that I have come to condole with you on the loss of your son, Colonel Howell-Price who died from a gunshot wound a few days ago. A gallant officer, he has died a gallant death. I am glad to say that he suffered little. He is an irreparable loss to the 3rd Battalion, and to the division. I have been so intimate with him the last two years that I feel as if I had lost a brother. Everyone has felt his loss. His brother, I am thankful to say is well, and behaving as gallantly as ever. I have just been talking to him. I am sure that you will bear your loss with the bravery of your family. I pray that you may not be called upon for any further sacrifice in this war.

With my kindest regards believe me, yours very sincerely.

H. B. Walker.[279]

Colonel Owen Howell-Price was further honoured in January 1917 when his gallantry was Mentioned in Despatches twice by General Haig and with the posthumous award of the DSO. His remains are interred at Heilly Station Cemetery Méricourt-L'Abbé, France. He was 26 years of age.

The sixth son and the second of the Reverend and Mrs Howell-Price's sons to pay the supreme sacrifice was 2nd Lieutenant Richmond Gordon Howell-Price MC. He enlisted on 14 December 1914 at the age of 19 and was allotted to the 16th Reinforcements of the 6th Light Horse, but later transferred to the 1st Battalion, no doubt keen to be with his brother Owen as a member of the 1st Division. He was obviously an eager, intelligent young man, and although early promotion through the ranks was offered to him, he declined, perhaps because he felt too young to assume responsibility

Lieutenant Richmond Gordon Howell-Price MC.
Australian War Memorial, P00267.005

over older men. He spent almost a year at training depots, but a posting to Tel el Kebir in December 1916 saw him participate in the Battle of Romani in Egypt with the Light Horse. Subsequently, he was transferred to France and commissioned. Apart from attending a machine-gun training school in the early part of 1917, little else is recorded about him. Before the terrible Battle of Bullecourt, the Reverend and his family received another letter from General Birdwood, but on this occasion it provided inspiration to the still grieving hearts of the family. Dated 6 May, he wrote:

> My reason for writing to you now is to tell you how really proud I am to have been able to recommend your youngest boy, Gordon, for the Military Cross, which he has so thoroughly deserved and which has just been awarded to him. I recommended him for the honour, owing to his exceptionally fine work in our operations in the vicinity of Dernancourt on April 9, when his initiative and bravery in leading his platoon were of the highest order. On being holed up near his first objective by hostile machine gun fire, he placed his Lewis gunners and bombers on his respective flanks, and advanced to capture the position under their covering fire with very little loss to his platoon. Later he overcame similar opposition by his sound tactics, which he carried out with great determination and resource, and which

largely contributed to our success in the capture of the village. It is difficult to exaggerate the value of the fine example which he set for his men in a difficult operation. As I may not be able to see your boy for some little time, I am sending him a line of congratulation. I know how proud you must both be of your sons, as indeed, you have every reason to be.[280]

Having dispensed some joy to the Howell-Price family, the celebrations of all parties proved short lived. On 4 May, 2nd Lieutenant Richmond Gordon Howell-Price was killed at Bullecourt. On 10 May 1917 General Birdwood wrote again, this time with a heavy pen and a leaden heart:

I know I need not tell you with what deep sorrow I write to you by this mail. It was only last week that I was writing to congratulate you on the bravery of your boy, Gordon, which had won for him the much coveted Military Cross. I little thought then that he was to be taken from us so soon, and I cannot tell you how deeply I regret this, and how much I feel for you and his mother to whom I know it will come as such a very cruel blow ... I will only add how very sincerely and deeply I do sympathise with you on losing this very brave son.[281]

Again, Major General Walker also extended his condolences:

It is with the greatest of regret that I have to sympathise with you a second time for the loss of another of your gallant sons. It has been a great blow to me to think that another of your family under my command should have fallen. He had just been awarded the Military Cross for gallantry in a previous operation less than a fortnight before. I cannot tell you how much I deplore his loss. He was wounded by a shell, and died at the dressing station. He was cheerful to the last, and I hope and believe did not suffer very much.[282]

It had been a cruel 12 months for the Reverend and his family, but worse was to follow. The third brother to join the family casualty list was Major Phillip Llewellyn Howell-Price who won a DSO and MC before he was killed at Broodseinde near Passchendaele on 4 October 1917. He enlisted on 14 December 1914 and was allotted to the 1st Battalion. He went through the same training camp in NSW as his brother Owen, and embarked on the same fleet of transports. Having previously served in the militia, he too applied for a commission and was appointed 2nd lieutenant.

Major Phillip Llewellyn Howell-Price DSO MC.
Australian War Memorial, P00267.004

After training in Egypt, Phillip was attached to the machine-gun section of his battalion at Gallipoli, where his skill and leadership soon saw him promoted to lieutenant. He was severely wounded at the attack at Lone Pine on 8 August 1915, and was hospitalised at Mudros and Ras-el-Tin, Alexandria, with a bullet lodged in the base of his spine. Such a potentially crippling and life-threatening wound would have made a lesser man request a return to Australia, but not Phillip Llewellyn Howell-Price. After just three months' hospitalisation, he rejoined his battalion at Gallipoli a short time before the evacuation. Possibly, at the time, he enjoyed the proud distinction of being placed in command of one of the very last detachments to leave.

The return to Egypt and subsequent reorganisation saw Phillip promoted to captain on 28 January 1916 and he proceeded to France as Officer in Command of D Company, 1st Battalion. By August 1916 word had reached Australia that he had been awarded the DSO for 'Conspicuous gallantry in leading a successful raid on enemy trenches in the face of heavy opposition and against uncut wire entanglements. He carried out the attack with great coolness and resource, and saw every officer and man back into our trenches before he returned. He had previously been recommended three times in despatches, the last time by Sir Ian Hamilton himself.'[283] In the raid which earned Phillip his DSO, he left with a party of four officers and 58 other ranks from the 1st Battalion on the night of 28 June 1916. The group successfully raided the enemy's trenches near Waterfot. The raid was supported by the fire of the Divisional Artillery and also by a howitzer battery of the 2nd Division. The men discovered that the enemy wire had not been completely cut, but they nevertheless managed to find a way through. They then entered a German trench and killed 10 to 12 of the enemy, captured two prisoners and took various trophies. There was only one Australian casualty, while two officers and eight other ranks were wounded.

By September 1917 the Sydney press were further able to report that Captain Phillip Llewellyn Howell-Price DSO MC had been promoted to the rank of major and appointed acting Brigade Major of the 2nd Division. At the time of his promotion he was under 23 years of age and, having left Sydney as a 2nd lieutenant, was one of the few original men of the 1st Division still at the front. He had been wounded three times—once at Gallipoli and twice on the Western Front, and Mentioned in Despatches three times. In recording Phillip's death, Bean makes mention of the fact that General Birdwood had offered the young soldier a position on the staff of I Anzac Corps in an effort to preserve his life, but on hearing that his old battalion was going into action, Phillip begged to be sent back to it.[284] No evidence could be found of the letters of condolence that Generals Birdwood and Walker would most likely have sent to the shattered Howell-Price family. Major Phillip Llewellyn Howell-Price's sacrifice is commemorated on the Menin Gate Memorial at Ypres.

The eldest of the Reverend's sons was 29-year-old Captain John Howell Price, RN, DSC DSO. He had run away to sea aged 14 and served his apprenticeship in the mercantile marine on the two well-known clippers *Netsfield* and *Yallari*. He passed his officer's exams in London, finally taking

Lieutenant Commander John Howell-Price DSO DSC.
Australian War Memorial, C318954

the Board of Trade Certificate as Master. At the outbreak of hostilities he left Sydney as a 2nd Officer aboard a transport and promptly offered his services to the Admiralty. He was called for duty immediately and spent five weeks at Portsmouth School before being appointed as a sub-lieutenant on *Alcantara* in March 1915.

A former Royal Mail ship and passenger liner, *Alcantara* was requisitioned by the Admiralty in April 1915. She was armed with six 6-inch (150mm) guns, anti-aircraft guns and depth charges. At Liverpool on 17 April she was commissioned into the Royal Navy's 10th Cruiser Squadron, the squadron's mission to patrol the North Sea and Arctic Ocean to prevent German access to or from the North Atlantic. On 29 February *Alcantara* was north-east of Shetland when she intercepted the German merchant raider *Greif* disguised as a Norwegian merchant ship. When the Germans realised that their identity had been discovered, they quickly lowered the Norwegian flag. At this point, *Alcantara* initiated an engagement and, after a ferocious bombardment, both ships were sunk. The battle killed 230 men from *Greif* and 68 from *Alcantara*.[285] Lieutenant John Howell-Price was in the freezing water for two hours before he was rescued. For his courage and gallantry during the engagement he was awarded the Distinguished Service Cross (DSC).

Following this harrowing experience, John next applied for a post on a submarine. As these vessels were a relatively new addition to the Royal Navy, few sailors had much experience of submarine operations and warfare, so more training was essential before John could assume his next appointment. He obviously demonstrated a natural aptitude for the work as he was then promoted to lieutenant commander and selected by Admiral Keyes as navigator aboard the submarine C3 which made the famous but unsuccessful attack on the breakwater at Zeebrugge. This raid took place on 23 April 1918 and was designed to block the Belgian port and canal of Bruges-Zeebrugge which housed a large pen used by the German submarine fleet in the North Sea. With air support and massed marines, the plan was to sink obsolete ships in the canal entrance to prevent German vessels leaving port. In addition to the 130 ships that were despatched on the mission, two submarines, C1 and C3, also took part in the raid. The former failed to make the port and so the task was left to C3 which was packed with five tons of amatol in its fore-end. The crew of five, all volunteers, were to set the submarine on automatic pilot and steam towards a viaduct which, in exploding, would prevent German reinforcements reaching the breakwater from land. In spite of the numbers involved and the complexity of the plan, it was ultimately inclement weather and the deteriorating condition of the vessels that saw the operation fail. For their courage, Captain Sanders was awarded the Victoria Cross and Lieutenant Commander John Howell-Price received the DSO.[286] After the Armistice John returned to Australia to command submarine J3 and served with the Royal Australian Navy until 1921 before rejoining the Merchant Navy as a Master with the Federal Steam Navigation Co. Ltd. He died in Liverpool, England, on 13 November 1937.

Major Frederick Phillimore Howell-Price DSO, the third of the Howell-Price sons, enlisted as a private on 17 September 1914 and was allotted to the 6th Company, Australian Army Service Corps, as a driver. At 26, he was one of the more mature recruits and had worked as a clerk for the Commercial Banking Company of Sydney. His strong work ethic immediately drew him to the attention of his superiors. Accordingly, on 26 December 1914, he was promoted to 2nd lieutenant, leaving Sydney five days later with the 2nd Light Horse Divisional Train. After training in Egypt, Frederick served on Gallipoli from September to December 1915, promoted to lieutenant just prior to the evacuation. By March 1916 Frederick's company had been disbanded and the attrition rate of senior officers at Gallipoli demanded new appointments. Frederick had proved his worth and was appointed acting Adjutant of the Anzac Mounted Train in Egypt. His managerial skills next saw him promoted to captain in the Australian Army Service Corps and appointed Supply Officer to the 2nd and 4th Light Horse brigades.

Throughout the war, as a member of the Desert Mounted Corps, Frederick was to see service at the famous engagements at Romani, Beersheba, Jericho Valley and numerous Syrian operations. During his service in the Middle East, his appointments included Senior Supply Officer to the Australian Mounted Division, Deputy Assistant Director of

Major Frederick Phillimore Howell-Price DSO.
Australian War Memorial, AWM C41638.

Supply and Transport to the Desert Mounted Corps, Acting Commander of the Anzac Mounted Divisional Train, and Acting Assistant Director of Supply and Transport to the Mounted Corps. Like Colonel Edwin Leane, Frederick's wartime role perhaps lacked the glamour of those of his fellow family members but, also like Edwin Leane, his accounting and managerial skills found a valued niche during army operations. For his outstanding service, Frederick was promoted major in 1917 and awarded the DSO. His citation stated that he was 'A painstaking and remarkably efficient officer and is equally good at office or outdoors work. He has acted as SSC and OC Divisional Train and carried out the duties efficiently.'[287] He was mentioned twice in General Allenby's despatches. In 1919 he returned to Australia and married, the union producing two daughters and a son. He died in 1978.

The service of the Reverend and Mrs Howell-Price's five sons provides yet another example of the extraordinary contribution of one family in service for King and country. All the Howell-Price sons received commissions and were decorated for bravery. Between them they received four DSOs, one DSC, three MCs and six Mentions in Despatches, amounting to 14 awards in the one family.

How then does one compare the service and achievements of the Howell-Price men with the Leanes? Both families came of sound religious stock and were highly principled Christian men. The sons of both families were disciplined, intelligent and well educated. Both families paid a heavy price for their service. Furthermore, both families were feted by the press in their own cities and were publicly lauded for their sense of duty to the Empire and self-sacrifice. On 3 March 1983, 20 members of the Howell-Price family, ranging in ages from five to 75, travelled to Canberra from Britain, Hong Kong, Singapore and around Australia to attend a presentation in the AWM Hall of Valour. The Memorial's Director, Air Vice Marshal Flemming, declared, 'We are deeply privileged to accept and display the medals and memorabilia of this distinguished family of brothers. It is a unique collection. Their deeds and sacrifice are an example to us all.'[288]

Since the conclusion of World War I, many articles have been published on 'The Fighting Leanes of Prospect' and their place in the pantheon of Australia's military history. While the Howell-Price family's contribution and sacrifice have also received acclaim, their name is not so widely acknowledged. This may have been due to the fact that the family name was sullied by one of its less-principled members during those bitter war years and, in the post-war period, there was no-one left to resurrect it. This situation probably arose due to the nefarious activities of the first-born son, David Clayton Howell-Price. Born in 1881, David joined the 3rd NSW Mounted Rifles to fight in the Boer War. He rose to the rank of lieutenant and served as Assistant Adjutant for some 3500 men. Following his return from South Africa, David took up farming, but this was not a success. Instead, he decided to build on his military experience and chose to return to army service. He was subsequently appointed Area Officer of Newtown and Darlington, where his work was deemed highly satisfactory. In 1912 he was appointed to the Administrative and Instructional Staff, and in 1913 he assumed the position of Adjutant of the 9th Light Horse Regiment. When war was declared in 1914, David's responsibilities increased exponentially, and it is fair to say that financial matters under his purview were not as tightly monitored as they should have been.

This laxity proved a considerable temptation to Lieutenant Howell-Price and, fuelled by his increasing disenchantment with his wife and daughter, he sought his pleasures elsewhere. He began an affair with one Nellie Fotheringham and became a frequent patron at racecourses, apparently able to win large sums of money. In general, he began to live well beyond his means. Such a lifestyle and emerging high profile saw him invest in racehorses and motor cars. Of course all of this required funding, and the easiest access to large sums of money was through the pay of the soldiers of the 9th Light Horse Regiment. As Adjutant, he mistakenly believed that a necessary sleight of hand was easy and foolproof.

In 1916 the CO of the 9th Light Horse Regiment, Captain Walter Herbert Pridham, refused to sign two cheques presented by Lieutenant Howell-Price. The cheques were for the sums of £1000 7s 6d and £1061 7s. Frustrated at this failure to secure approval, David Howell-Price then forged Pridham's signature and cashed the cheques for himself. Not only had David committed fraud, but he was also guilty of uttering. Captain Pridham was soon alerted to this fact. He demanded a full audit of the 9th Light Horse Regiment's accounts, to discover that, of the £61,000 that had passed through his Adjutant's hands for payment to the troops, none had been disbursed to them. As the troops were never mobilised, Lieutenant David Howell-Price foolishly imagined that he could get away with this misappropriation.

In simple terms, David was a thief and he was caught. Following his committal on two charges of forging and uttering military cheques, David Howell-Price was also arraigned on four other charges. These all related to the camp pay lists of four troops of the 9th Light Horse Regiment to the Defence Department from July 1914 to December 1914. The pay was to be authorised only if the troops were mobilised, which they were not. Naturally, a theft of such magnitude from one in a position of trust and responsibility and with a name such as Howell-Price, generated intense publicity and media interest. Not only did the Reverend Howell-Price and his wife have to deal with the loss of their three sons during 1916 and 1917, they also had to suffer the ignominy and public humiliation of their eldest son's misdeeds. David Howell-Price was found guilty and, in passing sentence, Mr Justice Scholes highlighted the gravity of the crime given the current circumstances:

> We are trying in every way in our power, by the supply of money and men to assist in the protection of the Empire. This money was subscribed for this all important work and you stole it by uttering false cheques and defrauding the government. It is a matter of intense seriousness.[289]

Justice Scholes could have sentenced David Howell-Price to 10 years' imprisonment for the crime, but considered his previous military service as a mitigating factor. Instead, on 26 March 1917, he was sentenced to serve four years' imprisonment in Long Bay Gaol. It seems that David got off lightly, for surely during wartime such substantial fraud at the government's expense could be construed by some almost as treason.

The shame for David and the Howell-Price family was to continue throughout 1917. In April 1917 the decree nisi for his divorce was passed, as was an application for the sequestration of his estate. This was finalised in December following the declaration of his bankruptcy in October 1917. In 1927, six years after completing his sentence, David Howell-Price married Florence Ann O'Malley. He died suddenly in 1937.

Every family has a black sheep and clearly David fulfilled that role for the Howell-Price family. His name was rarely mentioned in family circles after the scandalous events of 1917. Yet, the Leanes had their black sheep too in Ernest Albert, who abandoned his wife and 11 children. In comparing the misdeeds of both men, it is evident that while Ernest's failure was to his family, David's reached beyond the family, to the nation itself.

14. TO FIGHT THE GOOD FIGHT

Prior to the war, The Reverend John Howell-Price and his wife, Isobel, had lost three sons in infancy. To then nurture five more sons, and have three of them perish in the Great War, must have resulted in utter devastation for them both. The conviction and sentencing of their eldest son, David, to Long Bay Gaol for four years could have only exacerbated their despair. Added to this misery, was David's ignominious divorce and eventual bankruptcy. Given these burdens, it is not surprising that the Reverend Howell-Price passed away suddenly in 1921, aged 68. Upon his death, his wife, Isobel must have felt utterly bereft. We know virtually nothing about how she survived the lonely decade until her own passing in 1931. Unlike Alice Leane, Isobel had not courted publicity during the war years, as her husband had assumed the role of family spokesperson. Following the death of her husband, the previous focus on the Howell-Price family lost its momentum, especially in the light of David's despicable crimes. With the passing of the years, the gallant Howell-Prices and their remarkable achievements, were simply lost against the backdrop of post-war austerity, unemployment and the Great Depression.

The opposite was largely true for Alice Leane in Adelaide. Having been widowed since 1900, her equanimity and independence sustained her spirit and faith during the war years and beyond. As the family matriarch,

Alice Leane, the mother who supported her five sons and six grandsons in their decision to serve King and country, not only lauded their commitment, but seemed to relish the publicity that accompanied it. From the outbreak of the war, she endorsed and embraced the Wesleyan teachings of the renowned preacher Sir Josiah Symons. In his appeal to maternal duty on the issue of enlistment he entreated, 'Mothers. I know the sacrifice, but mothers too have a sacred duty. That duty is to encourage their boys to go, to tell them to go. It is for the mothers to point to that roll of honour [in the church] and say in the spirit of self sacrifice, 'Go and do likewise.' It is a great opportunity, a glorious cause and the reward of victory will be a future of transcendent greatness and peace and happiness for the Empire and for Australia.'[290] It was a response which Alice Leane never regretted and of which she was immensely proud.

Like the Howell-Price family in Sydney, the Leane family's commitment to the defence of the Empire became just as widely known in Adelaide. While publication of personal correspondence from Generals Birdwood and Walker, heralded the Howell-Prices' achievements in Sydney, correspondence from dignitaries, and even royalty, publicly acknowledged the Leanes' commitment in Adelaide. One such item of correspondence was directed to Alice Leane from Government House, Adelaide, dated 27 May 1915:

> Madam
>
> His Excellency the Governor, having learnt that all your sons, eleven in number are serving in His Majesty's Naval and Military Forces desires me to convey to you his warm congratulations on what he considers to be a splendid example of a Mother's Self Sacrifice and love of country. His Excellency regrets to learn that one of your sons had been wounded and offers you, both his and Lady Galway's sympathy.
>
> They trust however, that your boy will soon be returned to health and so be able to render further valuable service to his country's cause.
>
> I am
> Yours faithfully
> Secretary[291]

This affirmation was confirmed by a letter from the Court of King George V, dated 15 October 1915. It read:

> Madam,
>
> I am commanded by the King to convey to you an expression of His Majesty's appreciation of the patriotic spirit which has prompted your five sons to give their service at the present time to His Majesty's Forces.
>
> The King was much gratified to hear of the manner in which they have so readily responded to the call of their Sovereign and their country and I am to express to you and to them His Majesty's congratulations on having contributed in so full a measure to the great cause for which all of the people of the British Empire are so bravely fighting.
>
> I have the honour to be Madam
> Your Obedient Servant.
> I. Winsentin
> Keeper of the Privy Purse.[292]

Obviously there were not many letters of that ilk circulating in the small city of Adelaide in 1915, and it was a source of personal pride for all the Leanes, instantly stamping the family with a cachet of celebrity.

This early acknowledgement of the family's support for the Empire was reinforced in the widely published bulletins over the duration of the conflict. Reports of the gallant service of family members, and in four cases their deaths, received extensive coverage in the daily papers. Alice's name, and those of her sons, trumpeted the Leanes' contribution and sacrifice. One such article under the headline 'SHE GAVE HER ALL' described Alice as an example of 'practical patriotism' in her belief that she

> had given them all my men-kind, given them to [her] country. Five sons and six grandsons, all bonny boys and much loved. Yet I would rather that they go out to fight and leave me in loneliness than that they should skulk at home when the Motherland has need of them. When they gradually went off to their companies, I felt despondent, and as though they would never more return. But better thoughts have come and I know they are in God's hands, doing their duty. I could wish nothing better for the last years of my life than this

knowledge. It was not easy to let them go, but it is not easy for any mother to send out her own flesh and blood to probable suffering and perhaps death. But it was my duty, just as it is the duty of every other right thinking mother.[293]

Clearly Alice's views and values reflected both her religious faith and the socially accepted perception of the male role at the beginning of the twentieth century. Due to distance and censorship, news was often scarce and unfortunately generally grim. As such, details of a local family whose gallantry and honour drew reward and acclaim proved a fillip to a city and state whose battalions had suffered grievous losses. Therefore, the Leanes had established a measure of fame long before Charles Bean coined his enduring epithet that they were 'Australia's most famous military family'.

This sobriquet has endured now for over a century and in that time has become elevated to the realms of myth. Certainly, for a new nation with a limited history and the stain of convict origins, the Great War was to prove a crucible of national identity. From time immemorial every culture has developed myths to explore and express a people's self-image. For Australians, struggling to come to terms with the enormous cost of the war in both the loss of their youth and their promise for the future, something had to be salvaged from the conflagration. The 'Fighting Leanes of Prospect' was an evocative image, suggestive of a journey, challenge and conquest, the typical characteristics of myth. It acknowledged that, like thousands of families across the land, the Leanes had responded to the call to duty. They had accepted the challenge in the ordeals they faced, resisted temptation, faced enemies, endured the dark night of the soul and, by and large, emerged with honour. Also implied was the fact that, if they had returned damaged, they remained undaunted, willing to yet again sublimate their own needs for those of the common good. On the grand stage of life, the Leanes embodied the long-held masculine ideals of the fearless warrior and protector of fragile females. Such an image made for a good story in a land that needed heroes.

From the previous chapter, it is obvious that the Howell-Price family could be considered equally worthy of Bean's claim. Why then has their reputation failed to achieve popular notoriety? There are a number of factors which provide feasible explanations. Certainly David Howell-Price's criminal activities, which received widespread press coverage in NSW, must have profoundly damaged the family name. This, combined with his parent's shame, and grief over their other sons' deaths, may have inhibited voluntary public comment, rather than embracing it, as they had willingly done in the past. Similarly, Isobel's grief at her husband's sudden death, so soon after the war, must have compounded her sense of loss. Unlike Alice Leane, she was perhaps drained of the emotional energy to continue to promote the gallantry and sacrifice of her sons. While there is public affirmation of Alice Leane's commitment to the war effort and her pride in her family, nothing is publicly recorded about Isobel's feelings about her family's sacrifice. Her silence after 1921, failed to ensure that her sons would not be regaled on the same stage as the Leanes.

Perhaps the most significant reason as to why the Leane name endured at the expense of the Howell-Price legacy, is evident in the post-war service of the men who returned. At the conclusion of the war, and before he had embarked on his seminal volumes of the Official History of Australia at War 1914-1918, Bean published a small volume, titled *In your Hands Australians*. In this, he exhorted his countrymen to create a nation worthy of the sacrifice of the AIF. Of the Leanes who returned, Colonel Edwin Leane and General Raymond Lionel Leane, appear to have embraced this imperative. Furthermore, the sensitive and optimistic correspondence of Captain Allan William Leane and Major Bennett Leane reflected their own vision for shaping a better nation had they survived.

After a century, perhaps the question needs to be asked. Is the legendary status of the Leanes an accurate reflection of the sort of men they were? Were they the epitome of the Anzac legend that Bean sought to popularise? Were they something more, or perhaps less?

Certainly, most attempts to classify a group of people under one umbrella term are fraught because of the sheer diversity and uniqueness of each individual. The very word 'fighting', with its connotations and associations of combat and savagery, must be closely considered in evaluating the truth. In considering the word in a purely physical sense, the previous chapters show that the Leanes did indeed enlist to fight. Yet, to view the Leanes in such a singular capacity seems not only risible, but inadequate in evaluating and appreciating the true measure of these men. To reflect on them purely as soldiers, brothers in arms, actually does their memory a disservice. It debases and demeans the very essence of their service. They were a far cry from the battlers and larrikins who impulsively enlisted in the AIF. They were even more remote from the gung-ho young men who wanted to give the Hun his due. Certainly, all expressed a desire to fight, but a moral imperative underpinned their collective resolve. They did not volunteer to serve for money, escapism or any such base motive. They chose to serve as an act of honour and duty, which can almost be described, rather anachronistically, as a kind of chivalry. Viewed from this perspective, with their equally Christian heritage and values, were not the Howell-Prices, similar to the Leanes?

Undoubtedly, all of the Howell-Prices enlisted for much the same reasons as the Leanes. All of the Howell-Price men fought in the physical sense of the word. They enlisted to kill or be killed. Sadly, we do not have access to their finer feelings and personal struggles as is so evident in the Leanes' diaries and letters. If we are to consider the Leanes purely as soldiers engaged in physical combat, it could be argued that not all could fit the stamp of 'Fighting Leanes'. Although all experienced front-line service, not all were combatants. Edwin Thomas and Ernest Albert, largely fulfilled administrative functions and it remains a remote possibility that neither ever fired a shot in anger. Their bodies had succumbed to the ravages of ageing long before the war and neither was able to engage in a combative role. Admittedly, both served in necessary, essential services behind the lines, for which both received recognition, but they did not 'fight' in the simplest physical application of the term.

If, on the other hand, we are to consider 'fight' in a broader context, embracing a personal psychological struggle, then hopefully the previous chapters will have demonstrated that the 'Fighting Leanes of Prospect' well deserved their sobriquet. Not discounting the family's soldierly mien and interest in all things military, each in his own way struggled with his personal and familial expectations in becoming a member of the AIF. In offering their service, they did not just fight the enemy without, but the enemy within. Throughout his deployment, each member of the Leane family fought an enormous struggle of will, a fierce psychological battle within himself, to which only a personal resolution could be found. Each man's struggle was unique, and proved a constant spectre that haunted him throughout his service.

From the writings of those whose diaries and letters survive, it is evident that their authors were all highly literate and intelligent men. They were sensitive to the expectations that their families held of them and were open and honest about their own strengths and failings. Colonel Edwin Thomas, as the eldest in the family, struggled as a protector and self-appointed patriarch to his nuclear and extended family. His early diary entries aboard *Medic* demonstrate that his excitement in going to war was tempered by his fleeting visits to his cabin to reflect on the photographs of his family left at home. His personal struggles were exacerbated by the fact that four of his sons had enlisted, as of course had his brothers.

It is evident from Captain Allan Edwin's letters that both he and his brother, Lieutenant Geoffrey Paul, were frustrated by their father's protective meddling in their deployment. Given that Edwin was declared unfit for active service and was placed in administrative roles, he no doubt struggled with the fact that he could not actively protect his sons. However, by encouraging and orchestrating postings for his sons as members of the 48th Battalion, he would have derived some reassurance that his brother, Colonel Raymond, as CO would assume the role of *loco parentis*.

It is not unreasonable to imagine that news of Allan Edwin's death, while Edwin was on leave at home, evoked an illogical degree of guilt in him, sufficient for him to believe that the absence of his protective aura was a contributing factor to his son's death. Stricken with such grief, it must have taken a supreme act of will for Edwin to leave his distraught family in Australia to return to his duties in London and France. The loss of his beloved eldest son must have pitted his duty against personal grief and paternal responsibility for his other sons. Whatever the magnitude of the struggle, Edwin resolved to return. In so doing, his authority in ordnance and later repatriation, were to prove vital contributions to members of the AIF and their families.

Edwin, at the end of such a tumultuous four years faced a period of uncertainty and dislocation. In the immediate post-war years, Edwin was restless and struggled with the routines of civilian life. He had lost his way. As the eldest Leane, he remained mindful that he wanted those who loved him to be proud of him. As a result of his war service he had achieved tangible success and substantial prestige. The new challenge was how to continue to fulfil those exalted expectations. With this goal to the fore, the position as Administrator of Norfolk Island must have seemed a perfect fit for his skills and ambition. Such a position was prestigious. It accorded him the kind of gravitas that he had experienced in the AIF. But, in spite of his determination to impose his will on the islanders and facilitate all manner of economic growth and prosperity, Edwin, like Canute, could not turn back the tide. His well-intentioned endeavours failed because he could not make the transition from a senior and highly respected military position to that of a civilian administrator on a remote Pacific island. Edwin failed because of his inflexibility. He failed because he could not reconcile the unique mores of the islanders with his conservative morality and his autocratic rule. The rigorous obedience to clearly defined rules that were so definitive in military life could not be replicated in an alternative civilian community and he floundered.

Edwin's brother, Warrant Officer Ernest Albert, also struggled during his service with the AIF. Like Edwin, age had restricted his participation largely to administration and a minor role which denied him the kudos of his more illustrious brothers. On his return to Australia, Ernest appeared unable to commit himself to the resumption of family life and its mundane domesticity. As a consequence, he possibly suffered a kind of post-war neurosis that caused him to remain estranged from his wife and responsibilities. Certainly, such aberrant behaviour was not uncommon among returned servicemen who found the transition from military to civilian life 'a bridge too far'. Edwin Thomas and Ernest Albert struggled with both their roles and personal expectations after their service in the AIF. From Edwin's perspective, his service had been lauded and publicly acknowledged. From Ernest's point of view, his service might have appeared somewhat ignominious in contrast to the lofty achievements of his brothers. However, on their return from war, both struggled to adapt to a world that had lost its former centre of gravity. Both proved poor examples of the Anzac legend, as their wartime skills failed to equip them for the promised peace ahead.

The letters and diary of Captain Allan Edwin and Major Benjamin Bennett offer us the most enlightening insight into the personal struggles of these highly sensitive young men when confronted with the horrors of war. Both were clearly keen to fight and felt that if they did not engage in active service, their time in the AIF would have amounted to nothing of worth. Both speak of their determination to bring honour to the Leane name and live up to the example of the senior family members. Allan Edwin struggled with the ever-present fear of failure. He was afraid that he would fall short of his parents' expectations, that he would let the side down. His service as adjutant and captain were motivated by a desire to prove worthy of the Leane name, and he was prepared to spare nothing of himself in order to live up to the lofty standards of the family. Allan Edwin struggled with his lack of confidence and maturity. He constantly unburdened his soul to his mother concerning his anxiety in both soldiering and romantic relationships, yet he maintained a positive vision and expectation for the future. Over his period of service he achieved considerable success, which was rewarded with promotion. His delight in his achievements is palpable. With it an emerging self-confidence developed and a critical perspective of his own worth. With increasing maturity, he was able to evaluate his own performance objectively and, before he was killed, it seemed to sit comfortably on his shoulders. Geoffrey Paul's letter to his father after Allan Edwin's death highlights the tragedy of that death. It seems to indicate that Allan Edwin was on the cusp of becoming the man he wanted to be. 'Oh dad, it eased the pain a lot to hear how those boys spoke of him ... and the piece of work he did was marvellous and he would have received some recognition had he come out of it alive.'[294]

Major Benjamin Bennett Leane, like his nephew, was also a highly sensitive and passionate pilgrim in life's journey. Initially, he too was depressed at the prospect of not engaging in front-line action, writing, 'every fibre of my being is aghast at the thought of inaction, and I'll guarantee I would suffer a nervous breakdown if I was left at the base.'[295] As much as he wished to fight, he struggled with the painful separation from his beloved wife and daughters, one of whom he had never seen, much less held. His diary is filled with the conflict between physical longing and a yearning for the delights of home, against the struggle to honour the family's military expectations. The diary is an expansive and detailed record of his daily duties which he hoped to share with Phyllis on his return. Yet the entries are as much a reverie and catharsis as a daily record. Whereas Allan Edwin limited the grim details of battle from his mother, Benjamin spared nothing of the horror of destruction in his chronicle. While he cautioned Phyllis that he could be killed, he was pragmatic and devoid of the performance anxiety that punctuated Allan Edwin's letters.

Behind the façade of these two intelligent, resourceful and sensitive men, both struggled with insecurities and longing. Both yearned for the opportunity to prove that they were the superior type of man that white civilisation venerated: tough, capable and resilient. Unless we read their letters and diaries, it is all too easy to identify Allan Edwin and Benjamin Bennett as just two soldiers of the 'Fighting Leanes'. Their psychological struggles and their efforts to overcome their personal demons are testament to their unheralded inner fortitude, as men and humans of the highest calibre.

Little is known about Corporal Arnold Harry, who was also killed, but his brother William Ernest and their father, Ernest Albert, found the alien world of military service an assault on their sensibilities. Both father and son went adrift in a world where the moral compass had lost true north. In a world where tomorrow might not come, illicit passions and fleeting moments of joy had to be grasped at every opportunity. William Ernest, like so many thousands of Australian servicemen, succumbed to the temptations of the flesh. In addition, William Ernest's undisciplined behaviour after 1917 suggests his frustration with the constraints of military life. This weariness must have been compounded by the pain of his brother's death. William's hasty and perhaps impulsive marriage in England did not result in happiness on his return to Australia. Here his will and capacity for fidelity crumbled, as illicit liaisons continued, resulting in two divorces before a third marriage.

Among the young cousins, Geoffrey Paul, Edwin Thomas' second son, may have won the MC, but in every way it proved to be a pyrrhic award. He too found post-war life a very difficult adjustment. He remained bitter over his employment options and an uncertain future. According to his son Edwin, his father's rare delight in post-war life was only witnessed at the outbreak of the Second World War when he promptly enlisted in the New Zealand military. From his son's perspective, it would appear that Geoffrey Paul was profoundly damaged by his brother's death, and lacked the strength of will to reassert his finer feelings after the war. He may have had three children, but it seems he remained emotionally crippled for the rest of his life, unable to show them the normal love and affection to which they were entitled.

In detailing the journeys that the best-known Leanes travelled in the course of their service, it is evident that all felt it their duty to serve. They wanted to serve God, their King and country, to prove themselves worthy of the family honour. Yet, that does not mean that they all fought fearlessly in traditional military combat against a visible enemy. The better-known family members did indeed engage in combat. Of greater significance however is their fight against the enemy within. All the Leanes fought their battles on these two fronts. Not all succeeded in both domains, but the integrity of the struggle illustrates that they were far more than just soldiers. From today's standpoint, they were men of a bygone era, of an age when honour, duty and conscience were the hallmarks of a decent human being. From Bean's observations of the Leanes and correspondence from Generals Birdwood and Walker to the Howell-Prices, both families appear to have been cut from much the same cloth.

Given the similarities between the two families, there remains one major distinction between them. That is, by virtue of his survival, and his commitment to honour Bean's dictum; to create a nation worthy of the sacrifice of the AIF, we must single out Brigadier General Raymond Lionel Leane. He remains, without a doubt, the lynchpin, and the family's shining star. His post-nominals alone prove that he was a courageous and exemplary leader. The 48th Battalion, 'made of all Leanes' and identified as 'the Joan of Arcs', stamped itself as a fearless and disciplined force. It drew its fame not from reckless courage, but its *esprit de corps*, its initiative and resilience. Given that the 48th Battalion fought in some of the bloodiest and most costly battles of the war, its men and morale could have crumbled. Yet the example and leadership demonstrated by its CO, Brigadier General Raymond Leane, imbued in his men a loyalty and devotion that was rarely matched by any other unit. While the men understood that anything short of total commitment was unacceptable, they in turn knew that the CO's commitment to them was absolute.

More importantly from an historical perspective is the fact that in surviving, Raymond was able to transfer skills from his wartime experience to his post-war employment. The acquisition of such skills empowered him to establish and maintain a prestigious peacetime career. Yet, to simply list him under the banner of the 'Fighting Leanes of Prospect' fails to acknowledge so many of the finer qualities of the man. To see him only as an illustrious soldier, fails to acknowledge the breadth of remarkable qualities seated in his huge frame. In periods of global and local crises he was able to harness his myriad strengths in order to address the dictates of his duty in a peerless manner. His integrity and courage were balanced with the compassion and sensitivity he held for his family and all with whom he served. Unknown to most, Raymond Lionel Leane had also struggled to overcome fear in his life. He once admitted to his son Geoffrey Malcolm, that as a child, he was afraid of the dark. He steadfastly worked to overcome this fear by pure will. He recounted how, if he was out alone at night, he would walk in the middle of the street, whistling loudly to keep his spirits high.[296] With every foray into the night, he strove to bolster his own will, to confront fear and thereby build confidence in his own ability to conquer.

Clearly, Brigadier General Sir Raymond Lionel Leane was a man for all seasons who could adapt to diverse situations and succeed because of his self-belief and indomitable will. Having toyed with the idea of becoming a clergyman, his redirected focus to military and civil service embraced a similar religious commitment. It was his character and his ability to master control of his most profound emotions in a crisis that enabled his willpower to prevail. All aspects of his life were dominated by his strength of character and will. He proved this on numerous occasions in both war and peace.

Winston Churchill's physician, Lord Charles Moran, described courage as a moral quality. He believed that, 'It is not a chance gift of nature, like aptitude for games. It is a cold choice between two alternatives, the fixed resolve not to quit, an act of renunciation which must be made not once, but many times, by an act of will. Courage is willpower.'[297] It was willpower that drove Sir Raymond Lionel Leane to the unparalleled heights of his monumental achievements and earned him a justifiable place in the pantheon of great Australians. He fought every obstacle that life presented, both physical and psychological. More to the point, he conquered them. If anyone is to be truly lauded as a 'Fighting Leane of Prospect', Raymond Leane remains the exemplar of Australia's most famous military family.

In evaluating the Leanes in the light of Bean's statement, it is evident that the family members are bookended by the careers of Edwin and Raymond. The contributions of other family members are housed between those two figures of success and failure, in descending order of merit. Both Edwin and Raymond would not have been appointed to their prestigious positions in the post-war period had they not proved their mettle in the AIF. Post-war government policy endeavoured to reward men who had served as compensation for their sacrifice. The subsequent appointments of both men charged them to confront the puzzle of peace. Yet the values of Edwin's military career could not be grafted easily onto civilian life. Ironically, the flower of his military success held the seeds of his own failure. Like Icarus, he flew too close to the sun and, to his eternal shame, his enduring legacy was to be indelibly etched in the words of a Royal Commission. In contrast, Raymond's outstanding courage and wartime command of the 48th Battalion saw his service documented for posterity by the likes of Father William Devine and other officers in the battalion. The sobriquet of the battalion as 'the Joan of Arcs' attests to its uniqueness as a battalion of Leanes, and implies that all family members were imbued with Raymond's qualities. From the diaries of Allan William and Benjamin Bennett, this appears appropriate. Their writings reveal Raymond's courage and that their commitment to the battalion and its CO was unequivocal.

The deeds and thoughts of other family members cannot be as confidently identified. We have no evidence of their immediate sensitivities to prove that they were worthy inheritors of the Anzac legend. In fact, in the case of Ernest Albert, William Ernest and Geoffrey Paul, their wartime experiences appear to have blighted their lives. The 'transcendent greatness and peace' promised by the Methodists and the 'salvation' promised by Prime Minister Hughes, represented a peacetime illusion that marked the Anzac legend as a burden for so many returned men.

Notwithstanding this, the damaging effect of the war on some of the Leanes does not alter the fact that the men of this family differed in many ways from Bean's quintessential digger. 'There [was] a distinct similarity of personality and physique among them all. They [were] of the big buoyant type of quick, intelligent thinkers.'[298] The men of the Leane family were conservative Christians, raised in duty to honour an old order. They were citizens of cities rather than the bush. They were sensitive and articulate, rather than illiterate larrikins. They were temperate and mostly chaste, which was a far cry from the reputation of the drunken and virile diggers. All willingly enlisted to fight and, while not all fought physically, it is evident from the four who were killed that they battled the enemy within as much as the enemy without. Furthermore, the Leanes soldiered in a particular way. Their stolidity and dependability provided an example of how the AIF could persist as a viable force during the years of bloody stalemate. The Leanes may not represent the quintessential diggers of the Anzac legend, but perhaps that is what made them unique and worthy of a legend of their own making.

During the twentieth century Australian troops have fought in diverse theatres of war. We had barely recovered from the devastating consequences of the First World War when we were plunged into the second. Then, for the sons of First World War veterans who took up arms, the Anzac legend probably still held true. Its currency no doubt proved a source of pride and motivation for a new wave of Australian soldiers who fought in Europe, the Middle East, the Pacific and indeed our own shores.

Korea and Vietnam proved watersheds in Australian military history and the erosion of the Anzac legend. Australia's commitment to America's involvement in Vietnam stirred the fire of a generation who would not fuel another war based on the hollow rhetoric of a dubious myth. In spite of the liberally vaunted fear of the domino effect, and the lies and obfuscation of both governments, the general consensus in Australia was that this was a war that we could not win; nor was it a war in which we should even be involved. American and Australian involvement proved a disaster. Mass troops were ineffectual against the guerrilla warfare of resourceful and resilient fighters in their own country.

Subsequent military engagement in Afghanistan and Iraq, have further proved that mass armies are ineffectual in limited asymmetrical wars. Some 400,000 allied troops in Iraq have proved insufficient to enforce stability. As soon as allied troops are removed from Afghanistan, the Taliban will inevitably resume control. Mass armies may manage to take control of a territory, but the expense of holding it against organised resistance is unsupportable.[299] These factors severely limit the useful scope of mass armies. Given the fragile balance of power between the USA, China, Russia and North Korea, all of which possess a nuclear capacity, there exists the potential for a nuclear Armageddon of world-ending capability. Even if nuclear engagement is eschewed, the lethal potential of drone warfare is just as insidious and fearful.

While Australia continues to deploy highly trained troops to world combat zones, the majority of the Australian Defence Force serve globally to protect and honour the values of the world's democracies. All personnel are rigorously trained and highly skilled in the use of sophisticated weaponry and equipment. Long gone are the days of patriotic, cultural or conscripted enlistment. Tradition might possibly encourage many young recruits to follow in the footsteps of fathers and grandfathers who have fought in previous wars. It is unlikely though, that brothers, fathers and their sons, as members of a single family, will ever serve concurrently in such numbers as the Leanes. Modern families are much smaller than those of yesteryear. Consequently, it would be highly unlikely that one family could provide multiple members across a broad age range with a similar inclination to enlist for active service should the need arise.

Modern life now offers so many diverse career paths that challenge and fulfil all manner of talents. Attitudes to military service have also changed. In some circles, it is seen as unfashionable and confrontational. Servicemen and women are not encouraged to wear their uniforms publicly for fear of upsetting minority sensitivities. Further concerns exist as a consequence of the unprovoked murder of a British soldier by a terrorist in London. Thankfully these concerns are not widely held in Australia. After the diminished respect afforded to Australian servicemen during the turbulent 1960s and 70s, the wheel has now turned full circle. The recent Invictus Games, hosted by Australia, witnessed a groundswell of support and public respect for our veterans and serving members. National television coverage ensured that the proud custodians of our heritage, and protectors of our future received the acclaim that service and sacrifice deserve.

Given the decline in Christian values, changing demographics and the potential for nuclear warfare, the age of massed armies has long passed. We cannot afford armies of occupation. As a corollary, it becomes self-evident that we shall probably never witness the likes of the 'Fighting Leanes of Prospect' again. They fought in numbers, passionately, not only for a fading Empire, but for personal integrity and a kind of duty that has little currency in families and society today. Fittingly, Bean's words remain apt. The 'Fighting Leanes of Prospect' were and are unique. They are deservedly enshrined in our nation's annals as the 'most famous family of soldiers in Australian history'. We shall never see their like again.

Family Grave of Thomas John Leane and Alice Ann Leane, Walkerville Cemetery. The inscription reads. She hath done what she could. Her children rise up and call her blessed.

ACKNOWLEDGEMENTS

As there were numerous accounts of the Leane family's military exploits, I felt drawn to explore the myth and, if need be, challenge it. I resolved to unearth the human face of the men behind the myth. In order to do this, I realised that I had to make contact with as many members of the Leane family as possible, in the hope of documenting oral history, letters and personal documents before they were lost forever.

I am indebted to Frank Leane for providing me with a comprehensive and very detailed family tree of all of the descendants of Thomas and Jenny Leane who first arrived in South Australia in 1852. Without this wonderful document I think I would have floundered for years, and would never have made the connections and contacts that have proved so valuable in capturing some of the oral history of the family. Trevor Leane also generously provided valuable material and kindly met with me in Adelaide to share interesting details on the family's religious heritage. Kingsley Leane wrote and spoke with me on a number of occasions and provided excellent photographs of his grandfather, Ernest Albert Leane. I am most appreciative of his time and support. Although living in Queensland, Judy Mercer gave willingly of her time, to both speak with me and send photocopies of material in her family archives about her great-grandfather, Allan William Leane, as did Glenda Rae Leane about her father, Raymond Ernest Leane.

Bruce and Loretta Leane welcomed me to their home and offered some very personal and interesting perspectives on Bruce's grandfather, Sir Raymond Lionel Leane, while his wife, Loretta, followed up by providing an introduction to Bruce's sister, Peggy Leane. Peggy and her daughter, Athena, made a significant contribution to the book, offering previously uncirculated photographs and marvellous anecdotal material. My discussion of Colonel Edwin Thomas Leane was greatly enhanced by the generous contribution of some of his wartime letters from Daryl and Melinda Hume-Cook. Those letters mellowed my initial perceptions of the man. In the same vein, his grandson, Edwin Leane, was able to draw on his personal childhood memories to flesh out a more rounded picture of his father, Geoffrey Paul Leane. All of the people with whom I spoke added this personal touch that provided the human traits behind the names. This considerably enhanced my efforts to look at the men behind the myth and I am indebted to them all.

My profound thanks are also due to Christine and Peter Leane who drove and traipsed with me around various Adelaide cemeteries in search of specific details. Their warm welcome and hospitality encouraged me to soldier on in spite of many obstacles. Sincere thanks are also due to Mark Richardson from the South Australian Department of Planning and Infrastructure for clarification of title searches, Moya Sharp for photographs from the Goldfields Historical Association and Helen Stein, Cemetery Historian of the North Road Cemetery.

A very special thank you must be accorded to Nola Russell who has worked tirelessly and meticulously as my research assistant. Whenever I have encountered a brick wall, or the need for further details, Nola has found a way to tap into fresh resource material and flesh out additional information.

I owe a debt of immense gratitude to Peter Newbury, historian extraordinaire. His support of my endeavours has sustained my enthusiasm and energy though frustrating periods. John Thorne and Anne McIlroy have also supported me, by offering critical and insightful perspectives which have added substance and a much broader horizon.

These acknowledgements would not be complete without singling out Kym Hardwick and the wonderful volunteer staff at the South Australian Police Historical Society. Having arranged my visit well in advance, Kym and his staff not only offered a warm welcome, but office space and photocopying facilities for my research. Kym and his staff made my task so much easier by sifting relevant material from their files in advance, and I extend to all, my most sincere thanks and deepest appreciation. To all of you, I hope that you find the end product worthy of your time and effort.

To my husband, Rick, my technical consultant and whisky provedore, my eternal thanks for your infinite patience. My love as always.

A manuscript would never be considered worthy of a published work without the guidance and amendments of a skilled editor. In Catherine McCullagh, I have been doubly blessed. Not only is she a masterly wordsmith, but an erudite military scholar. Cathy's sensitivity and expertise have guided this story through my nervous uncertainty into an affirmation of research and value. Without you Cathy, this project would never have come to fruition. You are a pearl of great price! My heartfelt thanks must also be extended to Joce Jenkins and Peter Gamble for their expertise and forbearance in pulling the final strings of this manuscript together.

Endnotes

Chapter 1

1   E.G. Wakefield, 'A Letter from Sydney', *Morning Chronicle*, 6 October 1829, under heading 'A letter From Sydney; Sketch of a Proposal for Colonising Australasia'.

2   Graeme L. Pretty, 'Wakefield, Edward Gibbon, 1796–1862', *Australian Dictionary of Biography (ADB)*, Vol. 2, Melbourne University Press (MUP), 1967.

3   E.G. Wakefield, *How to Select Migrants. A letter from Sydney*, Everyman, London, 1829.

4   'The British Government Accepts Wakefield's Arguments', Goderich to Darling, 9 January 1831, H.R.A.1.16, pp. 20–21.

5   C.M.H. Clarke, *A History of Australia*, Vol. 3, *The Beginning of an Australian Civilisation 1824–1851*, MUP, 1973, p. 42.

6   Ibid., p. 44.

7   Ibid., p. 46.

8   Ibid., p. 50.

9   D.H. Pike, *The Paradise of Dissent. South Australia, 1829-1857*, Longmans, London, 1957, p. 150.

10   See http/gotquestions.org./Wesleyans.html

11   *Statistics on Migration From the United Kingdom 1825-51*, Twelfth General Report of Colonial Land and Emigration Commissioners, P.P. 1852, XVIII, Appendix 3, p. 1499.

12   *South Australian Government Gazette* 1866, pp. 79–80.

13   See the Clipper Route at: https://en.wikipedia.org/wiki/Clipper_route

14   See The Shipslist.com/accounts/rules1849.shtml

15   *Ballina Chronicle*, Ballina, Mayo, Ireland, Wednesday 5 December 1849.

Chapter 2

16   M. Simons and G. Payne, 'Introducing the Leane Family History', Leane Family
     History Collection, State Library of South Australia, Adelaide, 1996. Material from
     family reunion provided by Kingsley Leane.

17   Ibid.

18   'Hundred' is an archaic word used to describe an administrative division of land,
     usually part of a shire.

19   Mark 10: 44–45, *New English Bible*.

20   *Property Directorate*, Department of Planning, Transport and Infrastructure South
     Australia, 1857.

21   Arnold Dudley Hunt, *The Bible Christians in South Australia*, Adelaide Uniting
     Church Historical Society, 1983, p. 3.

22   Ibid., pp. 6–7.

23   Simons and Payne, 'Introducing the Leane Family History'.

24   *Property Directorate*, Department of Planning, Transport and Infrastructure South
     Australia, Old System of Land Records, 1858.

25   Simons and Payne, 'Introducing the Leane Family History'.

26   *Property Directorate*, Department of Planning, Transport and Infrastructure South
     Australia, Old System of Land Records, 1853.

27   'PENOLA Anniversary of the Bible Christian School at Mt Torrens', *Observer*,
     30 April 1859, p. 3. See http://nla.gov.au/nla.news-article158127185 (accessed 6
     November 2016).

28   Judy Mercer, family history notes.

29   'COUNTRY NEWS', *South Australian Weekly Chronicle*, p. 6. See http://nla.gov.
     au/nla.news-article 91260303 (accessed 21 August 2017).

30   Simons and Payne, 'Introducing the Leane Family History'.

31   Ibid.

32   *Property Directorate*, Department of Planning, Transport and Infrastructure South
     Australia, Old System of Land Records,1867.

33   Trevor Leane, family history notes.

34   Ibid.

35   'OBITUARY: THE DEATH OF AGNES NEALE', *South Australian Register*, 27
     September 1892, p. 3. See http://nla.gov.au/nla.news-article 48532990 (accessed 17
     June 2017).

36   Trevor Leane, family history notes.

37   Ibid. The Court Marion was a branch of the Oddfellows Association.

38   While I have found it difficult to ascertain precisely what this refers to, my research suggests that, if the court found no evidence of theft or fraud, the certificate may have been issued in acknowledgement of sheer bad luck. As such, his character would not be impugned.

39   Frank Leane, 'Descendants of Thomas Leane, A Family History'.

40   'MATRIMONIAL JURISDICTIONS', *Express and Telegraph*, p. 3, 10 August 1881. See http://nla.gov.au/nla.news -article 208192882 (accessed 6 November 2016).

41   Ibid.

42   Ibid.

43   Ibid.

44   'MR. A. LEANE', *Observer*, 21 March 1896, p. 44. See http://trove.nla.gov.au/ newspaper/rendition/article161837179 (accessed 23 November 2016).

45   Ibid.

46   'SUPREME COURT – MATRIMONIAL CAUSES JURISDICTION', *South Australian Advertiser*, 25 July 1884, p. 3. See http://trove.nla.au/newspaper/article 73199255 (accessed 23 November 2016).

47   Trevor Leane, family history notes.

Chapter 3

48   'A PATRIARCHAL PREACHER, THE LATE WILLIAM SHORT', *Australian Christian Commonwealth*, 14 June 1912, p. 17.

49   DEATH CERTIFICATE No 1224, 1867, Fanny Eliza Leane.

50   'In Memorium Nellie. M. Clatworthy', *Australian Christian Commonwealth*, 27 July 1923.

51   See http://nthadelaideps.sa.edu.au

52   June Haggett and Monty Smith, *A Jam Tin of Mosquitos*, DPA Publishing, South Australia, 2013, p. 37.

53   Ibid., p. 38.

54   'FAREWELLS TO SOLDIERS. Social at Thebarton', *South Australian Register*, 30 April 1900. See http://nla.gov.au/nla.news - article 56553090 (accessed 5 November 2016).

55   Official Records of the Australian Military Contingents to the War in South Africa, compiled and edited in 1911 by Lieutenant Colonel P.L. Murray (retd), pp. 356–58.

56   'LIEUTENANT LEANE IN SOUTH AFRICA', *Advertiser*, 9 February 1901, p. 6. See http://nla.gov.au/nla.news-article 4818217 (accessed 10 November 2016).

57   Interview with Melinda Hume-Cook, 10 June 2107.

58   Interview with Edwin Leane, 17 June 2017.

Chapter 4

59   Arnold Dudley Hunt, *For God, King and Country: A study of the attitudes of the Methodist and Catholic Press in South Australia*, Salisbury College of Advanced Education, Salisbury, South Australia, 1979, p. 2.

60   Ibid.

61   'A CRAZY CAESAR', *Australian Christian Commonwealth*, p. 7. See http:nla.gov. au/nla.news-article 214056747 (accessed 19 June 2017).

62   Arnold Dudley Hunt, *Methodism Militant; Attitudes to the Great War, 1914-1918*, South Australian Methodist Historical Society, Clarence Park, South Australia, 1975, p. 1.

63   Hunt, *For God, King and Country*, p. 5.

64   The Reverend Octavius Lake. See Hunt, ibid., p. 3.

65   Ibid., pp. 5–6.

66   Ibid., p. 6.

67   'MR HUGHES ENTERTAINED: "WAR THE SALVATION OF THE EMPIRE"', *Barrier Miner* (Broken Hill), 20 April 1916, p. 1. See http://nla.gov.au/ nla.news-article 45376167 (accessed 22 January 2018).

68   Ibid., p. 3.

69   Ibid., p. 8.

70   Hunt, *Methodism Militant*, p. 34.

71   Ibid., p. 1.

72   Sir Josiah Symons, *Australian Christian Commonwealth*, 2 April 1916.

Chapter 5

73   Diary extract, Edwin Thomas Leane, 2 November 1914. From family records of Daryl and Melinda Hume-Cook.

74   Ibid., 3 November 1914.

75   Ibid., 28 November 1915.

76   Ibid., 30 November 1915.

77   Ibid., 3 December 1915.

78   Ibid., 14 December 1915.

79   Ibid., 13 December 1915.

80   Ibid., 25 December 1915.

81   See Australian War Memorial at: awm.gov.au/images/collection/bundled RCIG1011736

82   Charles Bean, *Official History of Australia in the War of 1914-1918*, Vol. VI, *The AIF in France 1918*, Angus & Robertson, Sydney, 1942.

83   See Australian War Memorial at: awm.gov.au/collection/R1614020

Chapter 6

84   Leane, Captain Allan Edwin, letters to family members, AWM 1DRL/0411.

85   Ibid.

86   Ibid.

87   Ibid.

88   Ibid.

89   Ibid.

90   Ibid.

91   Ibid.

92   Ibid.

93   Ibid.

94   Ibid.

95   Ibid.

96   Captain Clarence Thomas Fairley MC was adopted by Ethel Leane Taylor
while she was living in Kalgoorlie. Ethel had been friends with his parents
and knew their two children well. Clarrie virtually became an honorary
Leane and, when he enlisted in August 1915, Ethel was named as next of kin.
Although allotted to the 16th Battalion on 7 March 1916 in Egypt, he was
promptly transferred to the 48th Battalion the next day. In the family battalion
he quickly rose through the ranks to become a captain by February 1917. In
November 1916, as a lieutenant, he was awarded the Military Cross (MC)
for conspicuous gallantry. The citation acknowledged his work as a signals
officer during an operation in which 'he repeatedly went out under heavy shell
fire to repair breaks in the wire. By his energy and pluck, communication was
maintained almost continually.' As an adopted Leane, the kudos for the award
was readily associated with the meritorious service of the family. Captain
Fairley, like some of the other Leanes, did not escape unscathed from the
conflict though, and was seriously wounded, resulting in blindness in one eye.

97   Leane, Allan Edwin (Captain), letters to family members, AWM 1DRL/0411.

98   Ibid.

99   Ibid.

100   Ibid.

101   Ibid.

102   Ibid.

103   Ibid. The 48th Battalion was known as 'the Joan of Arcs' because it was considered
to be 'made of all Leanes', a pun on the Maid of Orleans.

104   'Ern's boy' refers to his cousin No 1055 Corporal Arnold Harry Leane of the 27th Battalion.

105   Captain Allan William Leane, Allan Edwin's uncle.

106   Aunt Blanche was Captain Allan William Leane's wife.

107   Leane, Allan Edwin (Captain), letters to family members.

108   Ibid.

109   Lieutenant Geoffrey Paul Leane, letter to family members.

110   No. 5839 Private Harry Hewish, 48th Battalion, War Service Records, NAA B2455.

111   Correspondence from Miss Vera Deakin, Red Cross Missing and Wounded Inquiry Bureau, AWM RCDIG1044118.

112   Captain Allan Edwin Leane, 48th Battalion, War Service Records, NAA B2455.

113   'THE FIGHTING LEANES OF PROSPECT', *Observer*, p. 6 at: http://nla.gov.au./nla.news-aqrticle 165897507 (accessed 29 January 2018).

114   Ibid.

115   Neville Browning, *The 48th Battalion*, Quality Press, Huntingdale, Western Australia, 2009, p. 169.

116   Lieutenant Geoffrey Paul Leane, War Service Records, NAA B2455.

117   Lines from *Clancy of the Overflow* by A.B. 'Banjo' Paterson.

118   Interview with Edwin Leane, 14 June 2017.

119   Ibid.

Chapter 7

120   Ronald Hopkins, 'Leane, Edwin Thomas (1867–1928)', *ADB*, Vol. 10, MUP, 1986.

121   E.T. Leane, Enquiry Regarding Employment, NAA A2487 1919/1109.

122   E.T. Leane, Administrator, Norfolk Island, NAA A5186241/32 – Part 1, reference dated 17 April 1924, Manager, New Business Department, National Mutual Life Association of Australia Ltd.

123   Norfolk Island, Administration, Public Seal, letter to Mr Quinlan, 6 September 1924, NAA A518S800/1/4.

124   'Administration of Norfolk Island, Col E.T. Leane Appointed', *Advertiser*, Friday 30 May 1924, p. 13, at: http://nla.gov.au/nla.news-article 36673357 (accessed 20 July 2017).

125   Report of the Royal Commission on Norfolk Island Affairs with Appendices, NAA A432 1929/45705, p. 14.

126   Ibid., p. 22.

127 'COLONEL LEANE ON HIS WAY TO DARWIN', *Northern Standard*, 20 February 1925, p. 1, at: http://nla.gov.au/nla.news - article 48017218 (accessed 16 June 2017).

128 Report of the Royal Commission on Norfolk Island Affairs with Appendices, NAA A432 1929/45705, p. 26.

129 Ibid., p. 21.

130 E.T. Leane, Administrator, Norfolk Island, NAA A5186241/32 – Part 1, Memo from the Administration to the Secretary, Department of Home Affairs and External Territories, 31 October 1924. Norfolk Island.

131 'HOW POO BAH LEANE RULES NORFOLK ISLAND', *Northern Standard*, 27 October 1925, p. 1, at: http://nla.gov.au/nla.news -article 4802 0332 (accessed 20 July 2017).

132 Report of the Royal Commission on Norfolk Island Affairs with Appendices, NAA A432 1929/45705, p. 49.

133 Ibid., p. 47.

134 Ibid., p. 48.

135 Ibid., p. 50.

136 Ibid., p. 49.

137 *Northern Standard*, 27 October 1925, p. 1, at: http://nla.gov.au/nla.news-article 4802332 (accessed 16 June 2017).

138 Ibid.

139 Report of the Royal Commission on Norfolk Island Affairs with Appendices, NAA A432 1929/45705, p. 51.

140 Ibid., p. 52.

141 Ibid.

142 Ibid., p. 53.

143 Interview with Mr Bruce Leane, 13 December 2016.

144 Report of the Royal Commission on Norfolk Island Affairs with Appendices, NAA A432 1929/45705, p. 54.

145 Ibid., p. 55.

146 Ibid., p. 56.

147 Ibid., p. 55.

148 Ibid., p. 57.

149 'NORFOLK ISLAND: ADMINISTATOR DISMISSED', Melbourne *Weekly Times*, 21 August 1926, p. 10, at: http://nla.gov.au/nla.new-article 223333935 (accessed 10 May 2017).

Chapter 8

150   Red Cross Documents on the Death of No. 1055 Corporal A.H. Leane, SLR No. SRG76/1/1644.

151   Ibid.

152   Ibid.

153   Heroes of the Great War. Family Notices, Adelaide *Chronicle*,10 November 1916. p. 13. See: http:/nla.gov.au/nla-news-page 8609217 (accessed 12 June 2017).

154   Heroes of the Great War. Family Notices, Adelaide *Chronicle*, 28 April 1917, p. 14. See: http:/nla.gov.au/nla.news-article 87440337 (accessed 12 June 2017).

155   Lillian Musselwhite, née Penfold, was a clergyman's daughter. She married a British soldier, Owen Musselwhite, in 1916, but he was killed in action in France in 1917.

156   'DIVORCE COURT. LEANE V LEANE', *Western Argus*, 14 December 1926, p. 9. See: http://nla.gov.au//nla.news article 34406205 (accessed 30 January 2017).

157   Interview with Glenda Rae Leane, 20 November 2017.

158   No. 1055, Corporal Arnold Harry Leane, 27th Battalion, War Service Records, NAA B2455.

Chapter 9

159   Marlene Simons, 'The Fighting Leanes of Prospect, South Australia', Leane Family History Collection, State Library of South Australia, Adelaide, 2003, p. 9.

160   Judy Mercer, family history notes.

161   'THE FIGHTING LEANES OF PROSPECT', *Observer*, 6 September 1919, p. 36. See: http://nla.gov.au./nla.news-article 165897507 (accessed 29 January 2018).

162   Peter Burness (ed), *The Western Front Diaries of Charles Bean*, New South Publishing, Canberra, 2018, p.217.

163   LIEUTENANT COLONEL LEANE KILLED. *Chronicle*, 13 January 1917. http://.gov.au./nla.newsarticle 87441064 (Accessed 10 December 2016).

Chapter 11

164   Simons, *The Fighting Leanes of Prospect*, p. 9.

165   Ibid.

166   Ibid., p. 10.

167   Geoffrey Malcolm Leane, Biography from 1907-1990, sole family copy in possession of Athena Leane.

168   Ibid.

169   'CAPTAIN R.L. LEANE', *Kalgoorlie Miner*, 26 July 1915, p. 6. See: http://nla.gov. au/nla.news -article 89066710 (accessed 20 January 2017).

170 Leane, Brigadier General R.L., AWM 3DR8042, Item 15.

171 James Hurst, *Game to the Last, The 11th Australian Infantry Battalion at Gallipoli*, Oxford University Press, Melbourne, 2005, p. 57.

172 Ibid., p. 60.

173 Ibid., p. 66.

174 Captain W.C. Belford, *Legs Eleven Being the Story of the Eleventh Battalion (AIF) In the Great War of 1914-1918*, Imperial Printing Coy., UK, 1940, p. 134.

175 Ibid., p. 170.

176 Ibid., p. 167.

177 Ibid., p. 180.

178 'THE COLONEL; AN IRON MAN', Major A.G. Moyes, M.C., 48th Battalion, *Reveille*, Australian War Museum, Canberra, October 1932.

179 C.E.W. Bean, *The Official History of Australia in the War of 1914–1918*, Vol. III, *The AIF in France*. Angus & Robertson, Sydney, 1941, p. 707.

180 Father William Devine, *The Story of a Battalion*, The Naval and Military Press, London, 1920, p. 81.

181 Australian War Memorial at: awm.gov.au/images/collection/pdf. RCDIG1068688.

182 J.C. Irwin, 'Smith, Louis Laybourne (1880-1965)', *ADB*, Vol. 11, MUP, 1988, p. 60.

183 Devine, *The Story of a Battalion*, p. 81.

184 Ibid., p. 84.

185 Ibid.

186 'THE COLONEL; AN IRON MAN', *Reveille*, October 1932.

187 Neville Browning, *Leane's Battalion: The 48th Battalion*, Quality Press, Huntingdale, Western Australia, 2009, p. 101.

188 Devine, *The Story of a Battalion*, p. 85.

189 'THE COLONEL; AN IRON MAN', *Reveille*, October 1932.

190 Australian War Memorial at: awm.gov.au/images/collection/pdf/ RCDIG1068733.

191 Australian War Memorial, biographical details of Brigadier General Raymond Lionel Leane.

192 Australian War Memorial at: awm.gov.au/images/collection/pdf/ RCDIG 1068129.

193 Geoffrey Malcolm Leane, Biography from 1907-1990.

194 'AUSSIE SOLDIERS. BEST SHOCK TROOPS', *The Daily Herald*, 6 November 1919, p. 8. See: http://nla.gov.au/nla.news-article 106484393 (accessed 15 February 2017).

Chapter 11

195 'A NEW COMMISSIONER. BRIGADIER-GENERAL LEANE', *Advertiser*, 20 May 1920, p. 7. See: http:nla.gov.au/nla.news-article 37517112 (accessed 2 July 2017).

196 Ibid.

197 Commissioner Sir Raymond Lionel Leane, 'A General at the Helm', p. 3. Commissioner Sir Raymond Lionel Leane, file, South Australian Police Museum.

198 Ibid., p. 6.

199 Ibid., p. 8.

200 Ibid., p. 6.

201 Ibid., p. 7.

202 Ibid., p. 8.

203 Ibid., p. 9.

204 Ibid., p. 11.

205 Interview with Bruce Leane, 25 October 2016.

206 Leane, 'A General at the Helm', p. 22.

207 'THE WINGFIELD CAMP. BREEDING GROUND FOR OUTLAWRY', *The Daily Herald*, 27 March 1923, p. 3. See: http://nla.gov.au/nla.news-article 106734369 (accessed 10 November 2016).

208 'ALLEGED CRIMINAL LIBEL', Adelaide *Register*, 2 June 1923, p. 10. See: http://nla.gov.au/nla.news-article 64114489 (accessed 16 February 2017).

209 'ALLEGED LIBEL. CROWN ABANDONS PROSECUTION', *The Daily Herald*, 10 November 1923, p. 4. See: http://nla.gov.au/nla.news-article 106714681 (accessed 22 February 2017).

210 'GENERAL LEANE CRITICISED', *The Daily Herald*, 17 August 1923, p. 2. See: http://nla.gov.au./nla.news- article.106704885 (accessed 23 February 2017).

211 Leane, 'A General at the Helm', p. 36.

212 Ibid., p. 38.

213 Geoffrey Leane, 'Biography from 1907–1990'.

214 Ibid.

215 Ibid.

216 Ibid.

217 Ibid.

218 Ibid.

219 Leane, 'A General at the Helm', p. 33.

220   Wallace Budd, 'Australian Police in the National Waterfront Riots 1928-1931', at: sapolicehistory.org/waterfront.html.

221   'SERIOUS RIOTS ON THE WATERFRONT - WORKERS ATTACKED', Adelaide *Register*, 28 September 1928, p. 3. See: http://nla.gov.au/nla.news-article 56762692 (accessed 14 July 2017).

222   'DEFENCE BRIGADE; APPRECIATION OF WORK', *News*, 2 October 1928, p. 4. See: http:// nla.gov.au/nla.news – article129228309 (accessed 17 July 2017).

223   Leane, 'A General at the Helm', p. 44.

224   'ANARCHY AT THE TRADES HALL', *Advertiser*, 12 January 1931. p. 6. See: http:// nla.gov.au/nla.news-article 29859043 (accessed 17 July 2017).

225   Leane, 'A General at the Helm', p. 50.

226   Ibid., p. 51.

227   'BRIG. LEANE URGES RALLYING DIGGERS' *Border Chronicle*, 6 July 1940, p. 1. See: http://nla.gov.au/nla.news-article212463919 (accessed 26 July 2017).

228   Geoffrey Leane, 'Biography from 1907 – 1990'.

229   Commissioner Sir Raymond Lionel Leane, 'Supplement to the *Police Gazette*', Commissioner Sir Raymond Lionel Leane file, South Australian Police Museum.

230   'MILITIA NOT A FAILURE', *News*, 27 September 1957, p. 3. See: http://nla.gov. au/nla.news-article127066754 (accessed 26 July 2017).

231   Interview with Bruce Leane, 25 October 2016.

232   Interview with Peggy Leane, 2 January 2018.

233   'DEATH AT 83 OF SIR. R. LEANE', *Advertiser*, 26 June 1962 (no page number). Commissioner Sir Raymond Lionel Leane file, South Australian Police Museum.

Chapter 12

234   Diaries of Benjamin Bennett Leane, 1915–1916, AWM RCD1G00010007, Vol. 1, p. 13.

235   Ibid., p. 31.

236   Ibid., p. 114.

237   Australian War Memorial at: AWM RCDIG1068223-32-pdf

238   Benjamin Leane diaries, Vol. 3, p. 176.

239   Ibid.

240   Ibid., Vol. 4, p. 134. Thomas Clarence Fairley (Clarrie) was the adopted son of Ethel (Leane) Taylor and her husband, William Taylor. Previously mentioned in endnotes to Chapter Six.

241   Benjamin Leane diaries, Vol. 1, pp. 20–24.

242   AWM Photostat Copies of the Diaries of Benjamin Bennett Leane 1915-1916 RCDIG0010007 Vol 4. p.144

243   Ibid.p. 146

244   Ibid.

245   Ibid Vol V p.98

246   Ibid. p.106

247   Ibid. p.125

248   Ibid p.140

249   AWM RCDIG1068752039-pdf

250   AWM Photostat copies of the Diaries of Benjamin Bennett Leane 1915-1916 RCDIG0010007 Vol 6. p. 98

251   Ibid., p. 123.

252   Postscript to Vol. 6, added by Phyllis Leane after the war.

253   Les Carlyon, The Great War, Pan Macmillan, Sydney, 2006, p. 203.

254   Devine, The Story of a Battalion, p. 75.

255   Australian War Memorial at: AWM RCDIG1043754-1-pdf

256   Australian War Memorial at: AWM RCD1G1068676-53-pdf

257   'LATE MAJOR BEN. B. LEANE', Observer, 28 April 1917, p. 37. See: http://nla. gov.au./nla.news - article 164188136 (accessed 20 November 2016).

258   AWM 43, Letter from Phyllis Leane, 20 March 1918, with reference to her late husband, Benjamin Bennett Leane.

259   Commonwealth War Graves Commission website at: https://www.cwggc.org.

Chapter 13

260   'Six of Seven Sons of Frederick and Maggie Smith Died in WW1', Herald Sun, 25 April 2014. See: https://www.heraldsun.com.au.died.ww1/13d76c7aa41c

261   'All the brothers and all the sons', The Australian, 23 February 2008. See: https:/ www.the australian.com.au/national-affairs/defence (accessed 10 February 2019).

262   Ibid.

263   Ibid.

264   'Three have been Decorated for Gallant Service', Sunday Times (Sydney), 30 July 1916, p. 6. See: https://trove.nla.gov.au/newspaper/rendition/nla.news-article121351211 (accessed 4 February 2019).

265   Ibid.

266   Ibid. The Battle of Flodden Field was fought between English and Scottish forces

in 1513. The Scots were massacred, losing 10,000 men with English casualties numbering only around 1500.

267 'Death from Wounds. A Military Cross Hero', *Sydney Morning Herald*, 14 November 1916, p. 6. See: https://trove.nla.gov.au/newspaper/rendition/nla.news-article15687066 (accessed 13 February 2019).

268 Ibid.

269 C.E.W. Bean, *The Official History of Australia in the War 1914-1918*, Vol I, *The Story of Anzac*, Angus & Robertson, Sydney, 1921, p. 442.

270 Bean, *The Official History of Australia in the War 1914-1918*, Vol III, *The AIF in France*, p. 12.

271 Peter Burness (ed), *The Western Front Diaries of Charles Bean*, NewSouth Publishing, Canberra, 2018. p. 93.

272 Bean, *The Official History of Australia in the War 1914-1918*, Vol III, *The AIF in France*, pp. 578–79.

273 'Bravery of Howell-Price', *Sydney Sun*, 10 June 1917, p. 8. See: https://trove.nla.gov.au/newspaper/rendition/nla.news-article 221974208 (accessed 4 February 2019).

274 Burness (ed), *The Western Front Diaries of Charles Bean*, p. 190.

275 Ibid., p. 198.

276 Ibid., p. 189.

277 Ibid.

278 Ibid., p. 190.

279 'Late Colonel Howell-Price DSO MC', *Glen Innes Examiner*, 8 February 1917, p. 8. See: https://trove.nla.gov.au/newspaper/rendition/nla.news-article 183272945 (accessed 14 February 2019).

280 'Fighting Family. Late Lieut. R.G. Howell-Price', *Sydney Morning Herald*, 4 October 1917, p. 8. See: https://trove.nla.gov.au/newspaper/redition/nla.news-article 15741130 (accessed 12 February 2019).

281 Ibid.

282 Ibid.

283 'The Howell-Prices', *Richmond River and Northern Districts Advertiser*, 4 August 1916, p. 7. See: http://trove.nla.gov.au/newspapers/rendition/nla.news-article 125927109 (accessed 11 February 2019).

284 Bean, *The Official History of Australia in the War 1914-1918*, Vol III, *The AIF in France*, p. 844.

285 RMS *Alcantara* at: https://wikipedia.org/wiki/RMS-Alcantara - 1913 (accessed 10 February 2019).

286 Zeebrugge Raid at: https;//en. Wikipedia.org/wiki/Zeebrugge_raid (accessed 10 February 2019).

287 War Service Records, Frederick Phillimore Howell-Price, NAA B2455.

288 'The Valorous Achievements of five Australians', *Canberra Times*, 5 March 1983, p. 2. See: https://trove.nla.gov.au/newspaper/rendition/.nla.news-article116371976 (accessed 19 February 2019).

289 'Howell-Price Sentenced', *Daily Telegraph* (Sydney), 27 March 1917, p. 3. See: https://trove.nla.gov.au/newspaper/rendition/nla.news-article 2392243183 (accessed 8 February 2019).

Chapter 14

290 *Australian Christian Commonwealth*, 2 April 1916.

291 Letter from the family memoirs of Peggy Leane.

292 Letter from the collected history of the late Don Taylor, brother-in-law to Ethel Flora (Leane) Taylor. Quoted in Simons, 'The Fighting Leanes of Prospect'.

293 'SHE GAVE HER ALL', *Register*, 26 May 1915, p. 9. See: http://nla.gov.au/nla. news - article59603563 (accessed 27 July 2017).

294 Lieutenant Geoffrey Paul Leane, letter to family members.

295 Benjamin Bennett Leane diaries, Vol. 1, AWM RCD1G00010007.

296 Geoffrey Leane, 'Biography from 1907 – 1990.'

297 Ibid.

298 'THE FIGHTING LEANES OF PROSPECT', *Observer*, 6 September 1919, p. 36. See: http://nla.gov.au./nla.news- article 165897507 (accessed 27 January 2018).

299 Interview with Peter Newbury, 20 January 2018.

BIBLIOGRAPHY

Primary sources

Documents in AWM Collection

Leane, A.E., letters, 48th Battalion, 1915–1917, AWM 1DRL/0411.

Leane, B.B., Diary of Major B.B. Leane, 48th Battalion, March 1915–November 1916, AWM RCD1G00010007.

Documents in family collections

Leane, E.T., Gallipoli Diary, Leane family collection.

Books

Bean, C.E.W. *Official History of Australia in the War of 1914 -1918, Vol. I, The Story of Anzac.* Angus & Robertson, Sydney, 1921.

_____, *Official History of Australia in the War of 1914 -1918, Vol. III, The AIF in France 1918,* Angus & Robertson, Sydney, 1929.

_____, *Official History of Australia in the War of 1914 -1918, Vol. VI, The AIF in France 1918*, Angus & Robertson, Sydney, 1942.

Belford, Captain W.C., *Legs Eleven Being the Story of the Eleventh Battalion (AIF) In the Great War of 1914 -1918*, Imperial Printing Coy., UK, 1940.

Burness, Peter,. *The Western Front Diaries of Charles Bean*, New South Publishing, Canberra, 2018.

Collett, H.B., *The 28th, A Record of War Service with the Australian Imperial Force, 1915-1919, Vol. I*, Perth, Western Australia, 1922.

Devine, Father William, *The Story of a Battalion*, The Naval and Military Press, London, 1920.

Neale, A. (Caroline Leane), *Shadows and Sunbeams*, Scrymgour, Adelaide, 1893.

South Australian Maritime Museum, *Passengers in History 1836*, n. p., n. d.

Wakefield, E.G., *How to Select Migrants. A letter from Sydney*, Robert Gouger (ed), Everyman, London, 1829.

Whysall, F., *Report of the Royal Commission on Norfolk Island Affairs with appendices*, Government Printer, Melbourne, 1926.

Secondary sources

Battye, J., *Cyclopedia of Western Australia*, Hussey and Gillingham, Western Australia, 1971.

Browning, Neville, *Leane's Battalion: The 48th Battalion, A.I.F. 1916-1919*, Quality Press, Huntingdale, Western Australia, 2009.

Carlyon, Les, *Gallipoli*, Pan MacMillan Australia, Sydney, 2001.

——, *The Great War*, Pan MacMillan Australia, Sydney, 2006.

Clarke, C.M.H., *A History of Australia, Vol. 3*, Melbourne University Press, 1973.

Curnow, E.A., *Bible Christian Methodists in South Australia 1850-1900: A biography of chapels and their people*, South Australia Uniting Church Historical Society, Black Forest, 1915.

Gill, L., *Fremantle to France: 11th Battalion A.I.F.1914- 1919*, Advance Press Pty Ltd, Myaree, Western Australia, 2004.

Haggett, June and Smith, Monty, *A Jam Tin of Mosquitos*, DPA Publishing, South Australia, 2013.

Hunt, Arnold Dudley, *Methodism Militant; Attitudes to the Great War, 1914 -1918*, South Australian Methodist Historical Society, Clarence Park, South Australia, 1975.

——, *For God, King and Country: A study of the attitudes of the Methodist and Catholic Press in South Australia*, Salisbury College of Advanced Education, Salisbury, South Australia, 1979.

——, *The Bible Christians in South Australia*, Adelaide Uniting Church Historical Society, 1983.

Hurst, James, *Game to the Last. The 11th Infantry Battalion at Gallipoli*, Oxford University Press, Melbourne, 2005.

Lloyd, G., Charles *Wesley and the Struggle for Methodist Identity*, Oxford University Press, Oxford, 2007.

Pike, D.H., *The Paradise of Dissent. South Australia, 1829 -1857*, Longmans, London, 1957.

Websites and online articles

Budd, Wallace, *Australian Police in the National Waterfront Riots 1928-1931*, at: sapoliceehistory.org/waterfront.html

Hopkins, Ronald, 'Leane, Edwin Thomas (1867–1928)', *Australian Dictionary of Biography, Vol. 10*, Melbourne University Press, 1986.

Pretty, Charles, 'Wakefield, Edward Gibbon, 1796–1862', *Australian Dictionary of Biography, Vol. 2*, Melbourne University Press, 1967.

RMS *Alcantara* at: https://Wikipedia.org/wiki/RMS- Alcantara-1913.

Zeebrugge Raid at: en.wikeipedia.org/wiki/Zeeebrugge_Raid

Other

Hyde, Loftus, 'Personalities Remembered', scripts from the radio broadcast series, broadcast from 5CL 10.30-10.50 am, Sundays 7 June 1970–26 December 1971.

Jamieson, Eric (ed), 'The Gumeracha Methodist Church. On Hundred and Twenty Five Years', State Library of South Australia, pamphlet.

Material from family reunion provided by Kingsley Leane.

Millbrook School Centenary, '100 Years at the School on the Hill, 1879-1979', State Library of South Australia, pamphlet.

Simons, M., 'The Fighting Leanes of Prospect, South Australia', Leane

Family History Collection, State Library of South Australia, Adelaide, 2003.

Simons, M. and Payne, G., 'Introducing the Leane Family History', Leane Family History Collection, State Library of South Australia, Adelaide, 1996.

Simons, M., Vince, W. and Vince, M., 'Agnes Neale: A Life's Work', Leane Family History Collection, State Library of South Australia, Adelaide, n.d.

'The Chain of Ponds Story', State Library of South Australia, pamphlet.

'Union Church in the City: 1972 Church Anniversary and Final Services in the Pirie St Methodist Church', State Library of South Australia, pamphlet.

Webb, P.J., 'Friendly Societies in South Australia, 1840–1892', State Library of South Australia, pamphlet.

Newspapers and Periodicals

Adelaide Country News
Adelaide Morning Chronicle
Australian Christian Commonwealth
Ballina Chronicle (Ireland)
Border Chronicle (Bordertown, South Australia)
Canberra Times
Christian Weekly and Methodist Journal
Daily Telegraph (Sydney)
Glenn Innes Examiner
Herald Sun (Melbourne)
Kalgoorlie Miner (Western Australia)
Northern Standard (Northern Territory)
Observer (Adelaide)
Reveille (magazine of the Returned and Services League of Australia, New South Wales Branch)

Richmond River and Northern Districts Advertiser

South Australian Advertiser

South Australian Register

South Australian Weekly Chronicle

Sunday Times (Sydney)

Sydney Morning Herald

Sydney Sun

The Advertiser (Adelaide)

The Australian

The Chronicle (Adelaide)

The Daily Herald (Adelaide)

The Express and Telegraph (Adelaide)

The Register (Adelaide)

Weekly Times (Melbourne)

Western Argus (Kalgoorlie)

INDEX

ABOUT THE AUTHOR

Carol Rosenhain is a Melbourne writer and historian. Educated at Monash University, she has been a passionate teacher of English and History at senior secondary school for many years. In her professional capacity, Carol has been Head of the English Faculty at Genazzano FCJ College and a State Examiner in VCE English. She has presented seminars at the Victorian History Teachers' conferences and is a regular speaker at library, Probus and Rotary Groups. Carol has written commercially for artists and galleries including, *The Art of Paul Margocsy; A Biography.* She also co-authored with Jill Fenwick, *South Africa: From Settlement to Self Determination.* Her latest publication in 2016; *The Man Who Carried the Nation's Grief,* was nominated for the NSW Premier's Award. In that year she was also the recipient of a prize in the Box Hill RSL Centenary of WW1 Short Story Competition. Carol is a keen researcher and traveller, with a penchant for all places of historical connection with the Australian military.

www.ingramcontent.com/pod-product-compliance
Lightning Source LLC
Chambersburg PA
CBHW060044100426
42742CB00014B/2691